# Changing children's services: working and learning together

## DATE DUE

| | | | |
|---|---|---|---|
| | | | |
| | | | |
| | | | |
| | | | |
| | | | |
| | | | |
| | | | |
| | | | |
| | | | |
| | | | |
| | | | |
| | | | |
| | | | |
| | | | |
| | | | |
| | | | |
| | | | |

Demco, Inc. 38-293

# Working together for children

This innovative series brings together an interdisciplinary team of authors to provide an accessible collection of ideas, debates, discussions and reflections on childhood, practice and services for children. The books have been designed and written as illustrative teaching texts, giving voice to children's and practitioners' own accounts as well as providing research, policy analysis and examples of good practice. These books are aimed at students, practitioners, academics and educators across the wide range of disciplines associated with working with children.

There are three books in the *Working together for children* series:

- *Connecting with children: developing working relationships*, edited by Pam Foley and Stephen Leverett

- *Promoting children's wellbeing: policy and practice*, edited by Janet Collins and Pam Foley

- *Changing children's services: working and learning together*, edited by Pam Foley and Andy Rixon

# Changing children's services:
## working and learning together

Edited by Pam Foley and Andy Rixon

The Open University

Published by

The Policy Press
University of Bristol
Fourth Floor, Beacon House
Queen's Road, Clifton
Bristol BS8 1QU
United Kingdom
http://www.policypress.org.uk

in association with

The Open University
Walton Hall, Milton Keynes
MK7 6AA
United Kingdom

First published 2008

Edited and designed by The Open University.

Typeset in India by Alden Prepress Services, Chennai.

Printed and bound in the United Kingdom by The Alden Group, Oxford.

This book forms part of an Open University course KE312 *Working together for children*. Details of this and other Open University courses can be obtained from the Student Registration and Enquiry Service, The Open University, PO Box 197, Milton Keynes MK7 6BJ, United Kingdom: tel. +44 (0)845 300 60 90, email general-enquiries@open.ac.uk

http://www.open.ac.uk

**British Library Cataloguing in Publication Data**

A catalogue record for this book is available from the British Library.

**Library of Congress Cataloging-in-Publication Data**

A catalog record for this book has been requested.

ISBN 978 1 84742 060 2

1.1

# Contributors

**Pam Foley** is a Senior Lecturer in Children and Families at The Open University's Faculty of Health and Social Care. Her practice background is in women's and children's health.

**Caroline Jones** is a self-employed educational consultant and has recently worked for the University of Warwick, The Open University, the British Council and various local education authorities. She is also director of a group of day nurseries in the Midlands.

**Stephen Leverett** is a Lecturer in Children and Young People at The Open University's Faculty of Health and Social Care. His practice background is in social care and social work in both the statutory and voluntary sectors.

**Andy Rixon** is a Lecturer in Children and Young People at The Open University's Faculty of Health and Social Care. His practice background is as a social worker and in local authority training and development.

**Bill Stone** works on a freelance basis as a social work consultant with a mixed portfolio of work including practice as a children's guardian and independent social worker, as well as research, training and consultancy. He also edits the journal *Representing Children* and is a consultant for the Churches' Child Protection Advisory Service.

# Other contributors

This series of three books forms part of The Open University course *Working together for children* and has grown out of debates and discussions within the course team working at the University. We would like to thank the following for their critical reading and invaluable feedback: Judith Argles, Brigitte Beck-Woerner, Sheila Campbell, Maurice Crozier, Hasel Daniels, Trevor Evans, Louise Garrett, Gill Goodliff, Glo Potter, Lin Miller, Kate New, Janet Seden and our developmental testers. We would also like to thank our focus group, our Editors Carol Price, Alison Cadle and Kate Hunter, our Course Team Assistant Val O'Connor, and our External Assessor, Denise Hevey, who has provided insightful and timely comments at every turn.

We should especially like to acknowledge the contribution of our Course Manager, Tabatha Torrance, who has guided, assisted and supported the course team throughout.

# Contents

# Introduction

Pam Foley and Andy Rixon

Attempting to analyse the changes within children's services at any one time requires grappling with trends and directions, both overt and underlying, in a shifting area of social and political thinking. The wellbeing of children remains a central concern for each successive government, and the evolution of children's services never seems to pause. New ten-year plans are launched and major policy initiatives implemented before current plans and past initiatives can be absorbed, and consequently little definite analysis takes place. Developments can even appear to be circular as old ideas are recycled to address modern concerns. Moreover, while the costs of significant changes can be calculated and appreciated from the start, the benefits of changes may only emerge later.

Both rhetoric and realities co-exist within modernisation programmes that periodically sweep through public services. For contemporary children's services, delivering on targets and reaching key outcomes has meant significant reorganisation across rather than just within traditional practice boundaries. The argument that improvements to services require the sweeping away of established patterns of working has become explicit. For some this is a vital shift to the integration of services for children and families which should never have become so divided, and is the only means by which to achieve real improvements. For others this is a strategy that could undermine existing roles, expertise and values. Agencies merging, teams integrating, practitioners expanding their range of responsibilities, taking lead roles in new teams, and the invention of new kinds of practitioners are all consequences of this position. However, no one would argue that even radical restructuring is the answer to many, let alone most, of the really important issues such as the protection of children and the promotion of children's wellbeing; many of the underlying dilemmas of work with children may continue to be unaddressed. Whatever the view of the practitioners involved, this drive to integrate services has dovetailed with a commitment to address some deep-rooted social, economic and political issues through early intervention in the lives of children. Inevitably such fundamental challenges continue to raise a host of issues and uncertainties about roles and responsibilities, workplace cultures, values, and ultimately people's own identities as practitioners.

Many changes that define the modern world, such as the internet revolution for example, are having a major impact upon children's lives and children's services with both good and bad consequences. Policy and practice directions and developments can be knocked off course by particular events involving children and are frequently taken up by the media where anxieties about childhood remain a major preoccupation. Perspectives on childhood will continue to influence the working practices within children's services, and are reflected, for example, in the extent to which children's services can become over-focused on futures and outcomes at the expense of measures that can improve children's present quality of life. Equally it is also important not to become wrapped up in the measurement of short-term outcomes, while more long-term concerns for children remain, including low social mobility in the UK (Blanden et al., 2005) and unflattering comparisons of children's wellbeing in the UK with children's wellbeing in other European countries (UNICEF, 2007).

What remains at the heart of all work with children and families is the ability to create and sustain good working relationships. The need for a range of communication and interpersonal skills is not always given sufficient priority in the education, training and qualifications of the many groups of practitioners now working with children. Connecting with children and developing good relationships highlights not only the value of relationship skills but also essential 'qualities' such as being respectful, being trustworthy, 'being there', and being, at times, able to form extraordinary relationships with children and families. Practitioners working across boundaries need these skills too – interagency working equally requires interpersonal skills.

Practice relationships are complex, each located in particular kinds of context or setting and reflecting the wider sphere of child–adult relations. Good working relationships can be enhanced by seeing children as a distinct social group and childhood as an important period of life in its own right. It can also be helpful to recognise children's agency and that they play a part in the shaping of children's services and in the development of the skills of practitioners. These views of children and young people are no longer either new or radical, and many of the changes underway in children's services are increasingly informed by these kinds of ideas. However, children's participation is still far from universally embedded in processes and structures, consultation is not always sufficient, and participation is not always meaningful.

This book explores and explains the emphasis on integrated working in children's services, and it also examines both the combining of skilled individuals and the development of skills within an individual. It also intends to raise some key questions. To what extent are the barriers to agencies and practitioners working together at all levels really being addressed? How sure can we be that there is more to be gained than to be lost? What in the education of teachers, social workers, family support workers, early years workers and the many others who work with children, prepares them for this kind of work and helps them to meet the expectations it gives rise to? Are there other skills that are more important and frequently absent? Do we really know that integrated working delivers better outcomes for children and their families? There are many critical questions for us to explore. If, for example, we are going to place our faith in schools as settings from which to deliver health and social care services, it seems all the more crucial to examine how they work with their communities and how they operate as institutions given the marginalisation and disaffection of particular children within the current school system. What effect do institutions such as schools have on people and the kinds of work that are possible within them?

This book also addresses the issue of the knowledge and skills needed by those working with children, and asks questions about where is the best place to find them and how best to teach and learn them. Multi-professional teams will bring multiple understandings of the issues to their work with children. Questions have arisen about addressing the divisions between different disciplines of key importance to work with children including sociology, psychology, childhood and family studies, health, social care and education. Is the answer to these questions a necessity for common skills and knowledge for everyone working in children's services in order for integration to work? Is integrated learning the key to integrated working? The nature of learning itself seems crucial here as theories of informal learning such as that of 'communities of practice' (Wenger, 1998) illustrate some of the limitations of formal learning and the alternative ways in which new knowledge and skills are generated.

Other potentially revealing questions are now being debated that centre on the contrast between children's services in the UK and those that are the result of the different social pedagogical practices in other parts of Europe. Once there is some disruption of current understandings of what certain groups of practitioners do, there is room for some creative and productive transformations of practice by both generalist and specialist practitioners, for the benefit of the children with whom they work.

This series of books focuses on the nought-to-twelve age group and throughout we have placed an emphasis on the value of children's voices. We have, however, omitted children's ages, unless they are particularly relevant, to avoid reproducing the 'age and stage' thinking that has often obscured children's individual capacities and capabilities. In fact, we hope to encourage people with an interest in childhood to look outwards and consider how this important period in people's lives connects with the rest of the life course. We also value the views of practitioners and have drawn upon their insights on the changing world of practice in which they find themselves. Writers and practitioners from a variety of disciplines have contributed to this book, and this is reflected in the diversity of language and terminology.

In the first chapter we look at change as a backdrop to the rest of the book. This chapter considers in particular the impact of change since a modernising tone was set by recent governments. This impact is explored from the point of view of voluntary as well as statutory services, and from the standpoint of children and families as well as of practitioners. This chapter also analyses broader sources of change beyond the political and policy arena. Highlighting a key theme of the book, there is a particular focus on the relationship between change and interagency working.

In the second chapter we look at how working together has involved supporting and working in partnership with parents and carers. This chapter focuses on the political context in which parenting is experienced and the impact of the social context including gender, social networks and inequality in relation to parenting. The concept of capital is debated, examining different forms – economic, human, emotional and social. These forms of capital are then explored in relation to how parenting support is defined and the ways practitioners can work with parents.

In Chapter 3 we again pick up on one of the key themes of this book, the accelerating move towards integrated ways of working in children's services. Interagency working has several notable features, including addressing health promotion and social care issues through community agencies, extended schools and community schools, and more sustained and focused work with and support for parents. This is now to be achieved through a range of practitioners working in interagency teams of various designs, often in common settings, although policy also sometimes simultaneously suggests this is best achieved through the multi-skilling of the individual worker. Starting from the perspective of children and families, this chapter outlines some of the range of drivers behind interagency working and how these changes manifest themselves, particularly in terms of partnership working, between agencies but also with children and families. It goes on to explore the challenges and issues that have been experienced by practitioners engaged in the process of establishing closer working together.

Chapter 4 analyses the trajectory of policy as it becomes re-contextualised within practice through the lens of four different perspectives: influence, policy production, practice and evaluation. The example of the Common Assessment Framework and its implementation in England is used to explore in detail the tensions and issues arising from this relationship between policy ideas and their application in practice. The realities of different kinds of practitioners working together using the same practice framework are explored.

In Chapter 5 one of the key issues raised in the previous chapter is examined – whether it can be said with confidence that interagency working produces improved outcomes for children. While there is a growing body of research on the process of interagency working, it is suggested that the answer to this question remains uncertain. The evaluation of some of the key examples of multi-agency working such as Sure Start and the Children's Fund are now able to provide some insight into this area and are explored in some detail. Using these examples and others, the chapter attempts to summarise emerging indications of how agencies and practitioners are able to more successfully work together.

It is the 'learning together' of the book title that is the focus of Chapter 6. While raising the level of education, training and qualifications across the children's workforce has been a major aim of policy, this chapter examines how it is that practitioners can and do learn. Learning is viewed from a range of perspectives exploring both formal learning and theories of social learning such as the concept of 'communities of practice'. The importance of learning from the expertise that children and families possess about their own lives is also emphasised here. The chapter continues the interagency theme, touching on the role of both pre- and post-qualifying education and training.

A different approach is taken in Chapter 7, where issues for learning and working together are explored using personal accounts from practitioners. A range of practitioners from different settings and agencies were asked to reflect and contribute their views and experiences of the changing working environment in children's services. We look here at the nature of work with children and families and at some alternative models for those working in the children's workforce such as that of the social pedagogue common in the European context. Through the personal accounts, the reader is asked to engage with debates about some of the dilemmas of contemporary practice, about the gains and losses of integrated working and about the skills, knowledge and values needed by practitioners.

# References

Blanden, J., Gregg, P. and Machin, S. (2005) *Intergenerational Mobility in Europe and North America: A Report Supported by the Sutton Trust*, available online at <http://cep.lse.ac.uk/about/news/IntergenerationalMobility.pdf>, accessed 22 November 2007.

UNICEF (2007) *Child Poverty in Perspective: An Overview of Child Well-being in Rich Countries*, Innocenti Report Card 7, Florence, UNICEF Innocenti Research Centre.

Wenger, E. (1998) *Communities of Practice: Learning, Meaning, and Identity*, Cambridge, Cambridge University Press.

# Chapter 1

## Working with change

Andy Rixon

## Introduction

One of the defining features of working in children's services is change. Changing organisations, policies, procedures and expectations seem to be a constant feature of life for many practitioners. Government, national and local, constantly creates new policies, or recreates old ones, to try and deal with problems new and old. Political philosophies fluctuate in their beliefs about where solutions are to be found. As a result, resources grow, shrink and change direction. Practitioners with 'established' roles are expected to adapt; new practitioners' roles evolve or are created. At the same time, society and social relations do not stand still – relationships between service 'providers' and 'receivers' are less clear-cut. Even our understanding of children and childhood itself is subject to change.

Change is the theme of this chapter – its sources and its impact on practitioners and the children and families with whom they work. Amongst a variety of changes, we will explore in particular the interrelationship between change and interprofessional ways of working. While interagency and interprofessional working are not new phenomena, they are continuing to be a major theme in the organisation of early twenty-first century services for children in the UK. The creation of new agency structures, the emergence of 'lead professionals' and 'common' frameworks suggest that change in the direction of closer 'working together' for children is accelerating rather than slowing down.

### Core questions

- How is the landscape of children's services changing?
- What are the implications of change for practitioners, children and their families?
- What is the interrelationship between change and interagency and interprofessional working?

# 1 Continuous improvement – continuous change?

While the evolution of services for children is inevitable and in many cases highly desirable, the specific agenda of change is one that appears to have been actively encouraged – the government desire for 'continuous improvement' increasingly became equated to the need for continuous change. The tone for the start of the twenty-first century was set by such policy documents as *Modernising Government*:

> *What must change*
> ... The Government needs to ensure that public bodies are clearly focused on the results that matter to people, that they monitor and report their progress in achieving these results and that they do not allow bureaucratic boundaries to get in the way of sensible co-operation. We must make clear that additional investment comes with strings attached and is conditional on achieving improved results through modernisation. We must encourage a commitment to quality and continuous improvement, and ensure that public bodies know how to turn this commitment into results. And we must work in partnership with the independent audit bodies and inspectorates, so that we all focus on the goal of improving the value delivered to the public.
>
> (Cabinet Office, 1999, p. 35)

Public services were criticised for impeding the improvement in quality by sticking to working practices that were too 'traditional' when in fact: 'The world is changing too fast for that to be an effective approach' (Cabinet Office, 1999, p. 35). As well as reinforcing the need for change, this extract also suggests the mechanisms by which improvements were to be measured, such as regulation, targets, audit and inspection. The modernising theme was experienced across the UK as it was taken forward into new devolved governments and assemblies that in turn created their own currents of change. Change was experienced in other services – see, for example, *The New NHS* (Department of Health (DH), 1997) and the star ratings of the Modernisation Agency for the NHS which also placed 'continuous improvement' at the heart of the NHS (Pinnock and Dimmock, 2003). The NHS has since seen the rise – and in some cases demise – of GP fundholding, strategic health authorities, primary care trusts, and foundation hospitals to name but a few examples.

Partly as a consequence of these changes and the new initiatives and reviews that flowed from them, organisations which provide services for children often seem to be in a state of permanent internal reorganisation:

> We have no sooner settled down from the last reorganisation than they wanted to change the boundaries again and everything gets another shaking up.

> (Social worker, personal communication)

(See also the accounts of practitioners in Chapter 7.)

New councils or new directors of services may also want to 'make their mark' through changing the organisation and structure of service delivery.

Thinking point 1.1   What major changes are you aware of in children's services, either personally or professionally? What do you think has been the effect of these changes, both positive and negative?

While practitioners will support the principle of improving services, reorganisations can generate much cynicism amongst staff and have a substantial impact upon morale. The extent to which improvement is achieved through structural change, for example, is often unclear. A study of a major local government reorganisation of local authorities in Scotland, Wales and England in the 1990s identified a profound impact on the work undertaken by one of the agencies – social services. Little evidence of savings was found, compared to the upheaval in terms of loss of expertise and morale:

> The process of reorganisation was a bruising one for virtually every party involved in the provision of care services ... More than half the respondents within Welsh unitary social services departments reported declining morale, in many cases further accentuated by the prospect of a severe budgetary crisis looming, alongside perceptions of continuing increases in the levels of service demands. One authority reported a year after reorganisation that *'a recent trawl of expressions of interest in early retirement brought 350 responses (40% of the workforce)'*.

> (Craig and Manthorpe, 1999a, pp. 33–34)

A finding particularly relevant to one of the key themes of this book was the impact on interagency working. Significant redrawing of local authority boundaries meant that relationships with other agencies such as Health Authorities needed to be renegotiated. In addition to the disruption this caused, concerns about the shifting balance of power between health and social services were also raised, as the reorganised local authorities were usually smaller in size than before.

This reorganisation caused similar problems in terms of relationships with and within the voluntary sector. Craig et al. (2000, p. 94) found that the reorganisation was experienced by voluntary organisations as 'chaotic', 'turbulent', 'damaging', 'ill conceived' and 'expensive' with 'no obvious gains for users'. Funding cutbacks to the voluntary sector were a common consequence of such change, accompanied by difficult relationships where they were 'imposed not negotiated'. This often resulted in voluntary organisations implementing their own restructuring, including cutting jobs:

> For some voluntary organisations, such reorganisations and 'down-sizing' were immensely problematic: one wrote that such pressures 'had pushed it close to compromising its own organisational priorities'.
>
> (Craig et al., 2000, p. 93)

Changing geographical boundaries were again a source of difficulties, although in some instances the new, smaller, local authorities did develop closer and more creative working relationships with voluntary organisations (Craig et al., 2000). This highlights that while reorganisations of this nature are frequently experienced negatively, new opportunities are also created by change.

A changing environment inevitably calls for organisations to adapt. Banks (2004, p. 189) argues that some voluntary sector organisations illustrate a 'professional entrepreneurial' response where some 'private sector' approaches, for example in fund-raising, are blended with 'public service ideals'. The growth of social enterprise represents a further change in the landscape of the care sector and a new twist on this blend. While the forms that social enterprise have taken are diverse – ranging from registered charities and cooperatives to limited companies – the entrepreneurial response is explicit even if they have been defined as businesses with primarily social objectives – 'social enterprises are distinctive because their social or environmental goals are central to what they do' (Social Enterprise Coalition, 2007, p. 4).

## Practice box 1.1

### PLUS

PLUS (formerly Playplus) is a voluntary organisation based in Stirling that supports disabled children and young people aged 5–25 in play and social activities, and more recently in inclusion in schools. One of its founders who has written on the topic (Dumbleton, 2005) says that the project was 'born out of a chance remark' about the invisibility of disabled children in public play spaces – spaces which in fact were not all that appealing to non-disabled children: 'If public play areas were unattractive, unappealing and dangerous for non-disabled children, what of those who had additional support needs?'.

Several examples of their experiences are used in this chapter to highlight the evolution of such projects, the influence of funding, and changing relationships between agencies.

> The initial impetus for Playplus came from an informal group operating in a political climate in which local government had given legitimacy to the public funding of childcare. ...
>
> Partnerships with other agencies are the means by which as normal a life as possible can be achieved for children and young people whose needs fall outwith the norm. For Playplus, the positive political climate and, particularly, the existence of the play development officer were crucial. The presence of a council officer gave the project legitimacy with professionals and funders and facilitated the early interagency working – such as the use of school premises – on which the continued development of the organisation has depended.

However, funding for the project at this stage was uncertain and is described as coming 'through a number of departmental budgets' in 'one off' grants with broad outcomes resulting in '*ad hoc*' development.

(Source: Dumbleton, 2005, pp. 36–39)

Inclusive play activities are accessible through groups such as PLUS

In a study of family centres in England, Tunstill et al. (2007) found change to be a consistent feature of their work, pressures for change coming from three main sources (Tunstill et al., 2007, p. 122):

- 'pressures exerted by central government through new policy directions'
- 'pressures from local government through changing funding policies, including cuts in finance'
- the 'changing priorities of partner agencies in both the voluntary and statutory sectors'.

Of the 344 family centres reviewed, three-fifths reported experiences of organisational restructuring or a 'services review', or having completely changed the nature of their work (Tunstill et al., 2007). The direction of their work (between 1999 and 2003) moved towards more targeted and interventionist work with less open access provision. New services reflected shifts in government policy focusing on areas such as parenting education, homework clubs, support for teenage mothers and preparation to enable parents to return to work. This could again change the ethos of family centres as in some cases neighbourhood work decreased while that in assessment and child protection increased (Tunstill et al., 2007).

The funding arrangements to support these changes are often experienced as complicated and time-consuming, and seem to have become an area of expertise in their own right:

> 'Funding arrangements are becoming more complex and the expertise required to write funding bids and fill in complicated returns for different funding sources has also become more complex.'

> 'Funding can take up an eternity each year.'

> (Family centre workers quoted in Tunstill et al., 2007, p. 130)

As well as the funding complexity, all agencies have been required to demonstrate the success of their work in terms of outcomes, usually linked to explicit targets. Most areas of local government and the health service have had the experience of appearing in contentious league tables, exposing the extent to which their targets have been hit or missed. Banks (2004) links these developments to the emergence of a new form of accountability. Practitioners have always been accountable to both the children and the families with whom they work, and to the wider public. Banks argues, however, that the emphasis on public accountability has grown, 'requiring the production of quantifiable outputs and outcomes' in order not just to improve practice but 'to show a good job has been done' and value for money has been achieved (Banks, 2004, p. 151). This has been paralleled by an expansion in administration and proceduralisation.

A frequent criticism of outcome targets concerns the potential distortions that can arise as the focus of work shifts to meet them – creating some dilemmas for practice. MacBeath et al. (2007) noted a particularly serious version of this effect in their study of schools facing 'exceptionally challenging circumstances':

> As headteachers frequently testified, they had very short-term targets and some senior leaders saw this as a moral conflict that they wrestled with on a daily basis. Should they deploy the best

teachers and invest the greatest efforts on those young people most likely to pay dividends in terms of critical benchmark?

(MacBeath et al., 2007, p. 101)

In contrast to the experience of change as a result of a loss of funding, some family centres experienced change due to an increase in resources (Tunstill et al., 2007). Contracting resources in some sectors, new funding emerging in others, has been a pattern reflected throughout the sector. The most significant shift in government policy and funding has been towards preventative services based on the principles of early identification and intervention. The Children's Fund established in 2000 (funded until 2011) is one such example. This was established to deliver preventative services to five- to twelve-year-olds through Local Partnerships. (Aspects of the impact of the Children's Fund are discussed in Chapter 5.) Government gave clear direction that partnerships should preferably be led by voluntary sector organisations, enabling some large national organisations to expand. In turn, resources were given to many smaller local voluntary groups who could offer specific preventative services.

## Practice box 1.2

### PLUS and the preventative agenda

It was the emphasis on *prevention* that precipitated the most significant shift in Playplus's relationship with its local authority partners. In 2002/03 Stirling Council increased its funding allocation to Playplus by more than 50%. This increase came from the Council's share of the Changing Children's Services Fund [Scottish Executive, 2001] and ensured that Playplus moved from being possibly available to children, but with no commitment or obligation to provide a particular level of service, to an entitlement model – which was designed to 'prevent' some children from needing a formal social work assessment. ...

This funding development has meant a move to greater accountability for the organisation. The outcomes of the service are no longer measured in 'child hours' but in provision and uptake of each child's entitlement to support. Playplus's target is to work with 90% of the disabled children aged 5–19 in the Stirling Council area ...

This greater accountability has also 'bought' for funders a place on the Management Board ... Developments in the wider world of social care have also impacted on Playplus which is registered with the Care Commission as a support service and is inspected against the relevant care standards.

(Dumbleton, 2005, pp. 42–43)

However, rapidly evolving government policy still leaves voluntary organisations in an uncertain position as the related funding streams constantly change. When it was proposed that the dedicated budgets for the Children's Fund (and for other major initiatives such as Sure Start) were to move to the local authority, as this provision was 'mainstreamed', longer-term insecurity was generated. The National Evaluation of the Children's Fund (NECF) project commented on the impact of this 'change and uncertainty':

> Changes in rules imposed from the centre and the uncertainty resulting from the absence of guaranteed funding levels for the life of the initiative have had a de-stabilising effect and have been identified as barriers to effective planning and learning. This has also eroded the capacity building work undertaken with the smaller non-statutory stakeholders.
>
> (NECF, 2004a, p. 2)

Expansion, as well as downsizing, can raise questions about organisational priorities. Organisations are tied to the targets and outcomes that are linked to the funding provided. Prevention, as well as playing an important role in the welfare of children, can also require the early identification of potentially problematic families, or children at risk of offending.

Policy makers do sometimes acknowledge, in theory, that constant change is not always required:

> In creating a healthcare system fit for the 21st century we are not interested in change for change's sake and we are inclined to distrust structural change as a distraction from the key issues and challenges.
>
> (Scottish Executive, 2003, p. 9)

This statement seems to have been part of an attempt to establish a distinction between the Scottish and English approaches to the structure of healthcare. In this document this is located in Scottish 'collectivism' being a central feature rather than the key driver being 'choice' as in England. Hudson (2007) argues that this has led to an emphasis on developing 'networks' between services and professional groups rather than wholesale reorganisation. This distinction highlights the potential influence of broader national and political philosophies in shaping the way services are structured and practitioners work together.

## 1.1 Reacting and resisting

Thinking point 1.2    Can you think of the last significant change that happened where you worked? How did you respond?

Although change has positive as well as negative features, the discussion above acknowledges that some changes have a stressful impact on practitioners; issues of morale, for example, clearly emerged from the local authority reorganisations. A number of studies have tried to categorise in different ways how practitioners respond. Charles and Butler (2004), for example, argue that in the face of change practitioners are forced to adopt strategies that try to balance their work ideals with the realities of the working environment. They illustrate this through identifying the impact on social workers of factors such as deprofessionalisation, increasing bureaucracy and risk management, arguing that a cycle of 'accommodation' can become established which, by requiring the suppression of feelings, can have negative consequences for both workers and those they work with. The authors encourage the use of a more reflective form of practice that enables practitioners to be aware of this effect and seek other more positive strategies (Charles and Butler, 2004).

Troman and Woods (2000, p. 255) argue that there is a 'considerable body of work which links teacher stress with the wholesale restructuring of national education systems' due to factors such as the intensification of work and subsequent recruitment difficulties. Through a series of interviews with teachers, they identify significant points in teachers' lives where they responded to stress through choosing one of a range of strategies. Key strategies they suggest are submitting to imposed changes (retreatism), attempting to find ways of reducing workloads or stress (downshifting), or making the most of new opportunities (self-actualisation).

Other ways in which practitioners' reactions to change can be categorised have been suggested, for example that they can be seen variously as 'commitment', 'enrolment' and 'compliance' (Senge, 1990, cited in Rogers and Reynolds, 2003). Rogers and Reynolds focus on internal psychological processes and argue that it can be helpful to distinguish between change and transition:

> Change is external and transition is internal, although there are many external indicators of the internal states. People in transition may move through recognisable stages from denial and resistance, to exploration and commitment, although not always in that order.
>
> (Rogers and Reynolds, 2003, p. 104)

In interviews with a range of social care professionals, Banks (2004, p. 189) also identifies a range of possible responses to change, including similar categories such as 'reluctant conformity' and 'principled quitting', but she also stresses the strategies of resisting or challenging change both individually and collectively. Practitioners can resist change if they see it as having negative consequences for families, for example the closure of a particular resource, or if decisions have been made contrary to the conclusions of consultation with children and families. Advocates of the need to develop a 'new' form of professional practice suggest that this needs to incorporate collective action in the broader social context with users of the services they are involved in providing (Banks, 2004). Practitioners can also actively lead change where they see how services can be improved, including embracing targeted outcomes, albeit with a critical perspective.

Practitioners protesting alongside service users against hospital closures

Lack of change and challenge can lead to institutionalised provision and poor practice and values. Any group of practitioners, in certain circumstances, can become complacent about current practice or not understand the need for change. In the extreme, damaging practices can be maintained, illustrated by enquiries into the abuse of children in care (for example, Waterhouse, 2000).

Some target setting by the government has focused attention on areas where practice has been in need of improvement. The educational progress of Looked After children, for example, has long been identified as an area of concern (Jackson, 1987) and a government target for improvement (DH, 1998). Harker et al. (2003), noting that improvements had been slower than anticipated, interviewed children and young people in care about their educational experience and those who supported their progress. This research provides many positive illustrations of supportive practice, particularly from teachers, foster carers and residential workers. However, it also found that 22 per cent of children and young people interviewed could not give an example of a supportive person. There were still many examples of children experiencing teachers stereotyping them on the basis of being Looked After, and of education not being a high priority for many social workers: 'some children were disappointed with the level of interest social workers exhibited towards their education' (Harker et al., 2003, p. 95).

While there have been further legal and policy changes across the UK addressing this issue, this research is a reminder that change occurs at different levels, and beyond policy, structural and resource changes, a more fundamental change can also be required in the mindset of some practitioners.

The examination by MacBeath et al. (2007) of schools which faced challenging circumstances explored whether and how governments can change schools through externally-led initiatives. One issue they stress is that the key interface in terms of change and improvement is that between teacher and child in the classroom, whereas many initiatives focus on senior and middle leaders in the school that could not be guaranteed to penetrate through to student learning. This study also considers the relationship between initiatives focused purely on the institution rather than including the surrounding community, frequently marked in the case of these schools by deprivation being 'still by far the biggest determinant of educational success':

> The problem is that no matter how great the improvement in teaching or how enhanced the skills of senior leaders, middle leaders, teachers and SIGs [School Improvement Groups] ... these schools are located in the force field of external pressures greater than the impetus and capacity for internal school improvement.
>
> (MacBeath et al., 2007, p. 102)

Practitioners may sometimes feel at the mercy of constant policy changes; however, top-down change is of course mediated through the realities of organisational and individual practice. Practitioners can be relatively powerful in interpreting policy when working directly with children and their families (Lymbery, 2000). Change may not always have the consequences originally intended as various levels of reinterpretation are passed through. The idea of this 'policy trajectory' is explored further in Chapter 4.

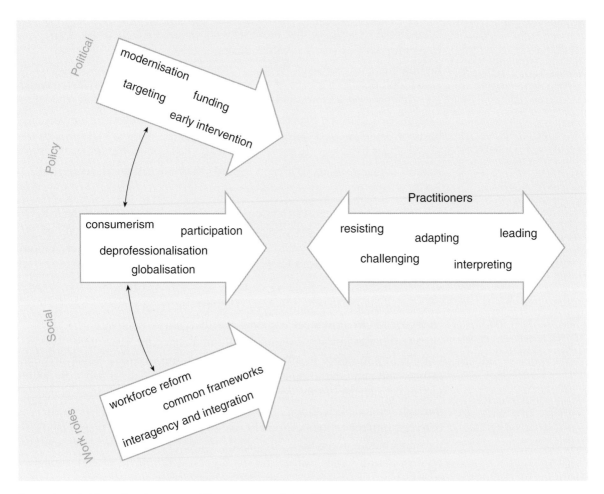

Examples of drivers for change and the response of practitioners

## Key points

1   The early twenty-first century has seen a concerted drive towards modernisation of the delivery of children's services, stressing the need for change and continuous improvement.

2   Organisational change can be a positive force to improve practice but is often experienced as destabilising.

3   Practitioners experiencing change can adopt a range of strategies which can be assisted by understanding the rationale for change and drawing on reflective practice.

# 2 Practitioners, families and the changing workforce

The experience of change is common across the children's workforce in virtually all settings, regardless of levels of training or history of professionalism. Any separation between the professional and the 'non-', 'semi-' or 'para-' professional will be largely artificial, but there can be particular issues for some groups of staff that have, or are aspiring to, the 'professional' label. The ideas of identity, ethics and culture are arguably more relevant to this second group. Changes and challenges to long-established practices and traditional ways of working will be felt more acutely by some groups of practitioners than others.

Thinking point 1.3   What do you think have been the main changes, over the last 5–10 years, in any *professional role* with which you are familiar in work with children (for example, for teachers, doctors, health visitors or social workers)?

Workforce structures in children's services have been changing significantly. Teachers, for example, have in the past had the classroom to themselves, but now they can expect to be sharing their working environment with other practitioners – teaching assistants and support staff (with a whole range of different titles), and volunteers. Between 1996 and 2006 the number of support staff providing additional learning resources in the classroom in England increased from 89,000 to 225,000 (National Statistics, 2007). This trend has been mirrored across the UK to varying degrees (see, for example, Scottish Executive, 2007). While approximately 85 per cent of teachers in primary and nursery education are women, the gender profile of support staff is also even more marked: it is estimated that only 1 per cent of teaching assistants are male (Open University, 2005). The same study also found recruitment from minority ethnic groups to be low at 1.8 per cent.

Teaching and classroom assistants have made a valuable contribution to children's education, including enabling the greater inclusion of disabled children within mainstream schooling. With schools managing budgets, there are also implications in the relative cost of different staff groups. The cost of resources is often an important factor driving change that may not be made explicit.

These changes are mirrored in other areas of practice with children. Social work assistants, once common, were significantly reduced in number as the emphasis on the importance of 'qualified staff' increased. Yet they have re-emerged in many teams in order to do tasks that are seen as not essential for social workers to undertake. Similarly, calls to the 'duty'

Head teacher   Class teacher   Parent helper

Teaching assistant   Caretaker   Learning support assistant

Children work with an increasing variety of practitioners in schools

social work team have increasingly been answered by a trained administrator rather than a social worker. In nursing and midwifery too, healthcare assistants undertake many roles that were previously the preserve of their more highly-trained colleagues, while some specifically trained nurses now prescribe certain drugs – a responsibility previously in the domain of doctors.

Thinking point 1.4   How well qualified do you think practitioners need to be who are working with children in children's centres and schools, teaching sports or listening to children read?

Closely tied into these changes are challenges to what it means to be a professional. What is it, for example, that distinguishes the teaching of a teacher from the 'helping' of others working in the classroom? Where are the clear boundaries? Does it matter whether or not they are maintained? Certainly this lack of clarity has been shown in a number of studies (for example, Russell et al., 2005) creating issues on both sides, with support staff, for example, feeling that their role is not fully recognised or rewarded in terms of status or pay:

> 'I would like to see an end to the two-tier system of support staff. Qualified and unqualified both doing the same job but with a huge difference in salary! I am responsible for the teaching of the groups I work with.'
>
> (Teaching assistant quoted in Russell et al., 2005, p. 185)

The emergence of such new roles can be both liberating and threatening. Teachers have broadly welcomed support staff, yet they have not in the past been trained for collaborative working (Open University, 2005). This pattern is repeated in other settings, leaving the complexities of working relationships to be sorted out in the front line of practice.

Fortunately children meanwhile seem to adapt without necessarily needing to distinguish the boundaries:

> 'Well the helpers seem to help out and do what the teacher does and the teacher seems to mostly teach children. But sometimes the helpers teach children.'
>
> (School pupil quoted in Eyres et al., 2004, p. 157)

Some commentators on the experience of teachers for example argue that they have experienced significant 'deprofessionalisation'. Professional judgement and discretion having been limited by prescribed methods, goals and learning outcomes, training has become more pragmatic and technical (Goodson and Hargreaves, 1996; Bottery and Wright, 2000).

This trend has been fuelled by the policies of successive governments, which have challenged working practices in health, education and social care. The agenda of 'modernising' the public sector which we explored earlier emphasised flexibility and choice to replace what were portrayed as old-style public service 'monoliths' (DH, 2002). New types of 'social care professional' were advocated that would also cross established divisions between professionals and knowledge bases:

> Family care workers combining the skills of the health visitor and the social worker to provide family support in times of trouble.
>
> (DH, 2002, webpage)

As equally significant as the promotion of this multi-skilled individual has been the acceleration of integrated teams within which professional identities can be renegotiated. At the same time, the idea of lead professionals (or key workers, designated professionals, etc.), who can be drawn from any discipline, has become increasingly central to new configurations of services advocated by government. The roles that professional identities play in interagency working are discussed in more detail in Chapter 3.

These trends can seem to be contradictory. In becoming a graduate occupation and having a regulatory body, social work has arguably increased its 'professional' status. At the same time, some commentators argue that it has been subject to these same forces of modernisation. As the emphasis on procedures, bureaucracy, managerialism and outcome targets has grown, so the ability of social workers to use independent professional judgement, or find creative solutions, can be reduced (Lymbery and Butler, 2004).

Practitioners without a 'professionalised' history or identity have become increasingly involved in acquiring training and qualifications as part of the drive to improve the skills level of the children's workforce. A central part of the modernisation agenda was the recognition that qualifications across the workforce varied but were at a low level in some sectors. Less than half of all staff working in early years, for example, were qualified to level 3 (A-level equivalent) (Children's Workforce Development Council (CWDC), 2006). The variety of qualifications and awarding bodies was also seen as confusing and led to the development of an integrated qualification framework. Again the aim was to shift the emphasis from:

> traditional professional boundaries to ensuring that the child's needs are met by someone with the right skills, whatever their job title or position in the organisation
>
> (DH, 2005, p. 43)

Virtually all practitioners have experienced the rising expectations of qualification and skills.

A further illustration of this change is the raising of the professional status of early years workers through the introduction of foundation degrees, and subsequently the explicit establishment initially in England of the early years professional. This role was seen as the mechanism by which the quality of early years provision was to be improved:

> They will act as an agent of change to improve practice in the settings in which they work. They will lead practice across the Early Years Foundation Stage (EYFS), support and mentor other practitioners and model the skills and behaviours that safeguard and promote good outcomes for children.
>
> (CWDC, 2006, p. 5)

The introduction and establishment of new professional groups to work in an arena where another group of professionals already operates can again be seen as a threat as well as an opportunity, as illustrated by one of the unions representing teachers in their initial responses to this development of a professional qualification to be seen as equivalent to their own:

> 'The Government has made it clear the early years qualification is not a substitute for a teaching qualification. Therefore, early years

## Fears new nursery staff will squeeze out teachers

*By Adi Bloom*

The new early years qualification may squeeze teachers out of nursery schools, the NUT fears. Steve Sinnott, the union's general secretary, has written to Alan Johnson, the Education Secretary, expressing concern that foundation stage pupils will not receive consistent support from qualified teachers.

"The foundation stage should have equal status with any other phase of the education system and for that to be so, it needs to be staffed by qualified teachers." Mr. Sinnott said. "The idea that teaching young children does not require the same degree of training must not be allowed to develop."

This year, 600 enrolled on the new three-month course to qualify to work with babies to 5-year-olds.

The Government target is to have one early years professional in every children's centre by 2010. But Mr. Sinnott believes this will undermine its target to have one teacher in every children's centre. He would prefer to see a teacher training programme developed to cover the birth-to-5 age range.

"The Government has made it clear the early years qualification is not a substitute for a teaching qualification. Therefore, early years professionals should not be substitutes for teachers. Their role needs to be clearly defined," he said.

Judith Pullen, the acting head of George Dent nursery in Darlington, employs a teacher in every class. "Nursery nurses are all very, very capable but they wouldn't argue their training covers planning and curriculum issues," she said. "It's a fundamentally important time in children's lives and you need to get the staffing right."

A DfES spokeswoman said the new early years professionals will not replace teachers, but high quality provision requires a well trained workforce with differing skills.

*The Times Educational Supplement; Friday December 1, 2006; No. 4713*

Restructuring of the workforce can generate new tensions

professionals should not be substitutes for teachers. Their role needs to be clearly defined'

(Steve Sinnott, quoted in Bloom, 2006, webpage)

## 2.1 Professionals in (late) modern society

The change and anxiety for all those working with children and families is also occurring within a broader social context where the 'status' of professionals is changing and being challenged. Scrutiny and criticism by the public and media can be intense: there are cases for damages in the court for negligence or 'failed' operations, or for compensation to children who were not protected from abuse. Professional claims to deploy 'expert' knowledge 'fairly' have been particularly undermined by high-profile enquiries (Frost, 2001). The trust in the ethics of professionals that they will always act in the best interests of their patients or clients is called into question.

High profile inquiries can lead to the loss of trust in professionals

We are all increasingly encouraged to see ourselves as 'consumers' of services with greater choice. Consumers have a different relationship with professionals than 'clients' or 'patients'. The drive towards modernisation discussed earlier made this shifting relationship a very explicit driver of change:

> People are becoming more demanding. Whether as consumers of goods and services in the market place, as citizens or as businesses affected by the policies and services which government provides.
>
> (Cabinet Office, 1999, p. 15)

'Patients' have in some cases been encouraged by government to become 'experts' on their own conditions (www.expertpatients.co.uk/public), and information available on the internet allows us all to believe that we can usefully acquire and apply information and expertise previously in the sole domain of the professional. This potentially enables a renegotiation of the power relationship between doctor and patient, teacher and parent, social worker and child.

Parents have been encouraged to have an increasing say in the running of schools, and parental 'power' has moved towards being equated with that of professional teacher. Of course in practice it is likely that this power will be easier to access for some parents, who have the appropriate **cultural capital**, than others. Without this, such changes are perhaps reinforcing rather than breaking down social, leading to educational, inequalities. Factors such as gender, ethnicity, class and social exclusion all influence the reality of this change. The importance of recognising these factors in work with parents and the role of different forms of capital is discussed in Chapter 2.

**Cultural capital** is a concept from sociology which refers to those forms of knowledge a person may have which gives them an advantage in society; for example, parents can give children the attitude and knowledge or 'cultural capital' that enables them to be comfortable and successful in the education system.

Most new developments in children's services require all practitioners to involve parents and children, encouraging accountability and greater participation. Their rights to be involved have been built into new partnership structures. This degree of participation can have many positive benefits, but shifting power relations clearly have an impact on practitioners and can create uncertainty if it is unclear what the shape of new relationships will be. Increasing participation is an issue not only of positioning people as consumers of services or even of children's rights, although fundamental, but also of changing and challenging perspectives on children themselves. Practitioners are increasingly recognising children's **agency** and that, if supported and enabled, children can, and want to, be involved in decisions that affect their lives (Leverett, 2008). The increasing adoption of schools councils, for example, supports children's rights and encourages active participation in schools (see, for example, Welsh Assembly Government, 2005). The extent to which this poses a challenge will fall differently on different professions and individual practitioners within them depending on their training, histories and value systems.

**Agency** is a term used in sociology to describe action by an individual or group that may transform the world around them.

Practitioners have also been directed to challenge each other's expertise. In analysing the inquiry into the death of Victoria Climbié (Laming, 2003), Parton (2004) argues that the inquiry report illustrates the breakdown of certainty over medical diagnosis:

> Not only does the report demonstrate numerous examples where 'erroneous' medical diagnosis and communications had a tragic impact on the way the case was handled by other professionals, but it also clearly argues that medical diagnosis and opinion must not be treated at face value and uncritically. Social workers, police officers and other doctors were all found culpable in this respect.
>
> (Parton, 2004, p. 87)

This led to the recommendation, in this instance to the police service, that:

> Training for child protection officers must equip them with the confidence to question the views of professionals in other agencies, including doctors, no matter how eminent those professionals appear to be.
>
> (Laming, 2003, p. 382)

The whole place of experts and expertise has been questioned more widely in a society seemingly infused with risk and uncertainty (Beck, 2004). The confidence that professionals have 'the answers' has been undermined not just as a result of challenges in the media but because of the multiplicity of other views and choices that now seem to have equal validity. A late modern or postmodern perspective would suggest that society no longer has the required shared value base:

> we could argue that dominant scientific values and the practices which harness scientific methods – such as medicine – have lost their privileged position as explanatory systems. They have become just one more set of claims about what is true and have to battle it out with other truth claims – for example, those of alternative therapies such as homeopathy or acupuncture.
>
> (Jones and Tucker, 2000, p. 10)

Professional expertise is not seen to have provided all the solutions to the problems experienced by society. In this sense all practitioners who have acquired professional status are operating in an environment where they experience a degree of deprofessionalisation.

This shift can be overstated; science and medicine continue to be powerful discourses in society and some professionals maintain privilege and power. In fact many of the social professions have sought to demonstrate clearer 'scientific' evidence for their decisions and judgements. An emphasis on 'evidence-based practice' has become increasingly significant for a wide range of practitioners. However, it is clear that relations between professionals and children and their families, and between professionals and other professionals, are on shifting ground.

Other social and economic phenomena impact upon professional practice. The increasingly complexity of family structures and relationships calls into question the skills of practitioners to engage effectively (Featherstone, 2004). Globalisation is radically altering society through economic change, labour force mobility, and more fluid and uncertain work patterns. UK society has become more ethnically and culturally diverse, reflected in practitioners themselves as well as those they work with. The reality of this changing context for practice is demonstrated by Nigel Parton (2004) in his comparison of two inquiries into child abuse thirty years apart. While superficially the inquiries into the deaths of the two girls Maria Colwell (in 1973) and Victoria Climbié, and the role played by the child protection agencies involved, may seem similar, Parton points out the radically different environments in which they took place. The Climbié inquiry reveals a social complexity marked by globalisation and individualisation not evident previously. Social workers, for example, themselves from a variety of countries, were working with large numbers of asylum-seeking families in organisations with increasingly complex procedures and systems of information technology (Parton, 2004).

Technological change has been equally profound, notably the broadening and speeding up of communication and access to knowledge particularly through electronic mediums. New initiatives are piloted but then often 'rolled out' by government as standard provision before there has been time to evaluate learning from the pilots. It can be this speed of change rather than change itself that can prove frustrating to practitioners.

> Further, and related to the issue of risk, the pace of contemporary change poses a problem for the professions ... Change is likely to have occurred in the legal structure in which they work, the organisation in which they work, and the technical detail of the specific field in which they operate. The claim to expertise then is doubly challenged – first, by the questioning of expertise by different social groups, and, second, by the pace of organisational and knowledge-based change they face.
>
> (Frost, 2001, p. 11)

## 2.2  The impact of change on children and families

---

**Practice box 1.3**

PLUS

Three major changes took place in 2006, demonstrating the ups and downs of funding arrangements, changing patterns of partnership working, and impact on disabled children.

Stirling Council cut the budget available to its Play Services, with staffed play sessions for 5–11-year-olds the main victim of the cuts. Play Services provision is now particularly focused on 'regeneration areas'. The reduction in Council organised opportunities has forced PLUS to offer more of its own provision for disabled children, which is inclusive only to the extent that siblings and friends are welcomed. Interagency work between PLUS and Play Services continues, but on a smaller scale.

The aim to establish school-based Circles of Support was met and funded for three years by Children in Need. A circle usually consists of 6–8 volunteers from the child's class who agree to meet weekly with the child and an adult facilitator, to work together to increase the child's social opportunities and choices. The circles are school-based and this project has led to a much closer relationship between PLUS and local 'mainstream' schools.

PLUS also introduced its Youth Inclusion Project in 2006, with a full-time project worker funded for three years by the Laidlaw Youth Trust. The Youth Inclusion Project works in partnership with youth organisations and after-school clubs to support the inclusion of disabled young people by offering information, advice, training and practical help to partner organisations. The project has already included work in support of Cubs, Brownies, Guides, Scouts, voluntary youth clubs, Council youth clubs and Out-of-School Care clubs.

Finally, there was a new project – the Networking Project – funded for two years by the Big Lottery Young People's Fund. This project offers tuition to members of PLUS aged 13+ to make use of electronic media such as social networking sites. There is a strong emphasis on personal safety on the internet as well as support and encouragement to make the most of the possibilities offered by sites such as Bebo and technologies such as instant messaging.

(Dumbleton, 2007)

Our focus so far has been on the challenges for practitioners of these currents of change but they inevitably affect the experience of children and their families as well. The evaluation of the impact of local government reorganisation discussed above also noted this effect. While services were on the whole maintained during the period of change, it nevertheless seemed to increase feelings of powerlessness:

> Users and carers, furthest removed from the process of reform, felt most vulnerable and least able to affect the way in which it occurred.

(Craig and Manthorpe, 1999b, webpage)

Even within the changing environment of user participation and 'parent power', large-scale change can be undertaken without participation, even clearly against the wishes of families using services. Major restructuring is rarely 'user-led'. Women, for example, may not feel they have any control over what they see as deteriorating health visiting services whatever the policy rationale for this and similar changes (Russell and Drennan, 2007).

Other trends affect the relationship between families and practitioners. While some parents are able to have a greater say in the running of schools, for example, other policies have arguably made them more responsible for their children's education. James and James (2001) suggest that developments such as contracts between home and school illustrate a 'narrowing of the gap' between education at school and in the family. However, any shift of power also implies a shift of responsibility. We may become 'expert patients', for example, but consequently we may also be increasingly taking on the responsibility for risk, and its associated anxiety (Beck, 2004).

While striving for 'continuous improvement' often results in constant change, research suggests that parents and children value the continuity of services and of individual workers:

> Several children and carers highlighted the negative impact of losing valued relationships with workers when time-limited interventions were withdrawn. Parents of children receiving mentoring support were concerned about the high turnover of staff and volunteers, which impacted on the relationships that the children were able to develop with their mentors.
>
> (Pinnock and Evans, 2007, p. 9)

Interviews in this study with children and parents in receipt of services from the Children's Fund reinforce the consistent finding that the establishment of trusting relationships with practitioners is a key element of effective service delivery, and that such relationships often require time to become established. Short-term services and staff turnover clearly work against this potential. Practitioners in the study were rightly concerned about whether long-term preventative services perpetuate dependency, and stressed the empowerment of families. However, given the policy emphasis on prevention, the study reveals the 'potential mismatch' between the views of practitioners and of children and their parents about the role of preventative services (Pinnock and Evans, 2007, p. 9).

The shifting funding and resource constraints that impact on projects and practitioners also affect the service delivery to children and their families in other ways:

> Some stakeholders from another partnership reported that resources had restricted the numbers of children and young people participating in various activities they had facilitated. A number of stakeholders also indicated that they felt that the rapidly changing policy context and atmosphere of uncertainty in relation to Children's Fund budget allocations had compromised levels of involvement of children, young people and families over the last year.
>
> (NECF, 2004b, p. 24)

Children's worlds are affected by these changes. For example, as we have seen, they have had to adapt to a range of adults being involved in supporting their learning in the classroom in addition to teachers. These trends may also result in children having the most contact with the least qualified staff – for example, children most in need of special assistance working primarily with assistants rather than teachers.

Children and their families can equally be agents of change, as they have been in relation to services for disabled children, for example, and may often be frustrated by the slow pace of it (Charlesworth, 2003). The national evaluation of the Children's Fund noted that children could see their involvement as bringing about change for other children, such as in the case of taking part in staff recruitment:

> 'I like doing the interviews and stuff because you know you are going to make a change for loads of different people, that you are going to make a good change for maybe some of the children that they are going to be working with and you are doing something good for someone, like you are giving them something new in their life and giving them change as well. It is like giving people a chance to change.'

(Child quoted in NECF, 2004b, p. 20)

Children and young people agreeing their feedback after interviewing candidates for the Group Director of Children's Services (Swindon Children's Fund)

Participation has the potential to include children and young people and can help overcome feelings of powerlessness. The same Children's Fund evaluation notes, however, that there is a lack of effective knowledge and practice in involving children and young people in a way that can bring about lasting change. Nevertheless attempts at 'mainstreaming' participation were felt to have had some impact on the prevailing culture, and the way in which organisations and practitioners can learn from this will be discussed further in Chapter 5.

## Key points

1   The composition of the children's workforce has been changing, causing a renegotiation of the boundaries between established and emerging roles.

2   Change has partially been fuelled by the desire to enhance the levels of qualifications and skills of the practitioners working with children.

3   Practitioners in 'professional' roles have also experienced challenges to their status and expertise as a result of broader social change.

4   Children and their families are creating change through their increased participation in the development of services – although not all are able to participate equally.

5   Families can experience changes within children's services as disruptive to relationships.

# 3 Change and interagency working

The developments in interprofessional and interagency working are an integral part of some of the changes discussed above. Breaking down existing boundaries between established roles is a central feature of many of the drivers for change. The increasing orientation of services around schools across the UK is just one example of major change in which more integrated services are central. Yet these policies can in themselves complicate interagency working as different government agendas can be competing rather than complimentary.

> 'I suspect it would be fair to say that one of the major changes in what's happening is the amount of legislation around at the moment. While it's always emphasising partnership, in many ways it's been destructive because people are so focused on delivering the agendas which they have been told they must do by their own agencies, that its kind of limiting some of the opportunities and choices and chances for partnership.'
>
> (Policy officer quoted in Charlesworth, 2003, p. 149)

Measuring the success or failure of these 'agendas' by performance targets and outcomes can also undermine more creative collaboration and establishment of trust between agencies and individuals (Charlesworth, 2003).

A number of the succeeding chapters will explore interagency working in more detail – its rationale, problems, effectiveness, and not least, its terminology – but our intention here is to focus on some of the issues raised by this aspect of change.

## 3.1 'Being confident enough to let go'

Just as there can be a multiplicity of roles operating in areas that were once the jurisdiction of just one practitioner, it seems inevitable therefore that changes arising from explicit requirements for interagency and interprofessional working will add an extra level of complexity. Practitioners bring with them a professional self-identity but also anxieties about their position and status. This seems particularly important if, as some commentators argue, one element of successful working together is the need for workers to each have confidence in their own professional identity.

> Another respondent argued that professionals need to be confident enough in their professional identity to let go of previous affiliations: 'People [in our team] don't seem to feel as though their

Teaching assistants can work with children using particular techniques drawn from those used by speech therapists

identity is just totally wrapped up with where they've come from, with their professional background. I think that [attitude] harnesses the strengths rather than identifies the weaknesses'.

(Anning et al., 2006, p. 72)

The alternative has been described as 'role-insecurity', which is much more likely to produce defensive responses, reducing the willingness to work across boundaries (Hornby and Atkins, 2000).

However, change can produce many more sources of threat and anxiety, and many things that practitioners may need to 'let go' of. One issue can be the erosion of what might have been seen as central elements of 'their role'. Anning et al. (2006), in their study of five multi-professional teams in children's services, cite the example of speech therapists training education staff to help children with language problems. This can be due to changes in children's services, for example, the increasing integration of children within schools, but is also influenced by a shortage of speech therapists.

Payne (2000) echoes the idea of 'letting go', using the phrase 'role release' to describe the idea that professionals can allow people from other occupational groups to undertake what would normally be seen as part of their primary role. Such blurring of roles can, however, be even more problematic if this is seen as a move from specialism to genericism:

'I still want to offer a professional service from a health perspective'

(Nurse quoted in Banks, 2004, p. 135)

> 'Yes I am a nurse, I don't write reports for court. Only stuff to do with health'
>
> (Nurse quoted in Anning et al., 2006, p. 66)

> 'You get a blurring of professional roles which I think is dangerous. Because at the end of the day social workers think they know what nurses and doctors do, but they don't. Similarly nurses ... think they know what social workers do, but they don't'
>
> (Social worker quoted in Davies, 2003, p. 203)

The emphasis placed on flexibility does not contradict the place of specialist knowledge; integrated teams often still value the contribution of different expertise.

The issue of labels can be particularly symbolic for some workers, both in terms of feelings about their own status:

> 'First of all we called ourselves project workers, which I absolutely hated, because that says we could be someone who had been employed as a volunteer you know, off the streets, without qualifications'
>
> (Practitioner quoted in Anning et al., 2006, p. 72)

and perhaps too for relationships with families they are working with:

> 'I feel happy with the label but I'm not sure that the community fully understands the label. I think it can be a little confusing'
>
> (Practitioner quoted in Anning et al., 2006, p. 73)

This perhaps mirrors the experience of practitioners labelling 'service users' – for both groups, how you are labelled may have important consequences not least for accessing resources.

Within the confusion of terminology, Banks (2004) argues that this 'letting go' could be characterised as the crucial distinction between multi-professional and interprofessional working:

> Carrier and Kendall (1995, p. 10) distinguish *multiprofessional* working, where the traditional forms and divisions of professional knowledge and authority are retained, from *interprofessional*, where there is a willingness to share and give up exclusive claims to specialist knowledge if the needs of service users can be better met by members of other professional groups. Many community-based teams are currently somewhere between multiprofessional and interprofessionals, with tensions apparent as they shift along the continuum.
>
> (Banks, 2004, p. 127)

Some of the research studies mentioned above do cite examples of professionals who were able to emerge from these challenges with a positive sense of a new identity and ultimately accept new labels. Anning et al. (2006) noted practitioners in a child development team who adapted to the change:

> 'I think myself and the physio do a lot of role blurring in terms of treating the child as a whole in certain aspects but I don't feel threatened by that. I know some people might.'
>
> (Anning et al., 2006, p. 73)

and practitioners in a Child and Adolescent Mental Health Service (CAMHS) team who were open to adopting such new labels and identities:

> 'I don't see myself as an ex-teacher or a counsellor. I see myself as a CAMH worker'
>
> (Anning et al., 2006, p. 73)

> Professionals who struggled through the pain of transformation to the gains of a new professional identity reported an enhanced sense of 'who I am'.
>
> (Anning et al., 2006, p. 75)

Thinking point 1.5   Can you apply any of these issues to your own role or the role of someone you know working with children?

## 3.2 Lead professionals and common cores

Given the significance of labels, the emergence of the 'lead professional' label seems a particularly important development. This is another strand of change within the reform the children's workforce.

Some of the impetus from this has come from children and parents who have argued that the professional system has been too complicated, requiring them to relate to too many people. This argument has long been advanced in relation to services for disabled children (Watson et al., 2002), but the principle of a single worker liaising between family and a network of practitioners has been adopted not just for disabled children (see, for example, HM Treasury/DfES, 2007) but more widely as a response to the coordination of services from a range of agencies (Scottish Executive, 2006; DfES, 2003a).

The importance of the family's perspective has also been preserved, at least in principle:

> You and your child will have a say in who should be the lead professional.
>
> (DfES, 2005c, p. 2)

However, the extent of this 'say' remains to be tested in the response of agencies, individuals and the rapid staff turnover experienced in areas of children's services.

This role may not be a radical departure from other incarnations of key workers or key professionals and link workers, but the scale of its use seems set to become much more widespread in children's services. This change is not necessarily a 'blurring' of roles as it is not anticipated that this 'lead' will provide all services but that they will be the initial point of contact, liaising with other professionals where necessary. However, in theory, and in practice, a wide range of professionals can perform this role.

> This could include (but is not limited to) personal advisers, health visitors, midwives, youth workers, family workers, substance misuse workers, nursery nurses, educational welfare officers, community children's nurses, school nurses and support staff such as learning mentors working in schools.
>
> Such practitioners could be drawn from voluntary sector organisations or from statutory services, depending on the agencies currently involved with the child or young person.
>
> (DfES, 2005d, webpage)

Similarly, in Scotland consultation on the proposal for lead professionals reflected the view that 'the lead professional should be appointed based on the needs of an individual child' and noted that 'the role should not automatically fall to social work' (Scottish Executive, 2006).

Nevertheless, specific skills may be needed for this role to work as it should, in forming relationships both with children and their families and with other professionals. Practitioners in this role have emphasised the importance of listening, empathy, counselling skills, and gaining confidence and trust, that is, core interpersonal skills rather than specialist knowledge (Halliday and Asthana, 2004).

These trends suggest a commonality of skills for those operating in this role, and government policies have also encouraged this development across children's services. In England a core of skills and knowledge was identified not just for lead professionals but for the whole range of practitioners working with children (DfES, 2005a). A common framework for assessing children was similarly designed to be used by any – whoever is the most appropriate – practitioner (DfES, 2005b). (The implementation of this framework is analysed in Chapter 4.) This again raises the issue of the increasing interchangeability of practitioner roles.

Here is one perspective on the core skills identified for success as a lead professional:

- Strong communication skills including diplomacy and sensitivity to the needs of others

- An ability to establish successful and trusting relationships with children, young people and families, and to communicate without jargon

- An ability to empower children, young people and families to work in partnership with other practitioners and to be able to make informed choices about the support they require and receive

- The capacity to support children, young people or parents/carers in implementing a range of strategies to enable them to achieve their potential

- An ability to establish effective and professional relationships with colleagues from different backgrounds

- An ability to convene meetings and discussions with different practitioners

- An ability to translate their own knowledge and understanding into effective practice

- An ability to work in partnership with other practitioners to deliver effective interventions and support for children, young people and families.

(DfES, 2005d, webpage)

## 3.3 Managing to change

There is a substantial literature on organisational change that it is not the intention of this chapter to summarise. Clearly, however, one key factor that emerges from the researching of change in children's services is the importance of the way change is managed. Various models of working with change are available, but they all usually stress the need for an understanding of the way people react to change and strategies for gaining the commitment of staff.

> 'I can see the importance of change and you learn from it ... It is important to acknowledge feelings and to help people by valuing what they have achieved: from that and their strengths change can come. People need time to look at what they are afraid of and to go through change with their feelings acknowledged.'

> ('Under-eights' project manager quoted in Seden, 2003, p. 112)

|  | Loss | Gain |
|---|---|---|
| **Personal** | Feeling deskilled | New co-training opportunities |
|  | Clarity of role | Interesting challenges |
|  | Current colleagues | Better communication with the practitioners with whom I mainly work |
| **Organisational** | Confusion | Better service for children |
|  | Reorganisation costs | Access to new resources |

A balance sheet for change: a simple way of working with practitioners to unpick the gains and losses they experience through the change process. (Adapted from Rogers and Reynolds, 2003a)

Recognition of the importance of the role of managers seems equally true of working across boundaries:

> Our work in this field suggests that perhaps the key variable in implementing effective practice is the leadership offered by managers. Effective leadership is an essential and challenging element in developing effective joined-up working. It involves individuals who can work in the new, ever-changing world of joined-up working that involves networking and boundary crossing.
>
> (Frost and Lloyd, 2006, p. 13)

Anning et al. (2006) suggest that a manager needs to be 'a chameleon', constantly able to adapt to change. Tronto (2001) has argued that this ability is true for all practitioners and that working within a constantly changing environment is a key element of professional competence:

> 'It also requires the capacity to act in a constantly changing world and be both cautious and confident about changing conditions'
>
> (Tronto, 2001, quoted in Banks, 2004, p. 182)

## Key points

1   Bringing practitioners together from different backgrounds can be challenging to established roles. Interprofessional working can also lead to the creation of new identities.

2   Government policy has increasingly stressed the common elements of skills and knowledge for all those working with children, including the development of lead roles.

3   The successful management of change is a key skill needed by practitioners and managers alike.

## Conclusion

Change is an experience common to all practitioners to varying degrees, which impacts on their work individually and their ability to work together. It may be that an understanding of change and its gains and losses can help practitioners reflect on and react to the forces impacting upon them. This can include the role that children and families play themselves in initiating and contributing to change. It is also important to recognise that all work undertaken with children, their families and carers takes place within the broad social arena, which will continue to throw up new and complex challenges in the future as in the past.

# References

Anning, A., Cottrell, D., Frost, N., Green, J. and Robinson, M. (2006) *Developing Multiprofessional Teamwork for Integrated Children's Services*, Maidenhead, Open University Press.

Banks, S. (2004) *Ethics, Accountability and the Social Professions*, Basingstoke, Palgrave Macmillan.

Beck, U. (2004) *Risk Society: Towards a New Modernity*, London, Sage.

Bloom, A. (2006) 'Fears new nursery staff will squeeze out teachers', *Times Educational Supplement*, 1 December, available online at <http://www.tes.co.uk/search/story/?story_id=2316493>, accessed 7 September 2007.

Bottery, M. and Wright, N. (2000) *Teachers and the State: Towards a Directed Profession*, London, Routledge.

Cabinet Office (1999) *Modernising Government*, London, The Stationery Office.

Carrier, J. and Kendall, I. (1995) 'Professionalism and interprofessionalism in health and community care: some theoretical issues' in Owens, P., Carrier, J. and Horder, J. (eds) *Interprofessional Issues in Community and Primary Health Care*, Basingstoke, Macmillan.

Charles, M. and Butler, S. (2004) 'Social workers' management of organisational change' in Lymbery, M. and Butler, S. (eds) *Social Work Ideals and Practice Realities*, Basingstoke, Palgrave Macmillan.

Charlesworth, J. (2003) 'Managing across professional and agency boundaries' in Seden, J. and Reynolds, J. (eds) *Managing Care in Practice*, London, The Open University/Routledge, pp. 139–164.

Children's Workforce Development Council (CWDC) (2006) *Early Years Professional National Standards*, available online at <http://www.cwdcouncil.org.uk/pdf/Early%20Years/EYP_National_Standards_July_2006.pdf>, accessed 3 September 2007.

Craig, G., Hill, M., Manthorpe, J., Tisdall, K., Monaghan, B. and Wheelaghan, S. (2000) 'Picking up the pieces: local government reorganisation and voluntary sector children's services', *Children & Society*, vol. 14, no. 2, pp. 85–97.

Craig, G. and Manthorpe, J. (1999a) *Unfinished Business? Local Government Reorganisation and Social Services*, Bristol, The Policy Press.

Craig, G. and Manthorpe, J. (1999b) *The Impact of Local Government Reorganisation on Social Services Work*, Joseph Rowntree Foundation, available online at <http://www.jrf.org.uk/knowledge/findings/government/999.asp>, accessed 2 January 2008.

Davies, C. (2003) 'Workers, professions and identity' in Henderson, J. and Atkinson, D. (eds) *Managing Care in Context*, London, The Open University/Routledge.

Department for Education and Skills (DfES) (2003a) *Every Child Matters*, London, The Stationery Office.

Department for Education and Skills (DfES) (2005a) *Common Core of Skills and Knowledge for the Children's Workforce*, Nottingham, DfES.

Department for Education and Skills (DfES) (2005b) *The Common Assessment Framework*, London, The Stationery Office.

Department for Education and Skills (DfES) (2005c) *Every Child Matters: What is the Common Assessment Framework?*, available online at <http://www.everychildmatters.gov.uk/_files/9C0FA5C9D5787362C313926CDD6D7E4F.pdf>, accessed 2 January 2008.

Department for Education and Skills (DfES) (2005d) *Every Child Matters: Lead Professional*, available online at <http://www.everychildmatters.gov.uk/deliveringservices/leadprofessional>, accessed 2 January 2008.

Department of Health (DH) (1997) *The New NHS – Modern, Dependable*, London, The Stationery Office.

Department of Health (DH) (1998) *Quality Protects: Framework for Action*, London, DH/The Stationery Office.

Department of Health (DH) (2002) *Speech by the Rt Hon Alan Milburn MP, 16th October 2002: Reforming Social Services*, available online at <http://www.dh.gov.uk/en/News/Speeches/Speecheslist/DH_4031620>, accessed 3 September 2007.

Department of Health (DH) (2005) *Report from the National Clinical Director for Children on the Development of the National Service Framework for Children, Young People and Maternity Services*, London, DH.

Dumbleton, S. (2005) 'Widening opportunities for disabled children in Stirling: a voluntary body initiative' in Glaister, A. and Glaister, B. (eds) *Inter-Agency Collaboration – Providing for Children*, Edinburgh, Dunedin Academic Press, pp. 36–46.

Dumbleton, S. (2007) 'Practice box 1.3, Plus' in Foley, P. and Rixon, A. *Changing Children's Services: Working and Learning Together*, Bristol, Policy Press/Milton Keynes, Open University.

Eyres, I., Cable, C., Hancock, R. and Turner, J. (2004) '"Whoops, I forgot David": children's perceptions of the adults who work in their classrooms', *Early Years*, vol. 24, no. 2, pp. 149–162.

Featherstone, B. (2004) *Family Life and Family Support: A Feminist Analysis*, Basingstoke, Palgrave Macmillan.

Frost, N. (2001) 'Professionalism, change and the politics of lifelong learning', *Studies in Continuing Education*, vol. 23, no. 1, pp. 5–17.

Frost, N. and Lloyd, A. (2006) 'Implementing multi-disciplinary teamwork in the new child welfare policy environment', *Journal of Integrated Care*, vol. 14, no. 2, pp. 11–17.

Goodson, I.F. and Hargreaves, A. (eds) (1996) *Teachers' Professional Lives*, London, Falmer Press.

Halliday, J. and Asthana, S. (2004) 'The emergent role of the link worker: a study in collaboration', *Journal of Interprofessional Care*, vol. 18, no. 1, pp. 17–28.

Harker, R.M., Dobel-Ober, D., Lawrence, J., Berridge, D. and Sinclair, R. (2003) 'Who takes care of education? Looked after children's perceptions of support for educational progress', *Child & Family Social Work*, vol. 8, no. 2, pp. 89–100.

HM Treasury/Department for Education and Skills (DfES) (2007) *Aiming High for Disabled Children: Better Support for Families*, London, HM Treasury/DfES.

Hornby, S. and Atkins, J. (2000) *Collaborative Care: Interprofessional, Interagency and Interpersonal* (2nd edn), Oxford, Blackwell Science.

Hudson, B. (2007) 'What lies ahead for partnership working? Collaborative contexts and policy tensions', *Journal of Integrated Care*, vol. 15, no. 3, pp. 29–36.

Jackson, S. (1987) 'Residential care and education', *Children & Society*, vol. 2, pp. 335–350.

James, A.L. and James, A. (2001) 'Tightening the net: children, community, and control', *British Journal of Sociology*, vol. 52, no. 2, pp. 211–228.

Jones, L. and Tucker, S. (2000) 'Exploring continuity and change' in Brechin, A., Brown, H. and Eby, M.A. (eds) *Critical Practice in Health and Social Care*, London, The Open University/Sage, pp. 3–24.

Laming, Lord (2003) *The Victoria Climbié Inquiry*, London, The Stationery Office.

Leverett, S. (2008) 'Children's participation' in Foley, P and Leverett, S. (eds) (2008) *Connecting with Children: Developing Working Relationships*, Bristol, The Policy Press.

Lymbery, M. (2000) 'The retreat from professionalism: from social worker to care manager' in Malin, N. (ed.) *Professionalism, Boundaries and the Workplace*, London, Routledge, pp. 123–138.

Lymbery, M. and Butler, S. (eds) (2004) *Social Work Ideals and Practice Realities*, Basingstoke, Palgrave Macmillan.

MacBeath, J., Gray, J., Cullen, J., Frost, D., Steward, S. and Swaffield, S. (2007) *Schools on the Edge: Responding to Challenging Circumstances*, London, Paul Chapman.

National Evaluation of the Children's Fund (NECF) (2004a) *Summary of Key Learning Points from NECF Reports on Participation, Prevention and Multi-agency Working*, Research Brief No. RBX11–04, London, DfES.

National Evaluation of the Children's Fund (NECF) (2004b) *Children, Young People, Parents and Carers' Participation in Children's Fund Case Study Partnerships*, Research Report No. 602, London, DfES.

National Statistics (2007) *Teacher numbers*, available online at <http://www.statistics.gov.uk/cci/nugget.asp?id=1765>, accessed 3 September 2007.

Open University (2005) E111 *Supporting Learning in Primary Schools*, Study Topic 1, 'Teaching assistants today', Milton Keynes, The Open University.

Parton, N. (2004) 'From Maria Colwell to Victoria Climbié: reflections on public inquiries into child abuse a generation apart', *Child Abuse Review,* vol. 13, no. 2, pp. 80–94.

Payne, M. (2000) *Teamwork in Multiprofessional Care*, Basingstoke, Palgrave Macmillan.

Pinnock, M. and Dimmock, B. (2003) 'Managing for outcomes' in Henderson, J. and Atkinson, D. (eds) *Managing Care in Context*, London, The Open University/Routledge, pp. 257–282.

Pinnock, K. and Evans, R. (2007) 'Developing responsive preventative practices: key messages from children's and families' experiences of the Children's Fund', *Children & Society*, available online at <http://www.blackwell-synergy.com/doi/full/10.1111/j.1099–0860.2007.00081.x>, accessed 22 October 2007.

Rogers, A. and Reynolds, J. (2003) 'Leadership and vision' in Seden, J. and Reynolds, J. (eds) *Managing Care in Practice*, London, The Open University/Routledge, pp. 57–82.

Rogers, A. and Reynolds, J. (2003a) 'Managing change' in Seden, J. and Reynolds, J. (eds) *Managing Care in Practice*, London, The Open University/Routledge.

Russell, A., Blatchford, P., Bassett, P., Brown, P. and Martin, C. (2005) 'The views of teaching assistants in English key stage 2 classes on their role, training and job satisfaction', *Educational Research*, vol. 47, no. 2, pp. 175–189.

Russell, S. and Drennan, V. (2007) 'Mothers' views of the health visiting service in the UK: a web-based survey', *Community Practitioner*, vol. 80, no. 8, pp. 22–26.

Scottish Executive (2001) *Changing Children's Services Fund*, Edinburgh, Scottish Executive.

Scottish Executive (2003) *Partnership for Care: Scotland's Health White Paper*, Edinburgh, Scottish Executive.

Scottish Executive (2006) *Getting It Right for Every Child: Proposals for Action – Analysis of Consultation Responses*, Edinburgh, Scottish Executive.

Scottish Executive (2007) *Classroom assistants*, available online at <http://www.scotland.gov.uk/Topics/People/Young-People/Early-Education-Child-Care/18096/11651>, accessed 3 September 2007.

Seden, J. (2003) 'Managers and their organisations' in Henderson, J. and Atkinson, D. (eds) *Managing Care in Context*, London, The Open University/Routledge, pp. 105–132.

Senge, P. (1990) *The Fifth Discipline: The Art and Practice of the Learning Organization*, London, Doubleday/Century Business.

Social Enterprise Coalition (2007) *Health Business: A Guide to Social Enterprise in Health and Social Care*, available online at <http://www.socialenterprise.org.uk/documents/Healthy_Business.pdf>, accessed 2 January 2008.

Troman, G. and Woods, P. (2000) 'Careers under stress: teacher adaptations at a time of intensive reform', *Journal of Educational Change*, vol. 1, no. 3, pp. 253–275.

Tronto, J. (2001) 'Does managing professionals affect professional ethics? Competence, autonomy and care' in DesAutels, P. and Waugh, J. (eds) *Feminists Doing Ethics*, Lanham, MD, Rowman & Littlefield, pp. 187–202.

Tunstill, J., Aldgate, J. and Hughes, M. (2007) *Improving Children's Services Networks: Lessons from Family Centres*, London, Jessica Kingsley.

Waterhouse, S. (2000) *Lost in Care: Report of the Tribunal of Inquiry into the Abuse of Children in Care in the Former County Council Areas of Gwynedd and Clwyd since 1974*, London, The Stationery Office.

Watson, D., Townsley, R., Abbott, D. and Latham, P. (2002) *Working Together? Multi-agency Working in Services to Disabled Children with ComplexHealth Care Needs and Their Families: A Literature Review*, Birmingham, Handsel Trust.

Welsh Assembly Government (2005) *The School Councils (Wales) Regulations 2005*, Cardiff, The Stationery Office.

# Chapter 2

## Parenting: politics and concepts for practice

Stephen Leverett

## Introduction

Throughout the twentieth century, the state progressively and simultaneously increased its level of support to, and its surveillance of, parents and carers (in bringing up children). Much of this centred on ensuring children were healthy, educated and safe. Although sometimes difficult to translate into practice, the ethos of *working together with parents* was usually maintained even in situations requiring more interventionist approaches such as child protection. This has continued into the twenty-first century when the expected outcomes for children from the perspective of the state have been more clearly defined and linked to the political and economic goals of the day (for example, children's rights, social inclusion, respect and citizenship, competitive economy). There has been a constant shifting of the boundaries between the state, families and the voluntary and private sectors (Wasoff and Cunningham-Burley, 2005) in terms of responsibilities for education and childcare, financial support for children and the management of children's behaviour. Consequently the expectations and demands placed upon parents and carers are more clearly stated (and open to scrutiny), extending their responsibility to promote wellbeing for their children to the wellbeing of society:

> an outsider tracking the thrust of policy and practice development over recent years might be forgiven for concluding that we as a nation had decided that almost any social ill – poverty, social exclusion, crime and anti-social behaviour, poor educational attainment, poor mental and emotional health – could be remedied by improving parenting skills
>
> (Moran et al., 2004, p. 14)

The willingness and ability of parents to fulfil these responsibilities can often be affected by where they and their children are positioned, socially, economically or culturally. In response there has been a dramatic increase in interagency support initiatives for parents, some of which are built around existing universal services, whilst others target, or even coerce, parents into fulfilling these responsibilities.

The purpose of this chapter is to examine how parents fulfil the state's expectations and make use of the support available to them. We introduce the theoretical concepts of economic, human, social and cultural capital, and consider ways in which the state can enhance these assets to support parenting.

## Core questions

- Whom do children and professionals identify as parents and carers?
- What inhibits or enhances parenting capacity?
- In which political context does support for parents operate?
- What are the concepts of economic, human, social, and cultural capital, and how can they help to analyse parenting and parenting support?
- How do different types of capital influence social policies and practice initiatives designed to support parents?

# 1 Defining parents and parenting

Thinking point 2.1  Who are parents/carers and what do they do?

If we were to write a job description for the role of parent or carer it would surely present itself as a complex and challenging task, subject to high levels of scrutiny and anxiety. Despite this, significant numbers of people in all populations continue to derive great pleasure and satisfaction from doing it. Attention has been drawn to the way in which those directly involved in the day-to-day care of children can be supported by agencies and adults (both formal and informal) located in a wider network. The African proverb 'It takes a village to raise a child' is often cited to reinforce this point. It has also been formalised in some policies, for example the Scottish Charter for Grandchildren:

> Families come in all shapes and sizes. Grandparents, aunts, uncles and cousins can all play an important role in nurturing children. While parents are responsible for caring for children and ensuring their needs are met, the wider family can play a vital supporting role.
>
> (Scottish Executive, 2006, p. 1)

It can be easy to overlook the wide diversity of relationships and cultures within which children are embedded, but children's own accounts reveal that they recognise the interconnectedness of the wider network of people who contribute in different ways to their wellbeing:

> 'People help little children – like teachers, dad, the bank, the big sister, mam, people, uncle, your grandma, grandpa, hospital, auntie'
>
> (Child quoted in Crowley and Vulliamy, 2003, p. 11)

Scotland has introduced a charter for grandchildren acknowledging the important role of grandparents in some children's lives

Yet they also reveal that children 'hold differentiated views of key people in their networks, with parents (particularly mothers) and friends usually being the main confidants' (Hill, 2005, p. 81). As we will discuss later, it makes sense to identify and work alongside adults who are the most closely involved in children's day-to-day care.

Definitions of parenting appear to centre on people who take the most significant role in this set of interrelationships within a home or family context 'including biological parents, step-parents, foster parents, adoptive parents, grandparents or other relatives' (Moran et al., 2004, p. 6). In this chapter 'parents' has been used as shorthand to include 'mothers, fathers, carers and other adults with responsibility for caring for a child, including looked after children' (DfES, 2006, p. 3). Carers acknowledged in this definition can include siblings, other family members and neighbours, as well as statutory and voluntary care provided by foster carers and residential care staff.

A distinction can be made between people who have *parental responsibility* for a child and people who provide care for the child. These may or may not be the same person or people. Parental responsibility is a term used across the UK to describe the legal relationship between parents and children. It governs all the rights, duties, powers and responsibilities which by law a parent of a child has in relation to the child. People who have parental responsibility for a child can take decisions about a range of matters such as education, religion and consent to medical treatment for the child. Birth mothers automatically have parental responsibility, as do married fathers or unmarried fathers who either are named on their child's birth certificate or legally acquire responsibility. Others, including local authorities, can acquire or share parental responsibility if this is agreed by a court. All parties with parental responsibility have to cooperate in making decisions on behalf of the child, using the court as a last resort to resolve disagreements. It is important for professionals to identify and work with the people who have parental responsibility for a particular child. As the following case illustrates, this can be complicated for some children; however, it is still possible for adults to work in partnership in the best interests of the child.

Teachers in a residential school for disabled children mostly discuss a student's day-to-day issues (homework and behaviour) with both the individual child and the school-based residential care workers. However, whenever teachers need to discuss broader curriculum issues (concerning religion, diet or sex education) they will consult with the child's parents. If one of the children is the subject of a care order, meaning parental responsibility is shared between the local authority and the child's parents, teachers have to liaise with both. All children in the Looked After care system have a regular statutory review, and through their attendance teachers can develop a good working relationship with the parents, the residential care staff and social workers. They are also able to contribute to the ongoing care plan.

Parenting is a multifaceted process requiring time, skills, knowledge and values. It often involves living with the child and performing discrete activities or physical tasks such as preparing food, buying and washing their clothes or liaising with health and education professionals. It also includes general behaviour such as being a role model, and providing encouragement and physical or emotional comfort. Underpinning all of these and making parenting unique, however, is mutual affection in an enduring, secure, trusting, responsive and loving relationship. The latter is particularly important; one young person's view on what will help you achieve your potential was:

> 'You need encouragement – someone behind you ... the love of your family, advice and help ... so you can believe you can do it'
>
> (Crowley and Vulliamy, 2003, p. 9)

There are several weaknesses in how parenting features in political and social debates and definitions. Frequently the gender and generational dimensions are down-played; the next section, for example, highlights how it is mainly women who are actively involved in parenting. But also the part played by children in parenting is overlooked. It is evident in the fact that although *parent* equates to *child* and *parenthood* equates to *childhood*, the act of *parenting* has no equivalent word, despite evidence that all children actively engage and contribute to the process of being parented. It could be argued that children make parents just as parents make children. Although all children develop skills and competencies in partnership with parents, their contribution is particularly evident in more specific situations such as where they live with an ill, disabled or drug-misusing relative and directly perform tasks associated with parenting.

## Key points

1   Children are embedded in a range of networks and relationships that includes people with and without parental responsibility.

2   Parenting is both a role and a process requiring a range of skills, knowledge and values.

3   Children are active social agents who contribute in many different ways to the role and process of parenting.

# 2  The politics of parenting

Parenting has variously been constructed as a vehicle of socialisation, as the root of inequitable life chances and as a resource or source of strength for children, practitioners and service providers. Attention has been drawn to the differences between parents in relation to factors such as gender, generation and social class. The state has maintained a relatively *laissez faire* attitude to families and parenting, intervening only when necessary to ensure children's safety and wellbeing. However, since 1997 the state has been more willing to intervene with a range of specific social and economic policy objectives related to anti-social behaviour, poverty, educational standards, revitalising the labour market, and so on, that directly involve or affect parents. In this section we briefly review some of the political debates that surround parenting and consider some of the implications for people working with children and families.

*Laissez faire* is a French phrase meaning 'leave alone'. In English it has been adopted as a political term to describe minimal interference by the state in people's lives. It is the opposite of an interventionist (or 'nanny') state.

Policy and practice with children have been directly influenced by, or had to contend with, debates concerning the suitability (or otherwise) of specific groups of parents or carers (including lone parents, lesbian and gay parents, Black parents for Black children). Subsequently there has been a continuation of the belief in the early twenty-first century that families are the places best suited for most children to be reared, as long as they are able to uphold the best interests of any individual child. Progress has been made in accepting the diverse ways families are structured and the way that parent–child or carer–child relationships are configured. For example, at the time of writing, legislation in England, Wales and Scotland makes it possible for unmarried partners, including same-sex couples, to adopt jointly, giving them the same parenting rights as heterosexual couples. One government report (PMSU, 2007, p. 21) clearly states that social policy should concentrate on improving 'educational attainment, the employment prospects of parents, and the strength of family relationships – rather than attempting to incentivise the creation of particular family types'. A key implication has been the need to ensure that practitioners overcome any preconceptions or prejudices and that services and agencies represent and seek to make welcome the rich diversity of parents and families.

Parenting is often presented as a gender-neutral practice despite the fact that the majority of childcare is carried out by women. Women rather than men are likely to spend more time with children and have direct contact with children's services such as GPs and schools. They are also likely to be the parents receiving more targeted provision. 'Consequently, it is primarily mothers who bear the brunt of initiatives and sanctions designed to promote 'good parenting' (Gillies, 2005, p. 841), including the more coercive policies. In a study of parenting programmes (Ghate and Ramella, 2002) carried out by the Youth Justice Board (which included parents referred by Parenting Orders), 81 per cent of participants were female.

Whilst the term *parent* or *parenting* in social policy may highlight the similarities between men's and women's experience of bringing up children, 'it can obscure the need to pay attention to their differing positions' (Daniel et al., 2005, p. 1344). Some commentators argue that child welfare policies should promote or mainstream gender equality (Daniel et al., 2005) and that some policies are unlikely to meet with total success unless gender inequality is fully addressed (Bradshaw et al., 2003). As an example they claim that attempts to eradicate child poverty should acknowledge that women are significantly more likely than men to be poor. Although the New Labour government provided more support and resources for working mothers and poorer families, and in 2007 introduced a duty requiring local authorities to promote gender equality and eliminate sex discrimination, it remains to be seen whether this is sufficient to address the covert or hidden causes of women's poverty identified by Bradshaw et al. (2003), in particular the unequal allocation of time, money and other resources within the domestic sphere. Familial and social pressures that construct women as primarily child carers create conflicts for some mothers who at the same time are being encouraged, or coerced, by the government into paid employment.

Some people argue for a more effective use of family and employment policy to encourage men into sharing childcare responsibilities, including adequately paid paternity leave (Women's Budget Group, 2005). Historically, attempts to attract fathers into support programmes such as Sure Start resulted in only 'low levels' of involvement (Lloyd et al., 2003). Subsequently in England the government has attempted to broaden the range of ways that children's centres can attract and involve fathers:

- as direct care-givers to their children ...
- in understanding children's developmental needs ...
- in demonstrating their emotional attachment to their children ...
- in developing and maintaining a positive, co-operative relationship with the mother of their children ...
- in developing their own support networks ...
- finding work, training for work or learning opportunities to enable them to better support their families, and financial support for such learning ...
- help with benefits, child support responsibilities, and entitlements, including housing; and
- during times of exceptional stress, for example following separation or on arrival in the UK as a refugee.

(Sure Start, 2006, p. 82)

Thinking point 2.2    In what ways, if at all, do these aims to involve fathers address gender inequality and the deep-seated reality that women rather than men look after children? What else could be done?

Some services actively encourage fathers to become more involved in caring for their children

The guidance document in which these aims are listed devotes only one chapter specifically to attracting fathers, which reinforces their position as 'other'. It also fails to make any overt reference to gender equality. Work with fathers will fall onto the shoulders of a largely female workforce, yet the guidance fails to address many of the factors considered by Daniel et al. (2005) that can impede work with men, such as:

- women practitioners' fear of violent men;
- lack of spaces within agencies to explore the fears and anxieties such work can engender;
- lack of a common belief system about what being a 'good' father means;
- different value systems in agencies and across user groups;
- the impact of social structures, and especially employment patterns.

(Daniel et al., 2005, p. 1351)

Parenting is widely constructed as a form of social duty and an aspect of citizenship devoted to a greater good for society and the economy. The state is willing to invest in child and family welfare in return for parental investment in wider social and economic projects. The government has chosen to emphasise that parenting involves rights and responsibilities (PMSU, 2007) and spelled these out in relation to parental work, life balance and children's behaviour and education.

**Neoliberalism** is 'a theory of political economic practices that proposes that human well-being can best be advanced by liberating individual entrepreneurial freedoms and skills within an institutional framework characterized by strong private property rights, free markets, and free trade. The role of the state is to create and preserve an institutional framework appropriate to such practices' (Harvey, 2005, p. 2).

Garrett (2006) highlights the extent to which New Labour social policy, in his view, is very much a **neoliberal** project. He identifies how welfare services promote specific 'material *and* cultural change', for example, the reshaping of policy and practice encouraging and enabling people to take up positions within a neoliberal workforce (Garrett, 2006, p. 10). Linked to this, Garrett argues, are the creation of new sites for capital accumulation (across health, education and social care) and the transformation of working practices in the public sector through mimicking traditional business models (setting outcomes and treating parents as customers). A good example of this has been the government's encouragement of the expansion of childcare. According to Ball and Vincent (2005, p. 558), 'childcare is seen as having the potential to bring women back into the workforce, thereby increasing productivity'. Ironically many of these women are finding jobs caring for other women's children. (For more on the commodification of care, see Chapter 7.) According to Blackburn (2004), the day nursery market is expanding and in 2003 was worth more than £2.66 billion. Consequently, like the residential care sector before it, the nursery market is likely to be consolidated via mergers into the hands of three or four major operators (Ball and Vincent, 2005). Parents and children are therefore exposed to market forces with parents requiring a certain amount of self-reliance, knowledge and skill to negotiate suitable childcare.

The government responded to such criticisms through its Ten Year Strategy for Childcare (HM Treasury, 2004). This showed more sensitivity toward the position of parents and children by making the parental leave system more flexible and increasing the availability of part-time free childcare for 3- and 4-year-olds. However, parents of younger children are still very much at the mercy of local market conditions which can vary greatly; some areas have a surplus of childcare in contrast to others which possess insufficient amounts to satisfy parental choice. The latter was particularly evident in comments gathered from parents by Ball and Vincent (2005) in London:

> 'couldn't find a nursery place – waiting lists'
>
> 'There just aren't many childminders, they are difficult to find'
>
> 'I was in the market too late at 6mths pregnant'
>
> 'sounds like a lot of choice but there isn't'

(Parents quoted in Ball and Vincent, 2005, p. 561)

The government suggests that the 'success of families is, first and foremost, down to the commitment and behaviour of those within them' (PMSU, 2007, p. 55). However, the above comments from parents illustrate how wider contextual circumstances can impact negatively on the parenting of even the most motivated and committed parent.

Thinking point 2.3    In your view is the success of families, first and foremost, down to the commitment and behaviour of those within them?

Of course, some choices and behaviours that impact negatively on children can be the result of parental agency, yet some of these (as we shall see later in the chapter) can be fully understood only by considering the wider context in which they are formed and enacted. Politicians sometimes find it expedient to be seen to be tough on behaviour without consideration of the wider social context:

> 'Society needs to condemn a little more and understand a little less.'
>
> (British Prime Minister John Major in an interview in the *Mail on Sunday*, 21 February 1993)

Butler and Drakeford (2001) remark that:

> there are some citizens who, through their behaviour, demonstrate their capacity to respond to the investment which the state might make in them and in their conditions. Then there are those whose behaviour demonstrates the opposite. To the first group, New Labour turns its generosity. To the second, it turns the stony face of authoritarianism.
>
> (Butler and Drakeford, 2001, p. 11)

Williams (2004, p. 419) suggests that the emphasis in education and welfare policy towards a 'responsibilization of parents' is unnecessary as 'most parents are acutely aware of their responsibilities to their children, even though they may differ in the ways they carry these out'. Other commentators are concerned that policy has become too focused on what it considers to be inadequate behaviour by parents (specifically mothers) whilst ignoring wider 'material factors' (Clarke, 2006, p. 718). An example used to illustrate this point is the Sure Start objective to support parents 'in caring for their children to promote healthy development before and after birth' (Sure Start, 2002, p. 19). Government targets to reduce maternal smoking and to reduce children's hospital admissions related to respiratory infections are clearly in the best interests of all children. Clarke (2006, p. 713) is concerned, however, that this may imply 'a belief that the care parents provide for their children is the reason for poorer child health among poor families' to the exclusion of wider social factors such as 'damp housing, overcrowding and inadequate incomes'.

In addition to individual causes of childhood morbidity and mortality there are wider social and environmental causes including poor housing conditions

Concern has been expressed by some commentators at the way inadequate parenting has always been seen as a moral issue closely linked, particularly within policies on social exclusion, to poverty, low aspiration and anti-social behaviour. 'Policy literature commonly cites the "condition" of exclusion referring to a disconnection from mainstream values and aspirations, as opposed to marginalization from material resources' (Gillies, 2006, p. 283). It is common to hear politicians praising 'hard working families' or encouraging parents through 'welfare to work' policies that 'work pays'. It implies that families where people do not work are in some way failing in their responsibilities as parents and as citizens. Sometimes it is children who are paying the price of their parents' hard work. As Williams (2004, p. 420) notes, these concepts are simplistic and contingent on wider social and geographical factors. Work does not always pay, for example 'because jobs, especially jobs open to mothers, are low-paid and insecure', or 'terms and conditions of local employment undermine their capacity to carry out their responsibilities in relation to the education of their children'.

As we shall discuss later, service providers and practitioners can help parents by assessing families and communities and providing them with support based on analysis of the wider familial, social, economic and political context. Practitioners can also reflect upon the negative impact of parental stereotypes and expectations promoted within the media and popular culture. Despite pressures to the contrary, it is important that practitioners position themselves as enablers rather than enforcers. As Williams (2004, p. 419) remarks: 'What parents need is time and support to follow their responsibilities through rather than reminders to carry them out'.

## Key points

1   The quality of parenting is considered more important than the configuration of family forms, but who judges this remains debatable.

2   Although parenting is presented as gender neutral, it is mainly mothers and female carers who access services and support predominantly provided by a female workforce.

3   Attempts to actively involve fathers in parenting cannot be considered separately from issues associated with gender equality.

4   Supporting parents can best be understood in relation to the wider social, cultural, environmental and economic context.

# 3  Using theory to conceptualise parenting

As we have already discussed, parenting cannot be understood without reference to each individual's wider context, which in turn implies that parents are different from each other. This section will introduce some theoretical concepts that help us understand the different resources (referred to here as different types of capital, under four main headings) that parents may or may not possess. These concepts will then be applied later in the chapter to what we understand as parenting capacity and the different ways of providing parenting support.

Thinking point 2.4    In what ways can a child's success be influenced by parental wealth, social contacts, skills or knowledge?

### Economic capital

This generally relates to financial physical and material resources available to parents that can be utilised to promote children's wellbeing. Within a capitalist society it is accepted that economic capital can be transformed into services and products. In terms of parenting this may involve obtaining a good education, good health or leisure for children. In a departure from previous welfare approaches, recent social policy has looked to support parents to generate economic capital for their children through work and saving rather than being provided directly with benefits. This change potentially affects the role, function and interrelationships of practitioners and services working with children and families.

## Human capital

This describes the skills and knowledge possessed by people usually associated with education or work. At the national level, investment by government in people (through, for example, promoting 'soft skills' within the education system) can result in economic returns (such as a skilled workforce who will contribute to a more competitive economy). Human capital can also refer to skills and knowledge acquired at the level of the individual. Parents can invest time in developing their child's human capital perhaps through supporting them with learning and helping them negotiate the education system. Practitioners and services for children and families may find themselves involved directly or indirectly in supporting parents with this task. One way of measuring the outcome of human capital for either individuals or nations is by examining the extent to which investment results in increased productivity or wealth.

### Practice box 2.2

The Step in to Learning approach has been adopted in some Sure Start projects to identify needs and support parents with their numeracy, literacy and language skills. By developing these aspects of their human capital, some parents are able to ultimately move from welfare benefits into work and subsequently improve their access to economic capital. The following account from the Team Leader at Sure Start Fleetwood describes how they work with other agencies:

> We have six key agencies who come to the drop-in, including Jobcentre Plus, Connexions, the local college, the NHS recruitment and retention officer. Parents can come in and have a cup of tea and a chat in an informal environment, and we look after their children for them, so they can relax and talk informally to representatives from the agencies.
>
> (Sure Start, 2007, p. 1)

## Social capital

This refers to the level of connectivity and reciprocity between individuals, through networks and within social groups. It consists of and helps maintain shared norms and levels of trust. It is multi-dimensional and can bring benefits at many ecological levels particularly within the family, the community or society as a whole.

Coleman (1991, 1997) identifies social capital as a resource that can be generated and employed within the family through parent–child relations and outside of the family through relationships within the local community. Social capital is considered important for some parents who wish to develop their children's human capital and educational achievement. 'Where you live and whom you know – the social capital you can draw on – helps to define who you are and thus to determine your fate' (Putnam, 1994, p. 14).

Bourdieu (1986) interprets this in a different way, highlighting how forms of capital represent resources and power which in turn are unequally distributed amongst a population. The possession of one form of capital can be used as an investment to acquire other forms of capital. The ability of some parents, but not others, to invest their financial capital in purchasing social capital (that is, access to new social networks for their children, including membership of sport and leisure clubs, and private education) results in some children receiving opportunities ahead of others.

Coleman (1997) identifies how obligations and expectations are built up and reciprocated over time within social groups. Families where members look after each other have social capital, as do groups of parents who might take turns to baby-sit or transport each others children to school. These social interactions can enable the sharing and acquisition of knowledge; for example, children may benefit from parental advice to help make life decisions related to relationships, education and choice of careers. Knowledge acquisition also occurs where parents come together informally (for example at the school gate) or deliberately (for example through participation in antenatal classes or parent and toddler groups). The types of knowledge related to their role as parents may include where the best deals are for buying children's clothing, what are the most beneficial after-schools activities in the area, and how to manage children's health and behaviour. Such relationships also help construct socially acceptable and unacceptable behaviour and norms. In some families this may involve prioritising children's education and the enhancement of their human capital above anything else. Parents may also learn prevailing norms and expectations through interaction with other parents in the community, for example encouraging them to volunteer to support their children's after-school clubs or discouraging them from leaving their children at home alone. Because social capital is unequally distributed amongst parents, the consequences for individual children vary considerably.

Three components of social capital have been identified (Woolcock, 2001). *Bonding social capital*, such as within families, helps create a sense of belonging and understanding. The importance of family interconnectedness and resource sharing is evident in a study by Bayat (2007) of families with autistic children. It suggests that adversity can promote bonding between family members which in turn can build resilience:

> 'My son's autism has made our family life tougher, emotionally and financially. Each member has to devote additional time and effort to help him, and learn how to live peacefully in such environment.

> Through working together, we all learned how to help my son together. In some sense, this also makes our family closer, because an individual cannot handle the toughness alone.'
>
> (Mother quoted in Bayat, 2007, p. 709)

Yet in order for this to not become too insular or detached it also requires *bridging social capital* or interactions of an outward character, such as with other families, which in turn help generate social norms and trust. Some parents find it helpful to join or develop mutual support groups for this purpose. Parents of disabled children 'often find that the most helpful sources of information and advice come from others with similar experiences' (Joseph Rowntree Foundation, 1999, p. 4). This is also true for disabled parents:

> One of the really great things I get out of my involvement and work with Disabled Parents Network is the support and contact with other disabled parents ... Other disabled parents can really understand so many of the issues, and offer empathy and emotional and practical support.
>
> (Baker, 2006, p. 1)

The final component is *linking social capital* which involves connections outside of the community enabling access to resources and opportunities, for example, formal parental support. This is evident in accounts given by disabled children and their families about support provided through Children's Fund projects (Pinnock and Evans, 2007). In particular they highlighted the importance of individually tailored, flexible, reliable and sustainable relationships with practitioners and service providers:

> 'If you have a problem ... if you tell them they can help you deal with it. And then if you want more help from, like, someone professional, they will give you numbers and stuff. And they will phone and take you there if you really want to.'
>
> (Disabled child quoted in Pinnock and Evans, 2007, p. 7)

> 'I still have contact with [the project worker] ... they don't just help you and leave you, they're there all the time ... I know that I've only got to say to [the project worker] I need help and I know that help is there.'
>
> (Parent of a disabled child quoted in Pinnock and Evans, 2007, p. 9)

One of the advantages of social capital as a concept within the context of interagency working with children is that it embraces the multi-layered formal and informal networks around and through which support for children is provided. Furthermore, it is a loose enough concept around which it may be possible to unify the energies of practitioners from different agencies and disciplines. The idea that social capital can serve the interests of the public good has proven particularly popular with policy makers, particularly as it has been linked to many contemporary problems including social exclusion and community regeneration. The Scottish Executive, for example, intends to make sure 'that individuals and communities have the social capital – the skills, confidence, support networks and resources – to take advantage of and increase the opportunities open to them' (Scottish Executive, 2002, p. 6).

Both Coleman (1988) and Putnam (1994) express concern that social capital over time has been eroded, appearing to coincide with government concerns about social exclusion and the apparent breakdown of social cohesiveness. Some commentators take issue with this view of social capital. Morrow (1999) suggests that the concept harks back to a glorious past that cannot be supported with historical evidence. By placing a strong positive emphasis on social connections, it glosses over the fact that although family and friends can be a source of support to parents, they are sometimes a source of stress (Quinton, 2004). It also fails to acknowledge gender, in particular the work of women in creating or sustaining social networks in relation to parenting (Morrow, 1999). Children's agency and ability to develop social capital is largely ignored, in particular by Coleman, who dismisses children's rights as a contributory factor in the decline of social capital by apparently reducing 'the strength of the parental role' (Coleman, 1988, p. 401).

Bourdieu (1986) suggests that like other forms of power, social capital is transmitted from one generation to another and leads to the reproduction of existing class inequalities. In other words social capital is something that you are more likely to inherit through existing social networks than anything offered through government social policies.

Thinking point 2.5    Do you agree that social capital is declining, or does it contribute to the reproduction of inequality from one generation to the next? Can children's services do anything in response to either of these concerns?

## Cultural capital

Two competing causal theories have emerged in academic literature to explain the ways that parents from different social strata raise their children (Chin and Philips, 2004). Firstly, parents differ in the aspirations and expectations that they have for their children. Secondly, inequalities of time and other material resources mean that some parents are more able than others to fulfil their own or wider society's expectations (Chin and Phillips, 2004). Bourdieu's concept of cultural capital goes some way to bringing together these different theories. As we have seen, social capital is *knowing who* can help parents achieve their goals to raise children; in contrast, cultural capital is *knowing how* to use these assets and other qualities to achieve goals (St Clair, 2005).

According to Bourdieu (Jenkins, 2002), cultural capital is a form of **legitimate knowledge** that individuals and families can use to secure some form of advantage. As we have seen above, knowledge and norms are often developed via social capital or contact with a particular social group. Of course, many parents are knowledgeable about many different things; in some cases this knowledge can be traded in to secure advantage for their children, yet in other cases it may appear to have no value. Knowledge has to be of a legitimate form in order to become cultural capital and secure advantage. This begs the question of who or what decides what kind of knowledge is legitimate. Bourdieu helps us understand how this works through the use of two further concepts which he refers to as *habitus* and *field*.

**Legitimate knowledge** is knowledge that is valued and useful within one context but not necessarily another. For example, an educational psychologist has a very good understanding of the Special Educational Needs Code of Practice. Outside of her employment this knowledge may have little relevance. However, if her son was having difficulty learning at school this knowledge may prove valuable. A parent without this form of legitimate knowledge may be relatively disadvantaged.

*Habitus* refers to the dispositions an individual has to feel, think, behave or understand the world in a particular way (Jenkins, 2002). '[T]he dispositions that make up habitus are ... so embodied in the individual that they can be identified in appearance, speech, behaviour, manners and tastes' (Tomanović, 2004, p. 343). Habitus is closely linked to the concept of *habit*, a way of behaving that is often learned through socialisation and experience and occurs without much prior thought. Certain dispositions found amongst some parents and not amongst others could potentially be explained through the use of habitus. Women's intention to breastfeed, for example, appears to be influenced by social relationships and prolonged participation (to at least age 18) in full-time education (Hamlyn et al., 2002; Bolling, 2005).

According to Bourdieu, a *field* is 'a social arena within which struggles or manoeuvres take place over specific resources or stakes and access to them' (Jenkins, 2002, p. 84). Fields vary in terms of how specific or concrete they are, and can include housing, education, land, prestige, life style or any other arena in which a person might wish to have a stake (Jenkins, 2002). In order to access or gain advantage within a particular field, it is necessary to have legitimate knowledge (cultural capital) specific to that field. The formation of habitus brings with it the possibility of inheriting, primarily through their family (Reay, 2000), cultural capital or knowledge about a particular field. 'When an individual's habitus is consistent with the field in which he or she is operating, that is, when the field is familiar to and understood by the individual, he or she enjoys a social advantage' (Lee and Bowen, 2006, p. 197). One way of thinking about the field is as a game or sport. As with any game, some people have a better understanding of the rules and tactics (the habitus) and therefore have an advantage. The concept of cultural capital has been utilised in explaining inequalities within the education system. Grenfell and James (1998) draw a comparison between cultural capital being used by some parents to enhance their children's education just as they might use their economic capital as power to purchase products. Although the parents in the following example have financial capital, it is insufficient to secure private education for all their children. But they do have legitimate knowledge (cultural capital) of school catchment areas that they employ in the interests of securing maximum educational advantage for their child.

> Katherine Bailey and her husband, Nicholas, are prepared to pay an extra £70,000 to move their young family a few miles south, into the heart of the catchment area for Henlow Middle School in Bedfordshire.
>
> 'We would have sent one child to private school but can't afford to send both, so this is the next best thing,' said Bailey. 'We have been absolutely rigorous about it: we have had long discussions with the local education authority and have got local gazetteer lists that show exactly which road is in which catchment area. ...'

> (Hill, 2004, webpage)

Thinking point 2.6    What are some of the advantages and disadvantages, linked to the different types of capital, for both the parents and children in making their house move?

Neoliberalism promotes the idea that advantage and success are down to individual effort and that disadvantage is the result of failure by individuals to take the opportunities open to all. Bourdieu's application of both social and cultural capital challenges this and helps us understand that institutions and processes essential to providing children with opportunities (such as education) are more accessible to particular parents than others, and often without realising it they reproduce rather than help eradicate social inequality. It is a reminder that parents' capacity to provide for their children can be understood only in relation to the wider social, economic and political context.

## Key points

1   Human and social capital are concepts that have been interpreted as beneficial to society, as well as individuals, and therefore have been influential in the design of children's services and the role and working relationships of practitioners.

2   Economic, human, social and cultural capital are concepts that enable us to understand resources unequally possessed by parents and unequally provided by parenting support.

3   The possession of one form of capital can be used as an investment to acquire other forms of capital.

# 4 Parenting capacity

All practitioners within the children's workforce are responsible for children staying safe, and this involves holistic assessment of children's lives including the capacity of their parents or carers. In England the dimensions of parenting capacity laid out in the *Framework for Assessment of Children in Need and their Families* (DH et al., 2000) have subsequently been incorporated into the *Common Assessment Framework* (Children's Workforce Development Council (CWDC), 2007) as:

**Basic care**: providing for the child's physical needs, and appropriate medical and dental care.

**Ensuring safety and protection**: ensuring the child is adequately protected from harm or danger.

**Emotional warmth**: ensuring the child's emotional needs are met and giving the child a sense of being specially valued and a positive sense of their own racial and cultural identity.

**Stability**: providing a sufficiently stable family environment to enable a child to develop and maintain a secure attachment to the primary caregiver(s) in order to ensure optimal development.

**Guidance and boundaries**: enabling the child to regulate their own emotions and behaviour – the key parental tasks are *demonstrating and modelling* appropriate behaviour and control of emotions and interactions with others, and setting boundaries.

**Stimulation**: promoting the child's learning and intellectual development through encouragement and cognitive stimulation and promoting social opportunities.

Contemporary assessment frameworks across the four nations now consider the wider ecological context in which the parent and child are located. In doing so they replace historic parenting models that, it has been argued, were constructed around the values of a dominant white middle class culture (Azar et al., 1998). Children's services as a result are now much better positioned to assess parents fairly without discrimination linked to factors such as age, sexuality, health status, social class or ethnic background. It is also recognised that the capacity of parents can be enhanced or undermined by factors and experiences, sometimes within their control sometimes not, located in family and wider social networks or created by the cultural, social, political and economic environment. 'Unfortunately, the social networks of parents and children, and the social capital of the areas in which they live, tend to reflect individual and area levels of disadvantage, often leaving those most in need of additional help with the most restricted social support resources' (Jack, 2006, p. 339).

Assessing parenting capacity within an ecological context helps practitioners understand and attribute explanations for parents' behaviour and attitudes, particularly where an act of omission or commission appears to be undermining a child's wellbeing. Thus concerns about a child coming to school hungry because they have had no breakfast, after investigation may reveal a parent who starts work early and leaves their child to get their own breakfast. On the other hand it may reveal a parent neglecting their child's needs as a result of a dependency on drugs or alcohol. Either case may be the result of a parent lacking sufficient social or cultural capital to recognise the problem or access, or negotiate access to, possible sources of support.

Thinking point 2.7   In what way can children's services help develop social and cultural capital to support parenting capacity?

The misuse of drugs and/or alcohol is a good example to consider here in more depth as it is widely considered to 'adversely affect the ability of parents to attend to the emotional, physical and developmental needs of their children in both the short and long term' (Social Care Institute for Excellence (SCIE), 2004, webpage). Children's accounts reveal the nature of their relationships with parents who abuse drugs and alcohol:

'My parents started giving me alcohol when I was 1 (year old) to put me to sleep. I got taken into hospital to have my stomach pumped.'

(Child quoted in Ayrshire and Arran NHS Board, 2002, cited in Scottish Executive, 2003, p. 15)

'I used to get really embarrassed at school when mum turned up drunk to collect me. I knew that I would have to make the tea when I got in.'

(Child quoted in Ayrshire and Arran NHS Board, 2002, cited in Scottish Executive, 2003, p. 15)

Other studies with children reveal that they often feel responsible for caring for a parent who misuses alcohol or drugs and they can become torn between love for their parent and dislike of the same parent's behaviour. In some cases children said that they would like to be involved in finding solutions to the problems. Some also found having a strong relationship with a support worker very helpful (SCIE, 2004).

Holistic assessment of parenting capacity entails gathering information about the influence of formal and informal support networks, access to education, childcare, and transport, housing and employment (CWDC, 2007). This information, along with knowledge of the child's own capital resources (Chin and Phillips, 2004) including resilience, self-care skills and willingness to work with others, is a good foundation for putting together a plan with the family. Attention would be paid to the kind of linking social capital already at the disposal of members of a family. For example, it may be possible to involve existing social networks such as the child's school (it may have extended provision) or introduce the family to a local children's centre or specialist services. In the following example, a plan is developed that involves exploring the potential use of bonding social capital within the extended family as well as linking social capital with a range of agencies.

## Practice box 2.3

A 20-year-old woman presented to hospital maternity services 12–16 weeks pregnant. She was injecting heroin and using diazepam, financed by prostitution. Her GP had been prescribing methadone but her behaviour in the surgery led to her removal from the practice list. Her partner, the baby's father, deals and uses heroin. They live in bed-and-breakfast accommodation. The specialist maternity service for pregnant women with substance misuse carried out other routine investigations and assessed her and the baby's father. She was prescribed methadone and her partner referred to a local community-based drugs project who provided an appointment within two days. A hospital social worker referred the couple to the area team for allocation. At 18 weeks the woman was admitted to hospital to manage detoxification from benzodiazepines. She was admitted again at 29 weeks having relapsed. The maternity service hosted a pre-birth case conference at 32 weeks' gestation, which recommended that the baby be placed on the Child Protection Register when born. Thereafter the mother used only prescribed methadone until her baby was born. She gave birth to a healthy but low birth-weight baby boy who developed withdrawal symptoms. He remained in the neonatal unit for treatment, and nursing staff carefully assessed how his mother was managing his care. She seemed to do well in the first few days but left the hospital with her partner and did not return for several days. When she returned she appeared drunk and when worried nursing staff refused to let her take her son home she assaulted a nurse and was arrested. The local authority sought a Child Protection Order and placed the baby with emergency foster carers. The local authority is now carrying out an inter-agency assessment and supervising the mother's contact with the baby in a family centre to see whether he can go home. Concurrently the social worker is assessing whether the maternal grandmother may look after the baby in the medium-term. Drug treatment services are working with the mother to stabilise her emerging chaotic substance misuse.

(Scottish Executive, 2003, p. 39)

The challenges presented in the above practice box illustrate the complexities of providing adequate and ongoing support for children and drug misusing parents. It could be particularly difficult for the various individual practitioners who become involved, some of whom may be unfamiliar with the practice skills and theoretical knowledge necessary to provide holistic support. It highlights the need for clear communication and information sharing between agencies and practitioners.

Sometimes basing practitioners from different disciplines and agencies together in teams or particular settings can enhance the effectiveness of support. Closer working proximity would enable individual practitioners to appreciate and develop a clearer understanding of each other's roles and working methods. The practice box below illustrates an innovative healthcare project involving cooperation between different agencies to provide holistic support to parents of preschool children. As well as promoting general issues such as healthy diets and exercise, it is also well placed to provide support with more complex issues including where parents misuse drugs. Although it is based within a universal service, it enables the development of linking social capital with specialist agencies. The emphasis on community capacity-building suggests the development of bridging social capital, and the educational emphasis is an opportunity for participants to develop cultural capital.

## Practice box 2.4

The Health Promotion Nursery is a pilot project funded by the North Hamilton Blantyre Social Inclusion Partnership. The project consists of a multi-disciplinary team from the partnership agencies: Health Promotion, Education and Social Work Resources. It is based within the Whitehill Parent and Child Centre and St Paul's Primary School and it focuses on the health and well-being of children, parents and professionals on the campus. The project is based upon the Pacific Institute Training: Steps to Excellence and consists of a rolling programme of training for staff, parents and children. The training has a strong community capacity-building theme. It concentrates on the promotion of health through building confidence and self-esteem, raising awareness and healthy lifestyles. This project is complemented by the Integrated Family Support Strategy and the multi-disciplinary team at Whitehill Family Centre who offer a range of family support groups at the nursery and school. This project supports children whose parents misuse drugs along with children with other problems.

(Scottish Executive, 2003, pp. 27–28)

Alcohol and/or drugs misuse is only one of many potential impacts on parenting capacity, including mental health, disability, domestic violence or previous history of abuse (Cleaver, 2006). It is important to acknowledge that none of these are absolute indicators of inadequate parenting, yet they do alert people working with children to potential situations where support may be needed. It has been noted, for example, that between 50 and 90 per cent of families on social workers' childcare caseloads have parent(s) with drug, alcohol or mental health problems (Kearney, 2003). Poverty is a further factor affecting parenting capacity. Access to financial capital, whether through regular employment, savings, benefits or tax credits, is a central factor for most parents and carers, in particular when related to the potential costs involved in bringing up children.

Quinton (2004, p. 181) argues that formal services should see themselves as part of the ecology of parenting: 'inter-agency working needs to be part of an effort to understand the whole of parenting ecology – not just a desire to see agencies work together better'. This is illustrated when one considers that some of the cost of bringing up children is forced upon parents by statutory agencies themselves. Education, even when provided by the state, is particularly expensive for parents in terms of transport, lunches and clothing, and may have a negative impact on children whose parents cannot afford it.

> 'People don't claim free school meals out of embarrassment. I would let people with money go ahead of me in the queue so they wouldn't see.'
>
> (Boy quoted in Crowley and Vulliamy, 2003, p. 15)

> 'Poor children can't buy the proper kit and if they didn't have the proper kit some people in the school were meanies and kept saying they haven't got the proper uniform, and they haven't got enough money to get sandwiches either.'
>
> (Boy quoted in Crowley and Vulliamy, 2003, p. 15)

> 'They bully you in school and go ha! ha! you can't go on the school trip and all that.'
>
> (Boy quoted in Crowley and Vulliamy, 2003, p. 16)

As the above accounts illustrate, the stigma associated with receiving free school dinners or not being able to afford the correct uniform, school trips or essential learning tools such as pens or calculators can impact negatively on children's experience and motivation within school (Children in Wales, 2006). Yet, as another account from Crowley and Vulliamy's research indicates, where schools are prepared to extend themselves even in very small ways, they can positively enhance parenting capacity amongst poorer and marginalised families. In the following account, a school ensures that a mother can develop cultural capital enabling her to stimulate and support her child's learning:

> 'My mum helps me to do the spellings, coz she's got a dictionary and she's Arabic but she doesn't know much English so we got an English dictionary from school and she borrowed it'
>
> (Boy quoted in Crowley and Vulliamy, 2003, p. 15)

This idea of schools extending their provision to support families in a wide and varied way is particularly evident from the New Community School Initiative in Scotland. Here parenting support, education and health promotion are integrated within schools. '[A] wide range of provision in parenting skills advice/courses including one-to-one support, confidence building and practical advice about support from different agencies' was evident in the early evaluation of these projects (Sammons et al., 2002, p. 10). Although such initiatives are still evolving, they demonstrate the potential role of schools as a form of social capital and as part of the ecology of parenting.

## Key points

1   Parenting capacity is a useful concept for assessing parent–child relationships and should be understood within an ecological context.

2   Different forms of capital may affect individuals' parenting capacity.

3   Children's services can strengthen parenting capacity through developing social capital between practitioners, agencies and families.

# 5 Parenting support

Our discussion on parenting capacity has inevitably led us to explore some of the ways in which parents are supported. We will now look more closely at parenting support in terms of how it is used and structured within social policy, in particular how it links to ideas of social capital. In one of its first Green Papers, the new Labour government stated its policy intentions regarding family support (Home Office, 1998), which in turn has featured on the agendas of a range of agencies:

- better services and support to parents
- better financial support to families
- helping families balance work and home
- strengthening marriage, and
- better support for serious family problems.

One definition of parenting support describes 'any intervention for parents or carers aimed at reducing risks and/or promoting protective factors for their children, in relation to their social, physical and emotional well-being' (Moran et al., 2004, p. 6). 75 per cent of parents say there are times in their lives when they would like more advice and support in their parenting role (Social Exclusion Unit, 2000). Although many parents seek support, they do so from a position of wanting to maintain their independence and retain control over how they deal with problems (Quinton, 2004). Parents show a preference for being provided with information to solve their own problems, and where this is not possible, to be provided with specialist advice (Quinton, 2004). Some parents prefer peer learning, particularly within the context of classes that provide parents with opportunities to develop cultural and social capital:

> 'Frankness and, um, the bond that we reached between the parents. We were not afraid to express our particular problems or issues and were there for each other and give advice and take advice. So, you know it is give and take.'

> (Parent discussing parenting programme in Barlow and Stewart-Brown, 2001, p. 121)

According to Moran et al. (2004), parenting support is provided as either a universal service (open to anyone regardless of need) or a targeted service (open to eligible people with an assessed need). Some forms of parenting

Parents attending a
parenting meeting

support are also compulsory. Three levels of parenting support have been
identified:

> primary ... intervening to prevent the onset of problems ...
> secondary ... intervening with high risk groups or where problems
> have begun but are not yet strongly entrenched ... tertiary ...
> when problems are already strongly present and require active
> treatment
>
> (Moran et al., 2004, p. 6)

The first two levels are very much preventative forms of support, whereas
although the third level may try to prevent further problems, it is also helping
people overcome or put right existing problems. This relates closely to the
tiers of need model (PricewaterhouseCoopers LLP, 2006). In this model
a fourth tier is included to represent the type of support being undertaken
with children mostly within the Looked After care system, enabling them to
return to live with their birth parent(s). Most support in tiers 1 and 2 is
received on a voluntary basis by parents. At tiers 3 and 4, support may be
provided on a compulsory basis, following a professional referral.

It is easy to assume that support is given and received willingly, yet it
cannot be divorced from the power relationships in which it operates.
Service providers and practitioners are endowed with power enabling them
to gate-keep resources and make judgements about parenting capacity.
Parents are sometimes disempowered by poverty, lack of information or
discrimination. In some cases what is presented as support may be
unwanted or experienced as an intrusion; on other occasions it may be
inadequate. In some cases something 'may need to be done against one
person's wishes in order to support the needs of another' (Quinton, 2004,
p. 179). This was illustrated in Practice box 2.3 where a nurse rightly made

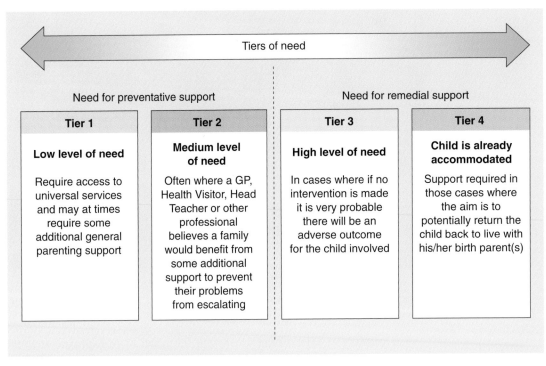

Tiers of need (PricewaterhouseCoopers LLP, 2006, p. 6)

a judgement in refusing to let a mother who appeared drunk take her child home. Even though 'providers still prefer to work with parents who are ultimately willing to receive their help' (PricewaterhouseCoopers LLP, 2006, p. 6), on occasions where it involves prioritising the best interests of the child, it can involve making hard and unpopular decisions. The nurse in the earlier practice box example was assaulted by the mother, an event that illustrates that practitioners need empowerment in the form of adequate resources and support when making these difficult decisions.

The terrain over which parents must pass in order to seek and find support can be difficult to negotiate. Seeking and requesting support may require aspects of cultural capital not available to all parents. In a government-funded piece of research, a wide variety of poorly coordinated parental support was identified, provided by statutory agencies, community groups, private providers and individuals (PricewaterhouseCoopers LLP, 2006). The following chart maps the type of provider against the four tiers of parenting support described above.

The types of service available to support parents in the community are sometimes diverse and disconnected from each other, and may exist only for as long as funding is available. This has resulted in services that protect their boundaries and fail to work beyond their own area of expertise (Quinton, 2004). Furthermore, 'what is available locally is not always known to professionals who meet parents and children in their day to day work' (Royal

Mapping provider types against different tiers of need (PricewaterhouseCoopers LLP, 2006, p. 9)

College of Paediatrics and Child Health (RCPCH), 2002, p. 22). Quinton (2004) suggests that there is a lack of cooperation between services providing support to parents, and where there is cooperation it can usually be attributed to energetic individuals rather than effective systems or structures. It could be argued that service providers need to develop their own social capital.

A distinction has been made between formal support (usually from statutory or mainstream services) semi-formal support (community or voluntary groups) and informal support (provided by family and friends) (Quinton, 2004). Sometimes a contrast is made between the capacity of formal services to provide specialist help and the capacity of informal networks to provide comfort, emotional and practical support. Parents appear to judge services on not only what is made available but how it is offered (Quinton, 2004). The key issue for success in providing support for parents is the quality of relationship developed by those providing the service; in some cases parents indicate that they feel not listened to or talked down to (RCPCH, 2002).

Thinking point 2.8    Who, if anyone, should be targeted for parenting support?

In a situation where resources are scarce, support targeted on people with the greatest need would appear to be the most efficient system. However, 'it is difficult to identify families at highest risk – there are no screening programmes with a high sensitivity and specificity'.

Consequently: 'There will always be parents who could benefit from services but do not receive them' (RCPCH, 2002, p. 23). Targeting is therefore more likely to happen in relation to particular communities (for example, poor neighbourhoods), particular children (for example, disabled children) or parents at particular points in the life course (for example, very young or first-time parents). However, issues requiring support do not always follow clearly defined patterns of distribution (for example, domestic violence) and therefore make targeting difficult to achieve.

A number of projects have targeted parents in the community in helping them support their children's education. Education is highlighted by governments in the UK as one of the key factors in achieving positive outcomes for children, and is increasingly providing support focused on issues such as health, social exclusion, financial capability and childcare. Educational attainment and achievement has become a key concern to create human capital suited to the changing economy and employment market. Education is also considered to be the main source of equality of opportunity and social mobility. Research, however, has revealed that equality of opportunity within education for children appears to be heavily influenced by parental background. Children in the Looked After care system compared to other children underachieve in the education system (Social Exclusion Unit, 2003). An influential study by Feinstein (2003) shows that at age as early as 22 months, distinct differences in cognitive development can be observed, with children from more advantaged backgrounds performing better than those from disadvantaged backgrounds. Significantly, these early scores can be used to predict (although not determine) final educational attainment. The research shows that the education system is better at promoting upward mobility for children from advantaged backgrounds than for children from less advantaged backgrounds.

One way to explain this is by attributing success to middle class parents' cultural and social capital enabling them to 'provide their children with the skills needed to perform well at school and ... use their social contacts for the benefit of their children's education' (Gewirtz, 2001, p. 376). Similarly Lee and Bowen's (2006, p. 213) finding that 'parent involvement at school and high educational expectations, which were most common among parents from dominant groups, showed the strongest associations with achievement suggests the better fit of these parents' habitus to the field of education'.

Policy responses such as the Peers Early Education Partnership (PEEP) Project target particular parents of children aged 0–5 in disadvantaged communities and encourage them to be more closely involved in their children's education. Activities promoted within the PEEP programme are shown in the following practice box.

---

Practice box 2.5

PEEP groups

- **Circle time**: parents, carers and children are led in a variety of carefully chosen songs and rhymes which are seen as 'a powerful interactive medium in relationships' (McColl, 2003). All families are offered an audiotape and a songbook containing the songs and rhymes used in the programme.

- **Talking time**: an opportunity for adults to discuss information and ideas, to share experiences and offer support.

- **Story time**: as daily sharing of books is a fundamental aspect of the curriculum, this is an integral part of every session. It is modelled by the leader who demonstrates stimulating ways of sharing books with children.

- **Book sharing**: books for parents to share with their children and to borrow.

- **Borrowing time**: a library of playpacks, that contain a book and play materials related to the story, are offered on a weekly basis.

- **Home activities**: practical suggestions for games and activities that are closely related to, and support the curriculum.

(Evangelou et al., 2005, p. 20)

---

The idea of targeting particular groups of parents at particular points has some disadvantages. Feinstein (2003) is concerned that the prioritising of early years intervention ignores the importance of providing support into and beyond middle childhood. There is also evidence that targeted interventions fail to reach their intended subjects. One evaluation (Sure Start, 2005, p. 8) concluded that 'parents/families with greater human capital were better able to take advantage of [Sure Start] services and resources than those with less human capital (i.e. teen parents, lone parents, workless households)'. It has also been shown in research that some groups of parents within a target population were particularly hard to work with, including looked after teenage parents, imprisoned fathers and emotionally abusing or rejecting parents (Quinton, 2004). In some cases, the barriers to engagement may be the result of differences in cultural capital between service providers and potential service users. In 2007 the NHS issued guidelines to staff on engaging with all fathers rather than those possessing a particular form of cultural capital. In support, the chief executive of Fathers Direct said: 'Staff are often good at engaging fathers if they are polite, articulate and middle class. But, if they are young or from an ethnic minority, they are regarded as too much trouble' (Carvel, 2007).

Communities develop their own ways of keeping safe by developing Home Zones in conjunction with statutory and voluntary agencies

An alternative to building community-based support is to encourage the community to identify its own needs and construct appropriate solutions with the help of different agencies. This is evident in the Home Zone initiative imported from the Netherlands and Germany. It seeks to create spaces in local neighbourhoods where children can play free from traffic. Although funding is targeted, communities must apply to a funding body. Consequently it relies on parents and other community members having sufficient cultural capital to be able to put together successful bids. However, such schemes, it has been claimed, encourage community cooperation and 'can reduce barriers to the development of bonding and bridging social capital between neighbours' (Aldridge et al., 2002). Projects are being piloted in England, Wales and Scotland.

## Practice box 2.6

Cavell Way is a residential area consisting of family houses and low-rise blocks of flats. 85 per cent of households receive Housing Benefit. It has a high child density, with over half the children aged under 11. Children make use of streets and open spaces for play. However, a number of traffic hazards exist including a lack of pavement in one area and roadways that fail to discourage speeding. The key organisations (Moat Housing Society, the Residents Association and Swale Borough Council) worked together enabling Cavell Way to become one of the country's first Home Zone pilot sites. Local people including children and parents were attracted into the project by holding a street party, and a visit was made to see similar projects in the Netherlands. This was followed by a period of consultation and the drawing up of a plan of action for the estate, including traffic calming measures and the creation of a ball game space for children.

(Source: Field, 2000, webpage)

Thinking point 2.9   What kinds of skills and knowledge are practitioners involved in this kind of project likely to need?

Universal support for parents is currently evolving at a rapid pace. In some cases, universal services are extending the type and scope of support available, including extra support to specific parents. At the time of writing, a pilot project with health visitors and midwives is being created in which they will be provided with 'training, tools and materials' enabling them to provide additional support to first-time parents who need it the most (DfES, 2007). Rather than targeting specific communities, there is a tendency to build parenting support into existing services such as schools or to build centre-based one-stop shops, like children's centres, in all communities. Small steps have also been made towards universal childcare provision, although as we have discussed this still does not adequately meet the needs of many parents, in particular women. There is also a need to ensure that universal adult provisions (for example, mental health services) are able to provide holistic support including help with parenting (Cleaver, 2006).

Parenting support provided to all parents would potentially have the advantage of lacking stigma and being available to people who are at risk yet who have not been identified. However, evidence exists from Sure Start evaluation that vulnerable families may be reluctant to use services dominated by 'affluent, assertive and confident parents' (Tunstill et al., 2007, p. 140). In contrast, the PEEP Project (see above) showed that carefully targeted support could be absorbed and disseminated beyond the original target population, generating social capital, knowledge and norms to support children's education. Parents are more inclined to try something that has been recommended by other parents in place of having it forced upon them by professionals. Many commonly encountered yet unhelpful parenting behaviours, such as smacking, shouting and criticising of children (RCPCH, 2002), could potentially be tackled in a similar way.

There is no guarantee that people will take up what is on offer from universal provision. One recent example of this has been the government's introduction in 2005 of the Child Trust Fund or 'Baby Bond'. This is an asset-based social policy, part of a national strategy to build financial capability amongst the population. By providing all children at birth with £250 (and a larger sum for poorer families) it aims to encourage parents to invest and save for their child's future. Gregory and Drakeford (2006) have shown that a lump sum could dramatically help young people from poorer families to plan their futures. However, by 2006 although 2.3 million vouchers had been sent out, 800,000 had yet to be cashed in (Jones, 2006). These figures suggest that some parents possess a greater degree of financial capability than others. The expectation that parents make choices between financial products (including equities) implies that they require a particular form of cultural capital not shared by large sections of the UK population. 28 per cent of UK households lack any kind of savings, with 49 per cent having less than £1500 in savings (Department for Work and Pensions, 2006). Lone-parent families and low-income families are over-represented in these figures, which may indicate that they lack sufficient income to put away as savings. It appears therefore that a universally available policy designed to help poorer parents accumulate financial capital for their children's future is failing to extend the role of many parents and is more likely to reproduce existing inequalities.

## Key points

1   Parenting support is presented in social policy as a solution to a range of diverse policy goals.

2   Parenting support can be understood in relation to human social and cultural capital.

3   Parenting support operates at different levels and can be formal or informal, universal or targeted.

4   Attention needs to be given to how agencies work together and provide support to parents.

# Conclusion

This chapter has encouraged practitioners to reflect on the political context in which parenting support operates. It is evident that most parents take their parenting responsibilities seriously and are willing to receive support. Different (sometimes imaginative) ways of providing support may work for some parents, particularly if presented as enablement rather than enforcement. Practitioners who provide support should be willing to positively embrace the wide diversity of family forms and understand parenting capacity within an ecological context. In Chapter 5 we consider how evaluation can be used to guide learning and improve services for children, yet as this chapter has demonstrated, theoretical knowledge can also play a part in this process. The concepts of social and cultural capital are useful thinking tools when supporting parents through social networking or when constructing fair, accessible and equitable services. Many new political issues will arise as parenting support evolves. There is a danger, for example, that the move towards common skills and knowledge may stifle new and innovative ways of working with children and their parents. Increasingly, parenting support entails encroachment by practitioners into the private terrain of the family. A further political issue for the twenty-first century is the extent to which practitioners from across a range of agencies are willing to take on these roles, and the extent to which parents and children are willing for this to happen.

# References

Aldridge, S. and Halpern, D. with Fitzpatrick, S. (2002) *Social Capital: A Discussion Paper*, London, Performance and Innovation Unit.

Ayrshire and Arran NHS Board (2002) *Needs Assessment of Alcohol and Drug Usage within Ayrshire*, Kilmarnock, Ayrshire and Arran NHS Board.

Azar, S.T., Lauretti, A.F. and Loding, B.V. (1998) 'The evaluation of parental fitness in termination of parental rights cases: a functional-contextual perspective', *Clinical Child and Family Psychology Review*, vol. 1, no. 2, pp. 77–100.

Baker, S. (2006) *Why I Volunteer*, available online at <http://www.disabledparentsnetwork. org.uk/cgi-bin/site/site.cgi?page=site/why_i_volunteer>, accessed 20 January 2008.

Ball, S.J. and Vincent, C. (2005) 'The "childcare champion"? New Labour, social justice and the childcare market', *British Educational Research Journal*, vol. 31, no. 5, pp. 557–570.

Barlow, J. and Stewart-Brown, S. (2001) 'Understanding parenting programmes: parents' views', *Primary Health Care Research and Development*, vol. 2, pp. 117–130.

Bayat, M. (2007) 'Evidence of resilience in families of children with autism', *Journal of Intellectual Disability Research*, vol. 51, no. 9, pp. 702–714.

Blackburn, P. (2004) *Children's Nurseries: UK Market Sector Report 2004*, London, Laing & Buisson.

Bolling, K. (2005) *Infant Feeding Survey 2005: Early Results*, London, Information Centre for Health and Social Care.

Bourdieu, P. (1986) 'The forms of capital' in Richardson, J.G. (ed.) *Handbook of Theory and Research for the Sociology of Education*, New York, Greenwood Press.

Bradshaw, J., Finch, N., Kemp, P.A., Mayhew, E. and Williams, J. (2003) *Gender and Poverty in Britain*, Manchester, Equal Opportunities Commission.

Butler, I. and Drakeford, M. (2001) 'Which Blair project? Communitarianism, social authoritarianism and social work', *Journal of Social Work*, vol. 1, no. 1, pp. 7–19.

Carvel, J. (2007) 'Maternity services urged to include fathers', *Guardian*, 4 June, available online at <http://www.guardian.co.uk/medicine/story/0,,2095080,00.html>, accessed 7 September 2007.

Children in Wales (2006) *Tackling Child Poverty in Wales: A Good Practice Guide for Schools*, available online at <http://www.childreninwales.org.uk/publications/ genpubdownloads/index.html>, accessed 4 September 2007.

Children's Workforce Development Council (CWDC) (2007) *The Common Assessment Framework for Children and Young People: Practitioners' Guide: Integrated Working to Improve Outcomes for Children and Young People*, Leeds, CWDC, available online at <http://www.everychildmatters.gov.uk/_files/ 0C734C7BC2984FA94F5ED0D500B7EF02.pdf>, accessed 20 January 2008.

Chin, T. and Phillips, M. (2004) 'Social reproduction and child-rearing practices: social class, children's agency, and the summer activity gap', *Sociology of Education*, vol. 77, July, pp. 185–210.

Clarke, K. (2006) 'Childhood, parenting and early intervention: a critical examination of the Sure Start national programme', *Critical Social Policy*, vol. 26, no. 4, pp. 699–721.

Cleaver, H. (2006) 'The influence of parenting and other family relationships' in Aldgate, J., Jones, D., Rose, W. and Jeffery, C. (eds) *The Developing World of the Child*, London, Jessica Kingsley, pp. 122–140.

Coleman, J.S. (1988) 'Social capital in the creation of human capital', *American Journal of Sociology*, vol. 94, Supplement, pp. S95–S120.

Coleman, J.S. (1991) 'Prologue: constructed social organisation' in Bourdieu, P. and Coleman, J.S. (eds) *Social Theory for a Changing Society*, Oxford, Westview Press.

Coleman, J.S. (1997) 'Social capital in the creation of human capital' in Halsey, A.H., Lauder, H., Brown, P. and Wells, A.S. (eds) *Education: Culture, Economy and Society*, Oxford, Oxford University Press, pp. 80–95.

Crowley, A. and Vulliamy, C. (2003) *Listen Up! Children and Young People Talk: About Poverty*, London, Save the Children.

Daniel, B., Featherstone, B., Hooper, C-A. and Scourfield, J. (2005) 'Why gender matters for Every Child Matters', *British Journal of Social Work*, vol. 35, no. 8, pp. 1343–1355.

Department for Education and Skills (DfES) (2006) *Parenting Support: Guidance for Local Authorities in England*, London, DfES.

Department for Education and Skills (DfES) (2007) *Government's Parenting Strategy – Putting Parents in Control*, available online at <http://www.dfes.gov.uk/pns/DisplayPN.cgi?pn_id=2007_0020>, accessed 4 September 2007.

Department for Work and Pensions (2006) *Family Resources Survey: United Kingdom 2005–06*, available online at <http://www.dwp.gov.uk/asd/frs/2005_06/frs_2005_06_report.pdf>, accessed 4 September 2007.

Department of Health, Department for Education and Employment, Home Office (2000) *Framework for Assessment of Children in Need and their Families*, London, The Stationery Office, available online at <http://www.dh.gov.uk/en/Publicationsandstatistics/Publications/PublicationsPolicyAndGuidance/DH_4003256>, accessed 20 January 2008.

Evangelou, M., Brooks, G., Smith, S. and Jennings, D. (2005) *Birth to School Study: A Longitudinal Evaluation of the Peers Early Education Partnership (PEEP) 1998–2005*, London, DfES.

Feinstein, L. (2003) 'Not just the early years: the need for developmental perspective for equality of opportunity', *New Economy*, vol. 10, no. 4, pp. 213–218.

Field, C. (2000) *Cavell Way – A Planning Zone*, available online at <http://www.homezones.org/homeZUKCavellWay.html>, accessed 4 September 2007.

Garrett, P.M. (2006) 'How to be modern: New Labour's neoliberal modernity and the *Change for Children* programme', *British Journal of Social Work*, available online at <http://bjsw.oxfordjournals.org/cgi/reprint/bcl345v1>, accessed 10 September 2007.

Gewirtz, S. (2001) 'Cloning the Blairs: New Labour's programme for the re-socialization of working-class parents', *Journal of Education Policy*, vol. 16, no. 4, pp. 365–378.

Ghate, D. and Ramella, M. (2002) *Positive Parenting: The National Evaluation of the Youth Justice Board's Parenting Programme*, London, Youth Justice Board.

Gillies,V. (2005) 'Raising the "meritocracy": parenting and the individualization of social class', *Sociology*, vol. 39, no. 5, pp. 835–853.

Gillies, V. (2006) 'Working class mothers and school life: exploring the role of emotional capital', *Gender and Education*, vol. 18, no. 3, pp. 281–293.

Gregory, L. and Drakeford, M. (2006) 'Social work, asset-based welfare and the Child Trust Fund', *British Journal of Social Work*, vol. 36, no. 1, pp. 149–157.

Grenfell, M. and James, D. (1998) *Bourdieu and Education: Acts of Practical Theory*, Bristol, PA, Falmer.

Hamlyn, B., Brooker, S., Oleinikova, K. and Wands, S. (2002) *Infant Feeding 2000*, Norwich, The Stationery Office.

Harvey, D. (2005) *A Brief History of Neoliberalism*, Oxford, Oxford University Press.

Hill, A. (2004) '£42,000: what parents pay for a place in a top state school', *Observer*, available online at <http://education.guardian.co.uk/schools/story/0,,1376960,00.html>, accessed 4 September 2007.

Hill, M. (2005) 'Children's boundaries: within and beyond families' in McKie, L. and Cunningham-Burley, S. (eds) *Families in Society: Boundaries and Relationships*, Bristol, The Policy Press, pp. 77–94.

HM Treasury (2004) *Choice for Parents, the Best Start for Children: A Ten Year Strategy for Childcare*, London, HM Treasury.

Home Office (1998) *Supporting Families: A Consultation Document*, London, The Stationery Office.

Jack, G. (2006) 'The area and community components of children's well-being', *Children & Society*, vol. 20, no. 5, pp. 334–347.

Jenkins, R. (2002) *Pierre Bourdieu*, London, Routledge.

Jones, R. (2006) '800,000 child trust fund vouchers are unused', *Guardian*, 3 March, available online at <http://business.guardian.co.uk/story/0,,1722387,00.html>, accessed 7 September 2007.

Joseph Rowntree Foundation (1999) *Foundations: Supporting Disabled Children and Their Families*, available online at <http://www.jrf.org.uk/KNOWLEDGE/findings/foundations/pdf/N79.pdf>, accessed 4 September 2007.

Kearney, P. (2003) *Alcohol, Drug and Mental Health Problems: Working with Families*, London, Social Care Institute for Excellence.

Lee, J-S. and Bowen, N.K. (2006) 'Parent involvement, cultural capital, and the achievement gap among elementary school children', *American Educational Research Journal*, vol. 43, no. 2, pp. 193–218.

Lloyd, N., O'Brien, M. and Lewis, C. (2003) *National evaluation summary: Fathers in Sure Start local programmes*, available online at <http://www.ness.bbk.ac.uk/documents/activities/implementation/160.pdf>, accessed 4 September 2007.

*Mail on Sunday* (1993) 'Interview with British Prime Minister John Major', 21 February.

McColl, C. (2003) in PEEP, *Annual Report 2002–2003*, Oxford, PEEP.

Moran, P., Ghate, D. and van der Merwe, A. (2004) *What Works in Parenting Support? A Review of the International Evidence*, available online at <http://www.dfes.gov.uk/research/data/uploadfiles/RR574.pdf>, accessed 4 September 2007.

Morrow, V. (1999) 'Conceptualising social capital in relation to the well-being of children and young people: a critical review', *Sociological Review*, vol. 47, no. 4, pp. 744–765.

Pinnock, K. and Evans, R. (2007) 'Developing responsive preventative practices: key messages from children's and families' experiences of the Children's Fund', *Children & Society*, available online at <http://www.blackwell-synergy.com/doi/full/10.1111/j.1099–0860.2007.00081.x >, accessed 26 October 2007.

PricewaterhouseCoopers LLP (2006) *DfES Children's Services: The Market for Parental and Family Support Services*, London, PricewaterhouseCoopers LLP.

Prime Minister's Strategy Unit (PMSU) (2007) *Building on Progress: Families*, Policy Review, London, Cabinet Office.

Putnam, R. (1994) 'Social capital and public affairs', *Bulletin of the American Academy of Arts and Sciences*, vol. 47, no. 8, pp. 5–19.

Quinton, D. (2004) *Supporting Parents: Messages from Research*, London, Jessica Kingsley.

Reay, D. (2000) 'A useful extension of Bourdieu's conceptual framework?: emotional capital as a way of understanding mothers' involvement in their children's education', *Sociological Review*, vol. 48, no. 4, pp. 568–585.

Royal College of Paediatrics and Child Health (RCPCH) (2002) *Helpful Parenting*, London, RCPCH, also available online at <http://www.rcpch.ac.uk/doc.aspx?id_Resource=1761>, accessed 11 September 2007.

Sammons, P., Power, S., Robertson, P., Elliot, K., Campbell, C. and Whitty, G. (2002) *Interchange 76: National Evaluation of the New Community Schools Pilot Programme in Scotland: Phase 1 (1999–2002)*, Edinburgh, Scottish Executive.

Scottish Executive (2002) *Better Communities in Scotland: Closing the Gap. The Scottish Executive's Community Regeneration Statement*, Edinburgh, Scottish Executive.

Scottish Executive (2003) *Getting Our Priorities Right: Good Practice Guidance for Working with Children and Families Affected by Substance Misuse*, Edinburgh, Scottish Executive.

Scottish Executive (2006) *Family Matters: Charter for Grandchildren*, available online at <http://www.scotland.gov.uk/Resource/Doc/112493/0027333.pdf>, accessed 4 September 2007.

Social Care Institute for Excellence (SCIE) (2004) *Research briefing 6: Parenting capacity and substance misuse*, available online at <http://www.scie.org.uk/publications/briefings/briefing06/index.asp>, accessed 5 September 2007.

Social Exclusion Unit (SEU) (2000) *Employment and the Policy Action Team 12: Report on Young People*, available online at <http://archive.cabinetoffice.gov.uk/seu/page864c.html?id=418>, accessed 7 September 2007.

Social Exclusion Unit (SEU) (2003) *A Better Education for Children in Care*, available online at <http://archive.cabinetoffice.gov.uk/seu/downloaddocdac1.pdf?id=32&pId=398>, accessed 20 January 2008.

St Clair, R. (2005) *Working Paper 1: Introduction to Social Capital*, available online at <http://www.gla.ac.uk/centres/cradall/docs/01workingpaper.pdf>, accessed 4 September 2007.

Sure Start (2002) *Sure Start: A Guide for Sixth Wave Programmes*, London, DfES.

Sure Start (2005) *Early Impacts of Sure Start Local Programmes on Children and Families: Report of the Cross-sectional Study of 9- and 36-month Old Children and their Families*, London, DFES.

Sure Start (2006) *Sure Start Children's Centres: Practice Guidance*, London, DfES.

Sure Start (2007) *Step in to Learning: Impact on Parents*, available online at <http://www.surestart.gov.uk/_doc/P0002145.pdf>, accessed 4 September 2007.

Tomanović, S. (2004) 'Family habitus as the cultural context for childhood', *Childhood*, vol. 11, no. 3, pp. 339–360.

Tunstill, J., Aldgate, J. and Hughes, M. (2007) *Improving Children's Services Networks: Lessons from Family Centres*, London, Jessica Kingsley.

Wasoff, F. and Cunningham-Burley, S. (2005) 'Perspectives on social policies and families' in McKie, L. and Cunningham-Burley, S. (eds) *Families in Society: Boundaries and Relationships*, Bristol, The Policy Press, pp. 261–270.

Williams, F. (2004) 'What matters is who works: why every child matters to New Labour. Commentary on the DfES Green Paper *Every Child Matters*', *Critical Social Policy*, vol. 24, no. 3, pp. 406–427.

Women's Budget Group (2005) *Response to 'Choice for parents, the best start for children: a ten year strategy for childcare'*, available online at <http://www.wbg.org.uk/documents/WBGResponsetoChildcareStrategy.pdf>, accessed 4 September 2007.

Woolcock, M. (2001) 'The place of social capital in understanding social and economic outcomes', *Isuma: Canadian Journal of Policy Research*, vol. 2, no. 1, pp. 1–17.

# Chapter 3

## Towards integrated working

Bill Stone and Andy Rixon

## Introduction

The expectation that agencies and their practitioners will work increasingly closer together has crossed all areas of children's services. This has ranged from closer strategic cooperation to bringing a range of practitioners together in highly integrated teams. This chapter explores the concepts of interagency and integrated working, and analyses the reasons why this trend has become such a major feature of policy and practice in work with children, and the problems and issues that have arisen in the process.

### Core questions

- Why, from the perspective of children and their families, are interagency working and more integrated ways of working important?
- What are meant by 'interagency', 'interprofessional' and the many other terminologies in this area?
- What are the policy context and the key drivers affecting the way practitioners work together?
- What are some of the key issues and difficulties arising from increasingly integrated working?

# 1 Starting with the child

## 1.1 The experience of children and families

A theme throughout several chapters in this book will be the exploration of whether, and how, different agencies and practitioners can work more effectively together to enhance the wellbeing of children. 'Working together' for children might sound a straightforward enterprise, and sometimes this may be the case. However, from the point of view of the child and their family at the centre of all this activity, things may look very different. We want to stress here therefore that any exploration of the subject should start with the experiences of children and families themselves.

> 'There are times that having all different people in my life is too much. I spend a lot of my time up the hospitals. I wish there were less appointments and less doctors to see.'
>
> (Child quoted in Turner, 2003, p. 21)

> 'At the beginning no-one explained that so many people would be visiting and phoning and that there would be so many appointments at the house. No-one told me what to expect, I'd like to have known more.'
>
> (Parent of disabled child quoted in Abbott et al., 2005, p. 231)

An example of the growing demand for better coordinated services has been that from disabled children and their families whose experience frequently lies at one end of the continuum of interacting with multiple

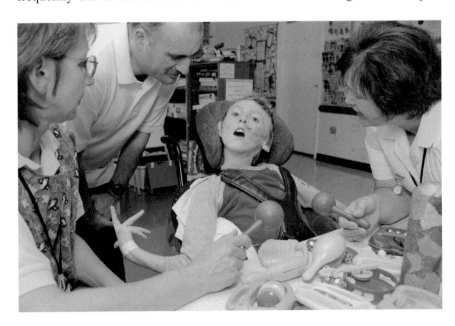

Some children and families have to deal with numerous appointments and assessments with many different practitioners

agencies and practitioners. In the past, families of disabled children have on average had contact with at least ten different professionals over the course of a year, and attended at least twenty appointments at hospitals or clinics (Care Co-ordination Network UK, 2001, cited in Townsley et al., 2004, p. 3). For disabled children with complex healthcare needs, these numbers can be much higher, leading to a bewildering situation:

> The sheer number of professionals who may be involved in supporting a disabled child in the community can often lead to a lack of continuity and coordination and may leave families uncertain about who to contact regarding specific problems
>
> (Townsley et al., 2004, p. 3)

It is clear that many disabled children understand the need to see a range of people and value the contribution they make to their welfare (Turner, 2003). However, their experience of fragmented services, the numbers of people involved and the lack of 'child-centredness' provide a clear example of how the work of different practitioners needs to be well coordinated (Turner, 2003). This can include, as discussed in Chapter 1, the value of having just one practitioner to liaise with, who in turn helps to coordinate services on their behalf (Abbott et al., 2005).

Analyses of what primarily drives the movement for the closer working together of different agencies and practitioners tend to be dominated by discussion of government policy and finance, so it is important to recognise that one force for change can and should originate from families themselves. Starting with children's views is also a reminder that, when asked, they can have plenty to say about their lives generally. They are not 'objects of concern' but, having expertise on their own lives, can be active participants in contributing to the shape of services and the construction of solutions. Supported by an emphasis on children's rights, this 'standpoint is to conceptualise children as agents, with specific views on the institutions and adult groups they interact with' (Mayall, 1996, p. 2). Research with disabled children and young people by Turner (2003) for the Welsh Assembly clearly demonstrated that they have a wealth of views on the type of practice they would like to experience and the sort of services they would like to see. Consultation with children and young people in care in England similarly illustrated how they can comment on issues directly relating to interagency service delivery (DfES, 2007). For example, while the increased sharing of information about children is widely seen in policy terms as important to enabling better working together, children clearly express their concerns about who has access to this information. They were equally able to comment on the idea of lead professionals and the proposal that they should hold their own budgets (generally positively on both proposals) (DfES, 2007).

Discussion about the difficulties for practitioners from different agencies or professionals working together usually focuses primarily on structures or issues of knowledge base, workplace and professional cultures, values and attitudes. But the way in which different practitioners view children – and construct their ideas of childhood – adds an additional layer. How children's services are constructed depends in part on how childhood is constructed (Moss and Petrie, 2002). Positioning children as more than only 'in need' of such things as care, control and education can call into question the current configuration of services and promote the ability of children to participate. The context of organising services is not just about different relationships between services but also about 'a new relationship with children themselves' (Cohen, 2005, p. 10).

While 'child-centred' practice is key, it is also important to ascertain the perspective of parents and carers, who will usually be there for the child when all the professionals have gone home. Their ongoing participation in the development of services is also crucial. The partnership structures discussed below that require the inclusion of parents in most new development have gone someway towards recognising this, although the extent to which this has impacted on services is variable.

## 1.2 Services for children at risk

The complexities of a multiplicity of practitioners working to enhance the welfare of a child (in addition to the tendency for 'child-centredness' to be lost) are clearly illustrated in the arena of protecting and safeguarding children. Ineffective interagency working may not just result in unsatisfactory services but can have serious consequences for children.

This is a long-standing issue. A report into the death of a child (referred to as Paul) through neglect (Bridge Child Care Development Service, 1995) included a diagram showing the family at the centre of a complex spider's web of professional and agency networks (see the figure below). It was estimated that his family had contact with over thirty different professionals from at least ten major agencies, offices and departments. Bearing in mind the rate of movement of staff between jobs and departments in a period of constant organisational change, Paul's parents and the practitioners involved must have found this network extremely complex to negotiate, with tragic results.

The challenge for practitioners and their agencies has long been to be able to work together in an effective way, sharing information and concerns, and planning in a coordinated way to meet the needs of children. In the case of vulnerable children, where the stakes may be very high indeed, working together is even more critically important. In a complex, modern society where there is a whole range of services available to help and support children, this is inevitably difficult.

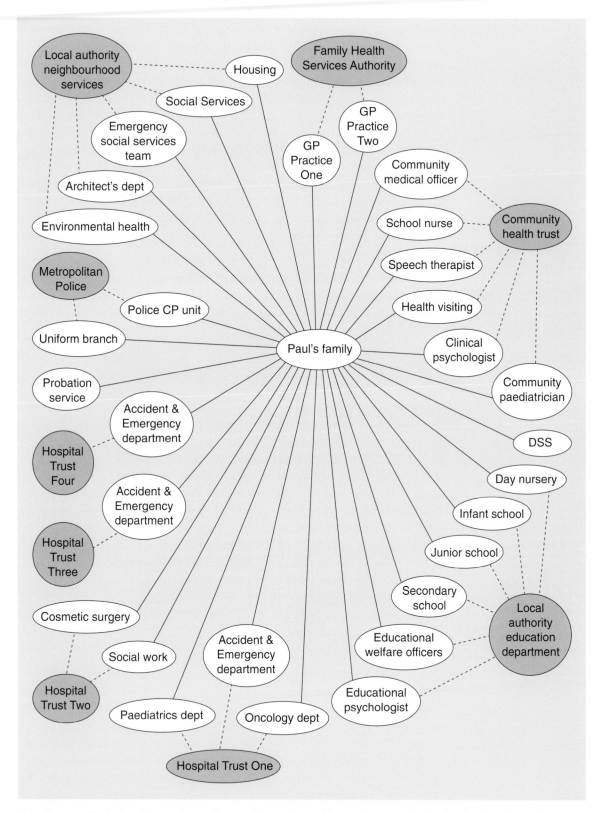

This diagram illustrates the numbers of agencies and practitioners that can be involved with a single family in complex situations (Bridge Child Care Development Service, 1995, p. 160)

The death of Victoria Climbié (Laming, 2003) several years later provided another example of how the network of agencies was not able to successfully protect a child. It is estimated that Victoria and her carers had contact with over seventy different professionals in the short period of time between her arrival in London from Paris and her death less than twelve months later. Numerous factors contributed to the inability of the child protection 'system' to intervene successfully in Victoria's life, including poor individual practice and lack of training and resources. However, the ineffective communication between agencies was identified, as in many inquiry reports before, as a significant contributor to the problem (Laming, 2003). Crucially, the inquiry report highlights the fact that the starting point for practitioners was rarely the child or her perspectives on her experience – Victoria was rarely seen as the central client in this case and rarely spoken to directly.

> Good communication, checking with partner agencies at the point of referral, and talking to the child as appropriate, must be the main way to decide how best to safeguard and promote a child's welfare.
>
> (Laming, 2003, p. 365)

## 1.3  The context of children's lives

There are many different perspectives on what children need and how best their wellbeing can be promoted. Despite this diversity of views, most practitioners would agree that all aspects of children's lives are inextricably linked. A child is a whole person whose life cannot be divided up into different segments, with each segment considered separately. A child's social and emotional development cannot, for example, be easily split off from her or his physical health. There has been a growing body of evidence in child development theory demonstrating that children's overall development is influenced by a whole range of other factors in the wider environment in which they live (Aldgate, 2006; Fawcett, 2000). These influences range from immediate family relationships through school to broader elements of the community and wider society. This 'ecological' model, developed in particular by Bronfenbrenner (1979), has become highly influential and provides a useful theoretical framework for understanding the interrelatedness of all these factors.

One of the most striking things about looking at children's development in this way – both holistically and in an ecological context – is the implication that each practitioner's perspective on children's lives is valid and all their contributions are potentially important. Equally, this model suggests that no one profession has all the answers and no one perspective is definitive. In turn, these different sources of knowledge and practice need to be coordinated if the whole child is to be supported effectively. Here lies one of the key challenges.

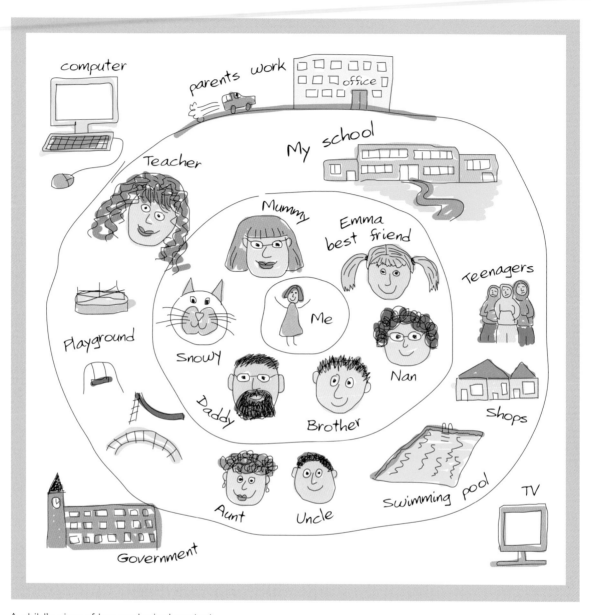

A child's view of her ecological context

The contribution of different perspectives can be seen at the level of theory. The education and training of a range of practitioners involves becoming acquainted with a different body of theory and underpinning knowledge derived from one or more of the academic disciplines. Health visitors and early years workers, for example, will draw on child development theory to a greater extent than other practitioners. Social workers are likely to have knowledge of theories about family relationships such as systems theory, and may be informed by sociological theory more than other colleagues in the children's workforce. This knowledge and theory is inevitably selective and partial; no one discipline claims a complete or definitive understanding of the complexity of children's lives. These theory bases, however, are not necessarily easily compatible or amalgamated.

In addition, at the level of practice, those adults who are working with children are based in a multitude of different settings: schools, health centres, play settings, children's centres, social work offices and community projects of all shapes and sizes. They are also employed by a variety of different agencies or working in a voluntary capacity. This obviously highlights the issue of communication and coordination, as summarised by Frost (2005):

> the complex division of labour suggested by a professionalised society ... creates problems of co-ordination. How can we ensure that all the professionals working with the same child know what each other is doing, and that they are pulling in the same direction? The same child might be known to a social worker, a nursery nurse, a general practitioner, a health visitor and a paediatrician, to name but a few. These professionals will also probably work for a wide range of agencies. Here we have the essence of the 'working together' problem – specialisation leads to fragmentation and can lose sight of the 'whole' child.
>
> (Frost, 2005, p. 12)

To achieve anything substantial in terms of children's wellbeing, this diverse, scattered and somewhat fragmented children's workforce needs to be joined up around each individual child and his or her family. It is this difficult process of joining up, with all the potential for conflict, rivalry, miscommunication and misunderstanding that the process inevitably entails, that is explored in the rest of this chapter.

## Key points

1  Explorations of the way practitioners work together should be informed by the voices of children and families and start with the realities of their lives.

2  A holistic view of children's lives provides a clear basis for the need for practitioners from different disciplines all having a contribution to make to children's wellbeing.

# 2 The context for working together: discovering the key drivers

## 2.1 Defining our terms

We have already used the words 'interagency' and 'interprofessional'; before proceeding any further, some reference to the terminology problem is required.

Any discussion of the difficulties and complexities of practitioners 'working together' is not helped by the proliferation of terminology used to describe it. The entire field is characterised by what one commentator has called 'conceptual hybridity', that is, one concept being grafted onto another concept in a confusing way (Taylor et al., 2006, p. xi). Just some of the key words to be found in the writing on this subject are given below.

- Multi-agency/Cross-agency/Interagency/Trans-agency
- Multi-professional/Interprofessional/Interdisciplinary/ Trans-disciplinary
- Coordination
- Cooperation
- Collaboration
- Partnerships
- 'Joined-up thinking' and 'Joined-up working'
- Cross-cutting
- Cross-boundary working
- Networks
- Integrated working

Thinking point 3.1   Can you define some of these terms in simple language? For example, what might be the difference between interprofessional, multi-agency and integrated working?

Even the language struggles to express with any clarity the complicated way in which concepts are being joined together, hence the proliferation of hyphens. Maybe that is also one explanation for the bewildering array of acronyms that one encounters in writing about this subject. We will not attempt to define the list of terms above, even if that were possible given the inconsistent way in which they are used; however, some could be usefully explored further. We should also clarify the terms adopted for this book to avoid adding to the confusion!

'Working together' and 'working across boundaries' are useful catch-all phrases; however, clearly many of these words are implying differing degrees of 'working together', and Frost (2005) suggests that some clarity can be brought to the subject by using the idea of a continuum of partnership. He argues that from all the possible terms that may be used, we can perhaps perceive a continuum from cooperation to integration, with partnership acting as an underlying theme:

- **no partnership**   uncoordinated, free-standing services
- **level one**   *co-operation* – services work together toward consistent goals and complementary services, while maintaining their independence
- **level two**   *collaboration* – services plan together and address issues of overlap, duplication and gaps in service provision towards common outcomes
- **level three**   *co-ordination* – services work together in a planned and systematic manner towards shared and agreed goals
- **level four**   *merger/integration* – different services become one organisation in order to enhance service delivery

(Frost, 2005, p. 13)

This model has the merit of showing that there are different degrees of working together that operate within structures and organisations. For any practitioner working with children it should be possible to place her or his agency somewhere on this continuum. A 'network', for example, is often used to describe one configuration of practitioners which could be placed within this framework, as illustrated here in relation to a preferred configuration of interagency relationships being developed in Scotland:

> A linked group of professions and organisations from health care, social care and other agencies working together in a coordinated manner with clear governance and accountability arrangements.
>
> (Hudson, 2007, p. 6)

However, such a continuum may tend to imply that there is a natural progression in working together from one end to the other, and that integration is the final, hoped for, outcome. Many government policies have fuelled this idea of the desirability of integration at all levels – organisational to individual teams (see DfES, 2004, for example). However, full integration may in fact be neither possible nor desirable in some cases. If it is the outcomes for the child and their family that really matter, then the question should be what is the best configuration for the development or delivery of a particular service.

'Partnership', a word we have already used, is often referred to both in the context of individual work with children and families and to describe more strategic arrangements. Its meaning in these different contexts will be discussed in a subsequent section, but it is in the strategic sense that the phrase has more recently risen to prominence. Following a change in government in 1997, partnerships increasingly became the mechanisms through which the government sought to deliver new initiatives. Developments like 'Sure Start', for example, required the establishment of partnership boards including all stakeholders in the statutory, voluntary and private sectors. Crucially, stakeholders were also to include, in this instance, parents and carers. We will return to analyse the idea of partnerships in more detail.

Terms such as multi-agency, interagency and even cross-agency working have been the most commonly used words to describe agencies working together to create better services for children and to ensure that none fall through 'gaps' in services provided separately. While 'multi' and 'inter' may not necessarily mean the same thing (see the suggestions of Malin and Morrow (2007) discussed below), these terms are often used interchangeably. Our preference will be to use interagency except when quoted authors use a different term, or when following government documentation as in Chapter 4. 'Integration' is usually used to describe a stage beyond collaboration. We will use the word in situations where agencies have been combined or practitioners from different backgrounds or disciplines work together in the same team.

The 'agency' in interagency working becomes blurred in situations where agencies are combined. Services for children and families across the UK are frequently reorganised. In England education and children's social services departments were brought together into a single 'children's services' designed in itself to lead to a greater degree of integration. Such reorganisations may enable the *structural* difficulties of two services working together to be overcome (although this is by no means certain), but not necessarily the *professional* or *disciplinary* ones. As we have noted, practitioners within organisations, however they are constituted, interact drawing on different knowledge bases and values, etc. The idea of 'interprofessional' working therefore remains a distinct issue, even where teams are otherwise fully integrated.

Malin and Morrow (2007), drawing on the work of a range of authors, suggest that distinctions can be made between the terms 'multi', 'inter' and

**ONE-STOP SHOP FOR THE JOINT STRATEGIC SOUTH-WEST REGIONAL COMMUNITY PARTNERSHIP TRUST'S INTEGRATED CHILDREN'S SERVICES SERVICE**

CLOSED TODAY FOR RE-ORGANISATION

Describing changing structures can be confusing

'trans' in relation to disciplinary areas of work. They adopt the terms 'multi-disciplinary' as referring to professionals 'working alongside but separately from each other' and 'inter-disciplinary' work as that involving professionals sharing information and deciding on service delivery together – these services are, however, 'implemented separately by members of the individual disciplines'. Finally, 'trans-disciplinary' involves 'sharing or transferring information and skills across traditional disciplinary boundaries to enable one or two team members to be the primary workers supported by others working as consultants' (Malin and Morrow, 2007, p. 447).

While the phrase 'interprofessional working' is also commonly used, it in turn implies an assumption that we are discussing a particular category of workers – those who have acquired the 'professional' label. Much of the literature and policy, particularly in the area of safeguarding (HM Government, 2006), does focus on some particular groups, for example teachers, educational psychologists, nurses, doctors and social workers. However, the children's workforce is highly diverse. It also includes people in roles such as teaching assistants, early years workers, childminders, family support workers, play workers and foster carers. Other practitioners might work in a voluntary capacity in children's clubs, as Cubs and Brownies leaders, or in provision run by faith groups; most of these have not traditionally been seen as professionals but they can nevertheless play a highly significant role in children's lives. They are also seen to be working in an increasingly 'professional' way as training and regulation have grown.

Issues around professionalism – who counts as a professional and why – are returned to later, but as the opening chapter made clear, our focus in this book is on the broader audience. Exploring 'working together for children' in this book is as much about 'interpractitioner' working as that implied by any other terminology used in work with children.

## 2.2 Politics and policy

The drive for agencies and their practitioners to work more closely together is not a new phenomenon. It has been around as long as there have been different groups of people providing services to children and families. But what is new is the extent of the emphasis on interagency, and increasingly integrated, working in recent approaches to the delivery of children's services. Although this approach has long been common in some areas, such as child protection (DH, 1989; HM Government, 2006; Scottish Executive, 2004; Welsh Assembly Government, 2006), its ramifications have become much wider and now impact on the whole of the children's workforce. This section looks at the context for this process and some of the overarching themes that have contributed to the unparalleled emphasis that has been placed on 'working together' for children.

Recognition of the need for agencies to working together has a long history in the UK. The Kilbrandon Report (1964), for example, as well as establishing the system of children's panels in Scotland, also highlighted the role played by a whole variety of people from different agencies, statutory and voluntary, in the juvenile justice system and the vital importance of effective relationships between them (Cohen, 2005). Lord Kilbrandon proposed the establishment of 'social education' departments, arguing that academic education and 'social living' could not be separated (Cohen, 2005). His arguments, though not acted upon at the time, prefigured thinking about restructuring many years later and the 'whole child' approach to children's services, central to the launch of New Community Schools in Scotland (Cohen, 2005).

Some commentators identify the Conservative administrations of the 1980s as a crucial phase in the recent history of interagency working (Percy-Smith, 2005). During the first administration under Margaret Thatcher there was increasing concern about economic inefficiency and the rising costs of the public sector. The welfare state was viewed as an inefficient bureaucracy with public services reflecting the priorities and interests of professional providers as much, if not more, than service users. The market was seen as a much more efficient vehicle for providing services than the public sector, and the government sought to 'open up' the public sector to competition and the economic disciplines of the marketplace; 'the role of identifying needs for services and planning to meet those needs could be separated from the role of delivering the services' (Percy-Smith, 2005, p. 9).

These ideas led to the 'contract culture' whereby local authorities were obliged to contract with a wide range of private and voluntary organisations, buying in services which they may previously have provided themselves. One of the results of this shake-up of the welfare state was to further increase the complexity of service delivery.

However, at the same time there was an increasing focus, at the highest level of government, on a range of complex problems such as urban regeneration, the environment, community safety and social exclusion.

> These issues were characterised by their 'cross-cutting' nature. In other words, they did not fall clearly within the remit of any one single organisation. Furthermore, they were seen as beyond the ability of any single organisation working alone to solve ... As a result the 1990s saw the development of multilateral partnerships involving the public, private and voluntary sectors, in part stimulated by the availability of central government funding, especially in relation to regeneration.
>
> (Percy-Smith, 2005, p. 10)

While the government changed in 1997, concerns about the public sector remained. New Labour thinking about public services centred on the need to modernise. Education, health and social care were thought of as being in dire need of reform, and a more rigorous, rational and 'scientific' approach to managing the public sector was introduced. This consisted of ensuring that public sector organisations were set clear targets and outcome measures as a means of evaluating how successful they were in achieving their stated objectives (Lister, 2005). The argument for this approach was partly about the efficient use of taxpayers' money, but also about the perceived need to drive up the quality of public services. An emphasis on joining up and working together is an explicit strand within this 'modernisation' agenda (Lister, 2005).

Social exclusion and the work of the Social Exclusion Unit played a central role in providing some of the underpinning theory for this new approach to social policy.

> The principal driver of integration was, from the outset, the six cross-cutting reviews set up under the Labour Government's Comprehensive Spending Review initiated in 1997. The seeds of the children's cross-cutting review can be discerned earlier, in the Labour manifesto pledge to set up Early Excellence Centres. Among its terms of reference was 'to consider whether the multiple causes of social exclusion affecting young people could be more effectively tackled at the family and community level by using a more integrated approach to service provision.' The Social Exclusion Unit was already highlighting the so-called 'wicked

areas' of public provision: cracks through which too many young people were falling.

(Clode, 2003, pp. 4–5)

The drive to work together across different departments, sectors and professional groups to achieve agreed outcomes became the conventional wisdom. 'Joined up thinking and joined up working' was the mantra as partnership arrangements became the vehicle for achieving the aims of government social policy right across the spectrum of public policy, including health, teenage pregnancy, drugs and youth crime – areas emphasised by the work of the government's Social Exclusion Unit. The key problems of delivering a service with many agencies and practitioners involved was restated at the start of the process of introducing *Every Child Matters* in England – including a recognition that some of the hurdles in the way of closer working together are caused by governments themselves:

> Our existing system for supporting children and young people who are beginning to experience difficulties is often poorly co-ordinated and accountability is unclear. This means that information is not shared between agencies so that warning signs are not recognised and acted upon. Some children are assessed many times by different agencies and despite this may get no services. Children may experience a range of professionals involved in their lives but little continuity and consistency of support. Organisations may disagree over who should pay for meeting a child's needs because their problems cut across organisational boundaries. Fragmentation locally is often driven by conflicting messages and competing priorities from central Government.

> (DfES, 2003, pp. 21–22)

## 2.3  Partnership

> Multi-agency working became a policy imperative when the Labour government fixed on 'partnerships' as an alternative ethos to the internal market and competition in services
>
> (Alexander and MacDonald, 2001, cited in Abbott et al., 2005, p. 229)

Thinking point 3.2    What do you understand by partnership in work with children and families? What might be some of the strengths and weaknesses of a partnership?

Partnership, rather like community, is a very nebulous term meaning different things to different people. In this context, partnership is used to describe the new strategic framework through which twenty-first century services were to be delivered. The launch of the Children's Fund in

England in 2000, for children aged 5–13, illustrated some of the key features of this approach:

> The programme aims to identify at an early stage children and young people at risk of social exclusion, and make sure they receive the help and support they need to achieve their potential.
>
> The Children's Fund provides a responsive approach to developing services that address the difficulties faced by some children and their families. It encourages voluntary organisations, community and faith groups to work in partnership with local statutory agencies, and children, young people and their families, to deliver high-quality preventative services to meet the needs of communities.
>
> (DfES, 2005, webpage)

The extract above reveals several things about the government's concerns with social exclusion and early intervention, but it is the summary of the way the service is to be developed that explains the nature of partnership. These developments were also frequently led by voluntary organisations rather than local authorities.

Strategic partnerships continued to be the way such service developments were taken forward in all areas of health and social care, in Scotland, Wales and Northern Ireland as well as England (Glaister and Glaister, 2005; Hudson, 2005). Hudson (2007) argues that these principles have been more explicitly pursued in Scotland, as in England they are complicated by the emphasis placed on the role of the market and competition in the provision of services.

Many local Children's Fund partnerships did succeed in involving small voluntary organisations with large statutory ones in a creative way, although the experience was variable; Chapter 5 will look in more detail at the evaluation of this and similar initiatives. The voluntary and community sector can be a major player at the local level, but because the sector is so diverse, communication with the statutory services for children can be problematic. Whereas the larger children's charities such as Barnardo's and the NSPCC may have an influencing voice at the 'top table' where strategy is agreed, there are many other charities working for children whose voices are rarely heard. The contribution these smaller organisations can make, through community projects or family centres, for example, to the welfare of children can be significant. (For an example of smaller organisations' contributions to the welfare of children, see the material on the voluntary group 'Plus' in Chapter 1.) Those within faith communities, for example, play a significant but often overlooked role, having contact with many of the most vulnerable and, in some cases, socially isolated children in the UK. Some families turn to these smaller groups because of a mistrust of larger or more statutory organisations. It is therefore important that they are included within partnerships working together for children.

Significantly, the extract above about the Children's Fund also refers to children, young people and their families as being part of these partnerships. This model was typical of new initiatives in its emphasis on consultation and representation on partnership boards. There was recognition that children and young people could actively engage in the development of policy. Government departments were starting on the process of 'learning to listen' (Children and Young People's Unit, 2001) and expecting everyone else to do the same. Subsequent policy initiatives have increasingly seen consultation documents such as *Every Child Matters* (Morgan, 2005), *Care Matters* (DfES, 2007) and *Telling Concerns* (Children's Commissioner for Wales, 2003).

> Children and young people's participation has never before been a more popular policy demand.
>
> (Tisdall and Davis, 2004, p. 131)

Partnership is not just about networks of professionals working together with children and families. It also refers to a style of working and an attitude towards working alongside others for the benefit of children. This attitude constantly questions power relationships 'with the lived experience of users, carers and students foregrounded, and the knowledge and status of "experts" challenged at all times' (Curran, 1997, in Taylor et al., 2006, p. 19).

An extensive body of literature around partnership working with children, parents and carers has appeared since a number of the studies reported in *Child Protection: Messages from Research* in 1995:

> Wanting partnership is a step in the right direction but achieving it is difficult. A positive attitude to partnership needs to underpin action, a fact emphasised by their finding that partnership with parents tended to follow from involving the child in the process
>
> (DH, 1995, p. 37)

The finding that it is important for professionals to be seen to be working *with* families is key to creating the right atmosphere for partnership working and is equally applicable to all settings. Partnership relations can be complicated when there are issues of power, status and respect, parents seeing professionals as being gatekeepers to scarce and much needed resources (DH, 2001). Empowerment of children and families is therefore a central strategy for promoting greater equality in the relationship between the service user and the practitioner and the service they work for.

The continued centrality of partnership working to the Children Act 2004 can be seen very clearly in the following table.

| Sections in the Children Act 2004 requiring partnership working | |
|---|---|
| **Section** | **Description** |
| Section 10:<br>The duty to co-operate | A duty is placed on local authorities to make arrangements to promote co-operation between agencies in order to improve children's well-being defined by reference to the five outcomes, and a duty on key partners to take part in those arrangements. It also provides a new power to allow pooling of resources in support of these arrangements. |
| Section 11:<br>The duty to safeguard and promote welfare | Creates a duty for the key agencies who work with children to put in place arrangements to make sure that they take account of the need to safeguard and promote the welfare of children when doing their jobs. |
| Section 12:<br>Information sharing | Allows further secondary legislation and statutory guidance to be made with respect to setting up databases or indexes that contain basic information about children and young people and their families. |
| Sections 13-16:<br>Local safeguarding children's boards (LSCBs) | Requires that local authorities set up statutory LSCBs, and that the key partners take part. |
| Section 17:<br>The children and young person's plan | Establishes a single plan to replace a range of current statutory planning. |
| Sections 18-19:<br>Director of children's services and lead member | To be appointed by local authorities, and to be responsible for, as a minimum, education and children's social services functions. Local authorities have discretion to add other relevant functions, such as leisure or housing, if they feel it is appropriate. |
| Sections 20-24:<br>Integrated inspection | Require an integrated inspection framework to be established by the relevant inspectorates to inform future inspections of all services for children. |

Sections in the Children Act 2004 requiring partnership working (Hudson, 2005, p. 9)

While partnerships appear to provide a participative and inclusive mechanism for the development of children's services and the tackling of social exclusion, Lister (2005) emphasises that the role of partnerships can also be seen as part of a changing model of governance. In effect they could represent a greater penetration of state power by drawing others in to the government agenda:

> The spread of an official and legitimated discourse of partnership has the capacity to draw local stakeholders, from community groups to business organisations, into a more direct relationship with government and involve them in supporting and carrying out the governments agenda ... Labour's emphasis on holistic and joined-up government, and its use of partnerships as a means of

> delivering public policy, can be viewed as enhancing the state's capacity to secure political objectives by sharing power with a range of actors, drawing them into the policy process.
>
> (Newman, 2001, quoted in Lister, 2005, p. 450)

This also potentially 'diverts attention' from resource issues, the need for more fundamental structural changes, and a return to focusing on redistribution:

> Fine words about social exclusion will come to little unless governments grasp the nettle of income redistribution. In a society characterized by a growing divide between rich and poor, talk of 'breaking the cycle of disadvantage' will amount to little.
>
> (Jeffs and Smith, 2002, webpage)

## 2.4 Early intervention

The extract above about the Children's Fund also promotes the importance of identifying '*at an early stage* children and young people at risk of social exclusion', and making sure 'they receive the help and support they need to achieve their potential' (DfES, 2005, our emphasis). This was another significant aspect of the development of New Labour social policy. There had been a growing consensus around the possibility of research identifying risk factors associated with subsequent social exclusion (France and Utting, 2005). Complex and seemingly intractable social problems such as teenage pregnancy or juvenile crime were seen to have their roots in early childhood and the quality of care given to a child before they even get to school, therefore the arguments for intervening early on in a child's life seemed to be inescapable (France and Utting, 2005).

The certainty with which such 'risk' factors can be identified has been controversial. Children could easily become labelled as potentially anti-social or proto-criminal from a very young age, while statistically this will be true for only a small percentage. However, while direct causation is impossible to predict, it was argued that reducing children's exposure to a range of risk factors would be a beneficial preventative strategy. This was supported by research indicating that where multiple overlapping factors are present in children's lives, 'the chances of later problems and problem behaviour increase disproportionately' (France and Utting, 2005, p. 79). This has been characterised as a paradigm that is preventative but also focused on risk:

> However, the underpinning paradigm can more accurately be described as 'risk *and protection-focused* prevention' since it embraces the concept of enhancing protective factors in children's lives as well as tackling risk. 'Protection' in this context is defined

as something other than the opposite of risk. It refers, specifically, to factors that have been consistently associated with good outcomes for children growing up in circumstances where they are, otherwise, heavily exposed to risk.

(France and Utting, 2005, p. 80)

This thinking also seems to underpin two key elements relevant to interagency working. These broader approaches were seen as appropriate for the involvement of whole communities within the partnership model. Tackling these multiple problems also required multiple agencies engaged with children and families focused at an early stage, highlighting the potential value of initiatives such as Sure Start, and informing all subsequent policy strategies.

The drive towards more integrated services for children in a range of differing configurations – extended schools, community schools, children's centres – sought to bring together co-located services and 'wrap-around' care. Any perceived barriers to communication between practitioners were to be dismantled by enabling shared assessment, the recognition of shared common skills, and the increased sharing of information.

## Key points

1   Terminology in this area can be imprecise and confusing but there are some distinct and important differences in what terms describe. One perspective on the way agencies work together is to view their relationships on a continuum of partnership.

2   Interagency working has been a constant theme in policy developments over the last twenty years, particularly in relation to safeguarding children and overlaps with other key ideas such as public sector modernisation and the benefits of early intervention.

3   Partnerships have been a central feature of much interagency working, involving the development of policy as much as its implementation.

# 3 Boundaries and barriers

The previous sections have focused on the various arguments, rationales and drivers towards agencies and their practitioners working more closely together – even changing their roles and structures. The reality of practice has shown that this is often a complex task. Problems have been identified with more integrated approaches to working, but acknowledgement of the issues can contribute to finding solutions.

## 3.1 Thinking about professionalism

If you were to ask a cross-section of the public to identify which occupational groups constitute the 'professions', it is likely that most people would include those traditionally associated with the label such as doctors and lawyers. Some might also include teachers, nurses, health visitors and social workers if asked about professionals working with children. But what about nursery nurses, classroom assistants, play workers, early years workers, childminders and foster carers? The more you examine the various groups of people who work with children, the more blurred the boundaries become between professional and 'non-', 'semi-' or 'para-' professional groups. The situation is also complicated by change, as can be seen in the creation of new roles such as the 'early years professional' as discussed in Chapter 1 or those with the word 'integrated' in the title.

Is professionalism about status and prestige or is it simply about economics? How important are expert knowledge, accountability, self-governance and professional ethics? Is professionalism related to whether one is managed or autonomous? Is there a distinction between acting in a professional way and being a professional? Many of these distinctions are not particularly helpful in understanding what it is that people within the children's workforce actually do. However, some discussion of professionalism is relevant here. The key knowledge bases that must be 'worked across', as discussed earlier, have become closely associated with professional disciplines. The 'professional' label and its history also has significance for hierarchy and power relations – crucial issues given that we are essentially discussing effective working relationships.

Thinking point 3.3   How might different ideas about what constitutes being a professional affect interprofessional working?

The thinking and writing about professionalism which developed in the first half of the twentieth century focused on establishing characteristics or traits that professions were expected to hold. These traits included such things as altruism, trustworthiness, expert skills and knowledge, self-regulation, membership of a professional association and a code of ethics. Members of the professions were contrasted with other occupational groups by the altruistic and ethical way in which their expertise was applied. Most occupations were seen as driven by economic self-interest, whereas professionals were also motivated by 'higher things'. Other perspectives suggested that professionals carry out tasks that are typically characterised by a high level of complexity and uncertainty requiring an equally high level of education, judgement and skill. From this standpoint the tasks carried out by other occupations are less complex and can be more easily standardised, therefore they require less training. Professions have to exercise discretion and judgement, and therefore professional knowledge is seen as more than a set of rules and procedures (Finlay, 2000).

Finlay (2000) suggests that this idea of 'expert knowledge' has remained a very powerful factor in the public acceptance of professions. This in turn has influenced historically 'newer' groups such as nursing and social work to seek to establish an expert knowledge base of their own.

> Some kinds of knowledge are seen as more valid than others. In general, scientific knowledge carries more weight and respect than practical, experiential knowledge. In an effort to gain recognition of their professional status, many 'newer' professions in recent years have driven to establish a more expert knowledge base and increase their academic and scientific credibility ... 'semi-professionals' have campaigned to extend existing diploma training to degree level and replace on-the-job training with university-based study. Turning away from common-sense knowledge, they have struggled to develop their professional research base to show the worth and value of their work.
>
> (Finlay, 2000, p. 77)

Also crucial to the debate on the position of professionals is the question of power and control over particular areas of work (Hugman, 2005). This can be reinforced by the use of language through jargon and defining and labelling people's needs and problems – labelling a child as 'special needs', for example. Professional power can both reflect and reinforce the relatively privileged positions some groups hold in the social and economic hierarchy. If control over areas of work is central to the identity of a professional group, then it is easy to see how working with other agencies in a way that might involve sharing an area of work might be problematic.

Power issues between groups of practitioners can also be seen in a variety of dimensions, notably class, ethnicity and gender. Finlay (2000) suggests that in relation to gender it is not just that women have been excluded from certain professions but also that those few professions dominated by women are defined in relation to those which are more traditionally

Professional power and status is also associated with issues such as gender and ethnicity

male-oriented. Care is not accorded the same weight as the application of knowledge even though the latter may be dependent on the former. (For more on care in children's services, see Chapter 7.) Some of the struggles between the relative professions of nurses and doctors can be perceived in this way (Finlay, 2000).

These critiques of professionalism have left many occupational groups working with children ambivalent about their professional status. On the one hand, they want to be seen as being 'professional' in the sense of having credibility (recognised by qualification), in terms of their specialised knowledge about children and their skills in working with children. On the other hand, it is obvious that elitism and professional language can act as a powerful barrier between the worker and the children and families with whom they are trying to build a relationship. Some practitioners have seen their role as forming radical alliances with people they work with, and have questioned why regulation and university-based education are essential to working in a professional way. Both social work and youth work, for example, have had anti-professional strands in their development (Banks, 2004). Similarly, why should new professions struggle to establish a more scientific knowledge base when the nature of professional knowledge is contested?

Some of this questioning of the basis of being a professional has led to the idea that a new form of professionalism could emerge. It has been suggested that this could take the form of more empowering and democratic relationships with service users, reflecting the participatory style of practice discussed earlier. At the same time there is a recognition of the difficulties of actually achieving this in the modern, pressured, managerialised working environment (Banks, 2004). In an article about what she calls the 'new multi-agency working', Edwards (2004) outlines her view of what could be a way of working together for children. Rather than being led by the needs of the service providers, Edwards argues that the new multi-agency working for children should be geared around the needs of the child and family:

> The characteristics of the new professional practice include:
> - a focus on children and young people as whole people, ie not as specific 'needs'
> - following the child's trajectory
> - an ability to talk across professional boundaries
> - an understanding of what other practitioners are able to offer the responsive package of protection that is built around the child or young person
> - acknowledgement of the capacity of service users and their families to help to tailor the services they are receiving
> - an understanding that changing the trajectories of exclusion of children and young people involves not only building confidence and skills but also a reconfiguring of the opportunities available to them – ie systems-wide change.
>
> (Edwards, 2004, p. 5)

There is no intention here to reach a conclusion about who is a professional and who is not; definitions are diverse and changing, and may be of limited value. The whole concept of professionalism is a fluid one as established professionals find their position challenged and new roles emerge and become more qualified or claim new areas of expertise. Other practitioners may adopt elements of working in a 'professional way' even if not any formal label. Nevertheless, even if unresolved, differing views about expert knowledge, established cultures and hierarchies will inevitably be an issue as workers are asked to cross established boundaries. Hudson (2002) argues that the sociology of professionalism suggests that there are three major features of interprofessional working:

- professional identity: how professionals understand themselves and their role including the more informal and implicit aspects of professional cultures
- professional status: how different professional groups are variously distributed along the continuum of power and influence in society
- professional accountability: the extent to which different professional groups have the ability to exercise professional discretion and the way in which they are supervised and managed.

As we discussed in Chapter 1, in research with a range of social care professionals (Banks, 2004), the most common themes that emerged from conversations with practitioners were perceived threats to professional identity, values and culture, a point illustrated by the following comment:

> 'I think you have to have a very good grounding in social work, as not just a profession, but as *a value base*, otherwise it is very easy to get sort of sucked into *the dominant culture* which social work is not in an integrated team.'

(Manager in a CAMHS team, quoted in Banks, 2004, p. 135)

It may be that any actual difference in values is less important than the fact that workers say that their values are different in order to distinguish themselves, for example as social workers and not nurses, or vice versa (Banks, 2004). Banks also argues that this can be threatening because being, for example, a social worker 'may contribute to part of what an individual thinks about as the deepest and most enduring features of their unique selves' (Banks, 2004, p. 138). Similarly, elements of a personal identity can contribute to an individual's whole approach to their working life.

A theme emerging from interagency working, particularly within teams, is that it is a process that needs to be worked through, individually and collectively. It is at the problematic points of this 'working through' that references to culture and values seem to be stressed by practitioners.

The drive towards increasingly integrated working therefore brings challenges to accepted professional boundaries and those that have worked within them. In multi-disciplinary teams, different specialisms, based on professional knowledge bases, can collide in uncomfortable ways:

> In multi-agency teamwork, professional knowledge boundaries can become blurred and professional identity can be challenged as roles and responsibilities change. Such changes can generate discomfort, anxiety, and anger in team members as they struggle to cope with the disintegration of one version of professional identity before a new version can be built. Moreover, the rapid pace of reform leaves little time for adjustment.

(Frost et al., 2005, p. 188)

While this process is problematic and presents barriers to effective working, there is evidence that such barriers can be overcome. Frost et al. (2005) explored the working of integrated teams in relation to the concept of 'communities of practice' – a concept of social learning (Wenger, 1998) that describes how people communicate, work and learn together. Their research suggests that whilst this process is never easy, it offers the opportunity for a great deal of learning and development as team members' knowledge and practice is enriched by mutual learning in a context of respect for diversity. New professional relationships can emerge that enable more successful learning and working together. The concept of 'communities of practice' is explored in more detail in Chapter 6.

Thinking point 3.4    To what extent do you think 'learning together' might overcome the problems of working together?

## 3.2  Barriers to collaborative working

While issues of knowledge and status are crucial factors to be addressed in enabling collaborative working, numerous other interrelated individual and agency factors have been identified as potential obstacles. Salmon (2004) notes the importance of the differing governing policies of agencies, their guidelines, definitions, eligibility criteria, budgets, reporting cycles, supervisory structures, salaries and career development. Salaries can undoubtedly be a sensitive issue:

> Joined-up work often means different professionals doing the same work; for example, in the emerging children's teams many staff will be expected to use the common assessment framework. Where they are on different salary scales and service conditions they may resent this, and ask why they are not being paid as much as another profession doing the same work.
>
> (Frost and Lloyd, 2006, p. 13)

In a review of interprofessional collaboration between professionals working with children and families in areas of high social need, significant areas of disagreement were found to be:

- Differences of view over the nature of the intervention that was required
- Differences of view over who was responsible for carrying out the intervention
- Poor communication or a breakdown in communication where the different services were prioritising liaison/collaboration itself differently
- Different time scales for action between different services and agencies, though this may be seen as mainly a resource issue
- Differences in prioritising cases and in what constitutes a 'crisis'
- Differences in the way the services were organised.

(Easen et al., 2000, quoted in Salmon, 2004, p. 158)

A large-scale study of the implementation of Children's Trusts in England reported some early findings based on the Pathfinder Trusts (O'Brien et al., 2006). The authors conclude:

> Our findings suggest that whilst professional communities are embracing a commitment to the education, health and care of the 'whole' rather than the 'sectoral' child, differences between professional discourses and traditions remain, particularly in relation to threshold and intervention decisions.
>
> (O'Brien et al., 2006, p. 394)

The study makes the point that a tension exists at the level of philosophy and policy about the overall shape of children's services around the balance between targeted and universal services.

Another study carried out over roughly the same time period looks at practical issues around the implementation of the Common Assessment Framework (CAF) and lead professional working (Brandon et al., 2006). An evaluation of the early piloting of these initiatives in twelve English local authorities found that there are a number of interlocking factors that either help or hinder implementation. Where there is enthusiasm for multi-agency working and a clear structure understood by practitioners on the front line, the CAF and lead professional role are helping agencies to come together much faster and enabling better follow-up services. However, hindrances included the lack of a local history of successful multi-agency working, breeding professional mistrust and fuelling anxiety about change (Brandon et al., 2006).

Sometimes it appears that there are fundamental issues of structure and philosophy that make desired change problematic. Cohen et al. (2004) analysed the reorganisation of early years services in England and Scotland to identify the success or otherwise of integrating the 'care' and 'education' aspects of early years provision. These different aspects of provision were developed in different departmental areas but were brought together under the department responsible for education in the late 1990s. The same integration occurred in Sweden, and the authors use this as a point of comparison.

The process of integration in England and Scotland has proved to be problematic from the most strategic level downwards. Amalgamating services under one department had not necessarily (five years later) resulted in a service that can be described as integrated, particularly in terms of philosophy. There was, for example, a problem with 'services formerly in the welfare system – "childcare" – adopting education principles' (Cohen et al., 2004, p. 188). Different element of provision in England and Scotland were increasingly 'linked' but could not be described as integrated where this is understood as 'merging or fusion'.

Integrating different philosophies into care and education in the early years can be problematic

The relative success of this experience in Sweden highlights some of the reasons why integration in the UK has proven so difficult. In England and to a lesser extent in Scotland, delivery of early years provision had become very fragmented after many years of a policy of a mixed economy of care. Drawing together these services here was always going to be much more complex than in Sweden, where the equivalent of the local authority was the main provider. Similarly, in the UK there is a history of a wide divergence between practitioners in the workforce of different aspects of early years work, for example in terms of training, pay and union membership; the differentiation between teachers and other early years workers is less marked in Sweden. Finally, the Swedish model is more focused on attaining a common view of children's learning and care (pedagogy being 'an integrating concept'), while in the UK the main drivers for change were concerns about solving long-standing social and economic problems. The employment agenda, for example, could be seen as 'a gravity field pulling childcare away from being fully integrated with education' (Cohen et al., 2004, p. 196).

There is no suggestion by Cohen and colleagues that the Swedish model can be easily copied; indeed, that would not be possible. Attempts to merge different services need to take account of their histories and cultures. The analysis of Cohen et al. (2004) provides a useful insight into why the stated desire for integration of services may not be achievable.

## 3.3 Communicating across boundaries

Worthy of specific consideration is the issue of communication. Communication is one of the most frequently reported problems of interagency and interprofessional work. Different groups of practitioners bring different terminology and meanings to any exchange, drawn from their specific training and worldviews. The most high profile failings of communication are those repeated in numerous child protection inquiry reports. When such concerns were reflected again in the Victoria Climbié inquiry (Laming, 2003), Lord Laming argued for more strategies to be employed to enable clearer communication. His report recommended the amalgamation of current guidance into 'one simplified document' that enables a 'common language':

> It must establish a common language for use across all agencies to help those agencies to identify who they are concerned about, why they are concerned, who is best placed to respond to those concerns, and what outcome is being sought from any planned response.
>
> (Laming, 2003, p. 373)

The twin solutions to practitioners working more closely together were to increasingly co-locate them, moving towards integrated teams, and to enable this process through a shared language. These are bold attempts to crack an important, recurrent and persistent issue. However, there have been questions raised about the logic of this approach. Does being physically in closer proximity automatically result in closer working relationships? Just because practitioners are saying the same thing, do they mean the same thing?

White and Featherstone (2005) observed communication in a child health team (paediatrics, CAMHS, child and family social work) who had recently moved to an integrated centre. The co-location did not automatically break down different agency perceptions of the same case. In some instances the visibility of certain practices – for example the time some groups spent in meetings – served to sharpen rather than reduce prejudices between certain groups. Interactions occur with long-established and ritualised ways of working and ways of viewing practitioners from 'other' groups:

> professionals working at the multi-agency interface operate with robust social identities, which they take for granted as members of particular occupational groups, organizations or teams. Co-location does not straightforwardly lead to more or better communication. People cannot communicate with proper openness to the 'other' (professional) whilst the aspects of their professional narratives that maintain ritualized ways of working are underexplored.
>
> (White and Featherstone, 2005, p. 215)

In the child protection arena there have been numerous examples of poor communication in terms of passing vital information on to the right person. However, even where this is good practice in this respect, information received is not always interpreted in the way it was intended. Reder and

Duncan (2003) argue for the need to focus less on a common language than on the actual process of communicating itself. They emphasise that communication is a sophisticated process that involves a great deal more than simply sharing information. A message has to be both given and received and then meaning attributed to it. In the complex and emotive area of child protection this process is highly problematic and there are lots of opportunities for messages to be distorted or lost in transition. Reder and Duncan (2003) point to numerous examples of such problems given in the evidence heard by the Victoria Climbié Inquiry (Laming, 2003):

> 'I cannot account for the way people interpreted what I said. It was not the way I would have liked it to have been interpreted.'
>
> (Paediatrician quoted in Laming, 2003, p. 9)

including conflicting versions of what was said:

> To get a better understanding of the medical concerns, Ms Arthurworrey telephoned Dr Rossiter. Dr Rossiter remembered a conversation with Ms Arthurworrey occurring some time that week, but their recollections of what was said are rather different.
>
> (Laming, 2003, p. 150)

Their conclusion is that the focus of successful interagency working should be less on structural change and more on the skill of communication itself.

> Some have argued that communication between relevant professionals would improve if agency boundaries were dissolved and they all worked together within the same organizational structure. This call for reorganization fundamentally misses the point about the psychology of communication: that individuals and groups create and recreate their own boundaries based on beliefs, attitudes, work pressures, and so on. Furthermore, each episode of communication has an interpersonal dynamic of its own, and clarity of understanding will not necessarily be enhanced by different organisational structures. In our view, efforts to enhance professionals' capacity to think, and therefore to communicate, would be more rewarding.
>
> (Reder and Duncan, 2003, p. 95)

## Key points

1   The idea of the professional and professionalism still has an important influence on the effectiveness of practitioners working across their traditional boundaries.

2   Research studies have highlighted a substantial range of issues that arise and must be understood when practitioners are asked to work in a more integrated way.

3   Communication is a particularly significant issue which may be partly enabled by closer integration of workers and the use of more common tools and language. Other aspects of this issue, however, may also need to be acknowledged, including practitioner skills in communication and their ability to reflect on practice.

## Conclusion

In exploring a topic that necessarily focuses on the nature of relationships between agencies and practitioners, this chapter has attempted to reinforce the importance of starting with the views and rights of children and their families and the context of their lives. The increasing drive towards interagency, interprofessional and integrated working has created complex issues with a huge range of potential barriers and surrounded by confusing terminology. In highlighting some of the most significant issues we hope to start the process of unravelling whether it is working and what might enable practice to develop further.

# References

Abbott, D., Watson, D. and Townsley, R. (2005) 'The proof of the pudding: what difference does multi-agency working make to families with disabled children with complex care needs?', *Child & Family Social Work*, vol. 10, no. 3, pp. 229–238.

Aldgate, J. (2006) 'Children, development and ecology' in Aldgate, J., Jones, D., Rose, W. and Jeffery, C. (eds) *The Developing World of the Child*, London, Jessica Kingsley.

Alexander, H. and Macdonald, E. (2001) 'Evaluating policy-driven multi-agency partnership working', paper presented to the UK Evaluation Society Annual Conference, 5–7 December, Belfast.

Banks, S. (2004) *Ethics, Accountability and the Social Professions*, Basingstoke, Palgrave Macmillan.

Brandon, M., Howe, A., Dagley, V., Salter, C. and Warren, C. (2006) 'What appears to be helping or hindering practitioners in implementing the Common Assessment Framework and lead professional working?', *Child Abuse Review*, vol. 15, no. 6, pp. 396–413.

Bridge Child Care Development Service (1995) *Paul: Death Through Neglect*, London, Bridge Publications.

Bronfenbrenner, U. (1979) *The Ecology of Human Development*, Cambridge, MA, Harvard University Press.

Care Co-ordination Network UK (2001) *Information sheet*, York, CCNUK.

Children and Young People's Unit (2001) *Learning to Listen: Core Principles for the Involvement of Children and Young People*, London, DfES.

Children's Commissioner for Wales (2003) *Telling Concerns: Report of the Children's Commissioner for Wales' Review of the Operation of Complaints and Representations and Whistleblowing Procedures and Arrangements for the Provision of Children's Advocacy Services*, available online at <http://www.childcom.org.uk/publications/Telling_Concerns.pdf>, accessed 2 January 2008.

Clode, D. (2003) *Integrated Working and Children's Services – Structures, Outcomes and Reform: A Briefing Paper*, London, Integrated Care Network.

Cohen, B. (2005) 'Inter-agency collaboration in context: the "joining-up" agenda' in Glaister, A. and Glaister, B. (eds) *Inter-Agency Collaboration – Providing for Children*, Edinburgh, Dunedin Academic Press.

Cohen, B., Moss, P., Petrie, P. and Wallace, J. (2004) *A New Deal for Children? Re-forming Education and Care in England, Scotland and Sweden*, Bristol, The Policy Press.

Curran, T. (1997) 'Power, participation and post modernism: user and practitioner participation in mental health and social work education', *Social Work Education*, vol. 16, no. 3, pp. 21–36.

Department for Education and Skills (DfES) (2003) *Every Child Matters*, London, The Stationery Office.

Department for Education and Skills (DfES) (2004) *Every Child Matters: Change for Children*, London, The Stationery Office.

Department for Education and Skills (DfES) (2005) *Every Child Matters: Children's Fund*, available online at <http://www.everychildmatters.gov.uk/strategy/childrensfund>, accessed 24 April 2007.

Department for Education and Skills (DfES) (2007) *Care Matters: Consultation Responses*, London, DfES.

Department of Health (DH) (1989) *Working Together to Safeguard Children*, London, The Stationery Office.

Department of Health (DH) (1995) *Child Protection Messages from Research*, London, The Stationery Office.

Department of Health (DH) (2001) *The Children Act Now: Messages from Research*, London, The Stationery Office.

Easen, P., Atkins, M. and Dyson, A. (2000) 'Inter-professional collaboration and conceptualisations of practice', *Children & Society*, vol. 14, no. 5, pp. 355–367.

Edwards, A. (2004) 'The new multi-agency working: collaborating to prevent the social exclusion of children and families', *Journal of Integrated Care*, vol. 12, no. 5, pp. 3–9.

Fawcett, M. (2000) 'Early development: critical perspectives' in Boushel, M., Fawcett, M. and Selwyn, J. (eds) *Focus on Early Childhood: Principles and Realities*, Oxford, Blackwell, pp. 49–64.

Finlay, L. (2000) 'The challenge of professionalism' in Brechin, A., Brown, H. and Eby, M.A. (eds) *Critical Practice in Health and Social Care*, London, The Open University/Sage, pp. 73–95.

France, A. and Utting, D. (2005) 'The paradigm of "risk and protection-focused prevention" and its impact on services for children and families', *Children & Society*, vol. 19, no. 2, pp. 77–90.

Frost, N. (2005) *Professionalism, Partnership and Joined-up Thinking*, Dartington, Research in Practice.

Frost, N. and Lloyd, A. (2006) 'Implementing multi-disciplinary teamwork in the new child welfare policy environment', *Journal of Integrated Care*, vol. 14, no. 2, pp. 11–17.

Frost, N., Robinson, M. and Anning, A. (2005) 'Social workers in multidisciplinary teams: issues and dilemmas for professional practice', *Child & Family Social Work*, vol. 10, no. 3, pp. 187–196.

Glaister, A. and Glaister, B. (2005) 'Space for growth' in Glaister, A. and Glaister, B. (eds) *Inter-Agency Collaboration – Providing for Children*, Edinburgh, Dunedin Academic Press.

HM Government (2006) *Working Together to Safeguard Children: A Guide to Inter-agency Working to Safeguard and Promote the Welfare of Children*, London, The Stationery Office.

Hudson, B. (2002) 'Interprofessionality in health and social care: the Achilles' heel of partnership?', *Journal of Interprofessional Care*, vol. 16, no. 1, pp. 7–17.

Hudson, B. (2005) 'Partnership working and the children's services agenda: is it feasible?', *Journal of Integrated Care*, vol. 13, no. 2, pp. 7–12.

Hudson, B. (2007) 'Partnering through networks: can Scotland crack it?', *Journal of Integrated Care*, vol. 15, no. 1, pp. 3–13.

Hugman, R. (2005) *New Approaches in Ethics for the Caring Professions*, Basingstoke, Palgrave Macmillan.

Jeffs, T. and Smith, M. (2002) *Social exclusion, joined-up thinking and individualization – new labour's connexions strategy*, available online at <http://www.infed.org/personaladvisers/connexions_strategy.htm>, accessed 5 September 2007.

Kilbrandon, Lord (1964) *The Kilbrandon Report: Children and Young Persons, Scotland*, Edinburgh, HMSO.

Laming, Lord (2003) *The Victoria Climbié Inquiry*, London, The Stationery Office.

Lister, R. (2005) 'Investing in the citizen-workers of the future: transformations in citizenship and the state under New Labour' in Hendrick, H. (ed.) *Child Welfare and Social Policy*, Bristol, The Policy Press.

Malin, N. and Morrow, G. (2007) 'Models of interprofessional working within a Sure Start "trailblazer" programme', *Journal of Interprofessional Care*, vol. 21, no. 4, pp. 445–457.

Mayall, B. (1996) *Children, Health and the Social Order*, Buckingham, Open University Press.

Morgan, R. (2005) *Younger Children's Views on 'Every Child Matters'*, Commission for Social Care Inspection, available online at <http://rights4me.org/content/beheardreports/14/young_views_on_everychildmatters_report.pdf>, accessed 10 September 2007.

Moss, P. and Petrie, P. (2002) *From Children's Services to Children's Spaces*, London, Routledge.

Newman, J. (2001) *Modernising Governance*, London, Sage.

O'Brien, M., Bachmann, M., Husbands, C., Shreeve, A., Jones, N., Watson, J. and Shemilt, I. (2006) 'Integrating children's services to promote children's welfare: early findings from the implementation of Children's Trusts in England', *Child Abuse Review*, vol. 15, no. 6, pp. 377–395.

Percy-Smith, J. (2005) *What Works in Strategic Partnerships for Children?*, Ilford, Barnardo's.

Reder, P. and Duncan, S. (2003) 'Understanding communication in child protection networks', *Child Abuse Review*, vol. 12, no. 2, pp. 82–100.

Salmon, G. (2004) 'Multi-agency collaboration: the challenges for CAMHS', *Child and Adolescent Mental Health*, vol. 9, no. 4, pp. 156–161.

Scottish Executive (2004) *Protecting Children and Young People: Framework for Standards*, Edinburgh, Scottish Executive.

Taylor, I., Sharland, E., Sebba, J., Leriche, P., Keep, E. and Orr, D. (2006) *The Learning, Teaching and Assessment of Partnership Working in Social Work Education*, London, SCIE.

Tisdall, E. and Davis, J. (2004) 'Making a difference? Bringing children's and young people's views into policy-making', *Children & Society*, vol. 18, no. 2, pp. 131–142.

Townsley, R., Abbott, D. and Watson, D. (2004) *Making a Difference?*, Bristol, The Policy Press.

Turner, C. (2003) *Are You Listening? What Disabled Children and Young People in Wales Think About the Services They Use*, Cardiff, Welsh Assembly.

Welsh Assembly Government (2006) *Safeguarding Children: Working Together under the Children Act 2004*, Cardiff, Welsh Assembly Government.

Wenger, E. (1998) *Communities of Practice: Learning, Meaning, and Identity*, Cambridge, Cambridge University Press.

White, S. and Featherstone, B. (2005) 'Communicating misunderstandings: multi-agency work as social practice', *Child & Family Social Work*, vol. 10, no. 3, pp. 207–216.

# Chapter 4

## Policy into practice: assessment, evaluation and multi-agency working with children

Caroline Jones and Stephen Leverett

## Introduction

The idea of different government or local authority agencies working together is not new. However, the drive towards integrated working which includes the entire children's workforce (that is, every individual who works, on an employed or voluntary basis, with children and their families across sectors such as health, education, early years and childcare, play work, social care, police, youth support and leisure services) under the 'interagency' umbrella is a more recent and ambitious innovation.

This chapter draws on the context of influence, the context of policy production and the context of practice (Bowe et al., 1992) as well as the context of evaluation. It uses these to take a closer look at the notion of multi-agency working from the perspective of individual practitioners and service users within children's services. It is important to note that the issues are complex and contentious, often involving deeply held values and beliefs. Even an acceptable discourse such as multi-agency working is subject to dilemmas in that individuals operate within unequal power relations. Policies and practices are subject to competing resources, choices and priorities and are, therefore, inherently political. The process of turning policy into practice reflects and is affected by this political context.

The first section focuses on the context of influence, in other words, the strategic overview enshrined in legislation and national policy (from across the four UK nations) which constructs multi-agency working as a means of improving outcomes for children. The next section looks at multi-agency work in terms of policy text production. As an example it focuses on the policy texts relating to the English Common Assessment Framework, which provides guidance on a common process to assess children's actual and potential 'additional needs', including the 'lead professional' role and guidance on information sharing. The third section examines the context of practice, highlighting multi-agency working as a practical evolving process of negotiation and communication between groups of practitioners, agencies and individual settings. The final section considers the importance of evaluation in order to assess whether multi-agency working is capable of achieving real change for children or whether it fails to penetrate beyond procedural issues.

## Core questions

- How does a government's strategic overview or vision reach practice through policy?

- What are some of the complexities and potential benefits of multi-agency working?

- Using the English Common Assessment Framework (CAF) as an example, what tensions and issues can be observed within policy texts and from their interrelationships with the realities of practice?

- How can evaluation provide evidence that multi-agency working leads to improved outcomes for children?

# 1 The context of influence: the policy trajectory

The drive towards multi-agency working is analysed here using a model which characterises the political process in terms of 'trajectories' (Bowe et al., 1992). This stems from a rejection of the linear or 'top-down' process of policy implementation, whereby legislation emanates from the top of a hierarchy and is implemented in a systematic way, in favour of institutional reinterpretation, claiming that in the context of practice, 'policy is not simply received and implemented' but can be interpreted and 'recreated' (Bowe et al., 1992, p. 22). Hence we focus on the individual practitioners who, to a greater or lesser extent, are crucial to the process of multi-agency working, as effective implementation may well be dependent on the cooperation of those individuals implementing the policy at the front line.

Thinking point 4.1   Think of an example of a widely promoted government social policy objective affecting children's services (for example, eradicating child poverty, disability rights, service user involvement). To what extent would it be fair to say this policy example has been interpreted and recreated by agencies and settings? What do you think has contributed to this variation?

Bowe et al. (1992) highlight the complexities of the policy process and challenge previous portrayals of policy generation as separate from implementation. Rather than regarding policy simply as something that is 'done to people', it is argued that policy is a continual process which emerges from and interacts with a variety of interrelated contexts. As in the traditional game of 'Chinese Whispers', what is stated or even intended at one end of the chain does not automatically equate with messages received at the other end. The bottom line is that all policies are 'implemented by individuals and those individuals will interpret them in their own idiosyncratic ways' (Goacher et al., 1988, p. 19).

The notion of multi-agency working can be analysed using three primary policy contexts. First, the *context of influence*, where policy discourses are constructed and key policy concepts – for example, partnership or multi-agency working – are established. Second, the *context of policy text production*, or the documents that represent policy. These are usually expressed in language which claims to be reasonable and for the 'general public good' (Bowe et al., 1992). They include texts such as the *SEN Code of Practice* (DfES, 2001) or the *Working Together to Safeguard Children* guidelines (HM Government, 2006). Such texts are then responded to within the *context of practice*, or what actually happens on the ground – for example, schools, childcare or health settings – as a result of a particular policy.

In addition to the contexts of influence, text production and practice, Ball (1994) added two further contexts which are particularly relevant to this chapter: first, the *context of outcomes*, which is concerned with effects on practice and on patterns of social access, opportunity and justice; second, the *context of political strategy*, or a cataloguing of a set of political and social activities 'which might more effectively tackle inequalities' (Troyna, 1993). Jones (2000) added a sixth context, the 'context of hidden values'. This is where, overtly, the policy outcome should have a positive effect; for example, most legislation promoting interagency cooperation in children's services aims to improve the wellbeing of children and protect their welfare. However, Jones suggests that there may be a range of hidden meanings and outcomes. At a central level, policy can be cleverly constructed to disguise a particular set of intentions, values and beliefs. Intentionally or otherwise, policy may be a 'wolf in sheep's clothing'. Legislation, for example that improving the availability and quality of childcare, may be part of a wider project to generate human capital and stimulate the economy by encouraging women into part-time flexible employment. There is also evidence that practitioners construct their own meanings related to policy, whether these are intended or not. Commenting on the tendency of policy makers to centrally design forms, e-templates and assessment tools (such as the Common Assessment Framework that we will examine in the next section), both Garrett (2006) and Axford et al. (2006) note how these are sometimes resisted by practitioners because they are 'perceived as exerting central control over hitherto fairly autonomous areas and suspected of being a cost-cutting device' (Axford et al., 2006, p. 172). Consequently, policy could actually sustain or create circumstances that maintain or exacerbate problems. Rather than being a solution to the perceived problem, the interaction between policy and practice may cause a new set of problems.

For the purposes of this chapter, the key point is that policy is enacted at three levels – central, local and front line. At central level the key ideas are made concrete, reflecting the dominant discourses and values. These are then articulated nationally and locally, in the form of texts. By the time policy enters a workplace involving children, such as a childminder's home or a children's centre, practitioners' perceptions and practice are inevitably affected. The question is: to what extent is the vision enshrined in central policy on multi-agency working likely to change as it travels on its journey from central government to individual practitioner?

Governments have a tendency to construct their vision for policy as a statement of aims or intended outcomes. Sometimes the vision is embedded within a wider framework; for example, governments in Scotland, Wales and Northern Ireland align themselves closely to the UNCRC.

The Scottish Executive (2005a) states that in order to become 'confident individuals, effective contributors, successful learners and responsible citizens', all Scotland's children need to be 'nurtured, safe, active, healthy, engaged in learning, achieving, included, respected and responsible'.

In Wales, the seven Core Aims are that all children and young people:

- have a flying start in life;
- have a comprehensive range of education and learning opportunities;
- enjoy the best possible health and are free from abuse, victimisation and exploitation;
- have access to play, leisure, sporting and cultural activities;
- are listened to, treated with respect, and have their race and cultural identity recognised;
- have a safe home and a community which supports physical and emotional wellbeing;
- are not disadvantaged by poverty.

(Welsh Assembly Government, 2004, p. 1)

In Northern Ireland, a Ten Year Strategy measures itself against the following outcomes framework, indicating whether children are:

- Healthy;
- Enjoying, learning and achieving;
- Living in safety and with stability;
- Experiencing economic and environmental well-being;
- Contributing positively to community and society; and
- Living in a society which respects their rights.

(Office of the First Minister and Deputy First Minister of Northern Ireland, 2006, p. 7)

In England, children's wellbeing was defined as the five mutually reinforcing outcomes originally presented in the *Every Child Matters* Green Paper (DfES, 2003, p. 6):

- being healthy
- staying safe
- enjoying and achieving
- making a positive contribution
- economic well-being.

The next stage in the process is to translate these visions into learning and action that can be adopted and implemented by people working directly with children. In Northern Ireland, the outcomes framework has been embellished with supporting themes which give direction to the way in

As well as policy makers sharing their vision with the children's workforce, it is also considered important that children have an awareness of intended policy outcomes. The Northern Ireland Children and Young People's Unit has attempted to do this by introducing the Super Six Cartoon Strip (NICYPU, 2006).

which children's services will be shaped. Notice how the fourth of these specifically relates to the particular Northern Ireland political context:

- the need to adopt a 'whole-child' approach ...
- working in partnership with those who provide and commission children's services ...
- securing and harnessing the support of parents, carers and the communities ...
- responding appropriately to the challenges we face as a society emerging from conflict ...
- making a gradual shift to preventative and early intervention approaches ...
- developing a culture where the views of our children and young people are routinely sought in matters which impact on their lives;
- ensuring the needs of children are fully assessed using agreed frameworks and common language and that the services they receive are based on identified needs and evidence about what works; and
- driving towards a culture which respects and progresses the rights of the child.

(Office of the First Minister and Deputy First Minister of Northern Ireland, 2006, p. 13)

In England, there was an attempt to embed the government's vision within training for practitioners. The five outcomes were integrated into the development of 'the common core skills and knowledge for the children's workforce' (DfES, 2005a) consisting of:

- Effective communication and engagement with children, young people and families
- Child and young person development
- Safeguarding and promoting the welfare of the child
- Supporting transitions
- Multi-agency working
- Sharing information.

Despite variations, all UK governments agree that children will benefit from closer working between practitioners and between agencies. This illustrates the extent to which their vision is often linked to the evaluation of existing policy, in this case both to recommendations from official reports into the failings of some children's services and to findings from research into the experiences of people accessing children's services (including parents). Both of these links suggest that different professions and agencies should communicate effectively and work together more closely in a coordinated way in the interests of children's health, wellbeing and safety:

> 'My child isn't cut into three pieces and I think there is a coordinated service between the agencies and I think that's important.'
>
> (Parent of a disabled child quoted in Sloper, 2004, p. 572)

> The social worker and health visitor who were supposed to visit Caleb [a baby subject to child protection procedures who later died] did so, but not often enough in the circumstances, even allowing for a gap between what was known about his home environment and what was the reality. What monitoring they did do was not jointly planned, or effectively co-ordinated.
>
> (O'Brien et al., 2003, p. 4)

> The agenda for ... [children's] services requires close joint working arrangements with other local government services including education, leisure, environmental services and housing ... Partnerships outside the authority with the private and voluntary sectors, the police and probation service are also of great importance.
>
> (Social Services Inspectorate for Wales, 2004, p. 3)

The political rationale for multi-agency working was based on the idea that 'joined-up' problems require 'joined-up' solutions. Commenting on interagency partnership relating to the establishment of Education Action Zones policy in 1997, Tony Blair, then Prime Minister, announced that:

> 'all too often governments in the past have tried to slice problems up into separate packages ... in many areas dozens of agencies and professions are working in parallel, often doing good things, but sometimes working at cross purposes with far too little co-ordination and co-operation ... Joined-up problems demand joined-up solutions'

(Tony Blair quoted in Power, 2001, p. 17)

The commitment is clear and stems from the belief that a child should be seen as a whole individual: not a pupil, a client or a patient, but an active person within a social and political environment. Many of the texts translating policy into assessment guidelines represent this ecological perspective (as we will see later in the discussion around the Common Assessment Framework) with the three domains (see figure below) of:

- the child's developmental needs
- the parents' or caregivers' capacities to respond appropriately
- the wider family and environmental factors.

**Elements within the three domains**

**Development of child**

- Health
  - *general health, physical development and speech, language and communications development*
- Emotional and social development
- Behavioural development
- Identity, including self-esteem, self-image and social presentation
- Family and social relationships
- Self-care skills and independence
- Learning
  - *understanding, reasoning and problem solving, participation in learning, education and employment, progress and achievement, aspirations*

**Parents and carers**

- Progress and achievement, aspirations
- Basic care, ensuring safety and protection
- Emotional warmth and stability
- Guidance, boundaries and stimulation

**Family and environmental**

- Family history, functioning and wellbeing
- Wider family
- Housing, employment and financial considerations
- Social and community elements and resources, including education

Elements within the three domains (Children's Workforce Development Council (CWDC), 2007a, p. 21)

Agencies and practitioners offer services that relate to one or more of these three domains and consequently can be effective by learning and working together.

Thinking point 4.2    Which agencies and practitioners should be cooperating and working together?

As previous chapters have highlighted, the drive towards 'partnership' working has gradually been replaced by a continuum of arrangements described variously as 'integrated', 'multi-agency' and 'interagency' working, terms which have been used interchangeably in policy documents. In England, the Children Act 2004, for example, required each local authority to make arrangements for multi-agency working through a Children's Trust (HM Government, 2004). Here services work together at central and local policy level as well as on the front line.

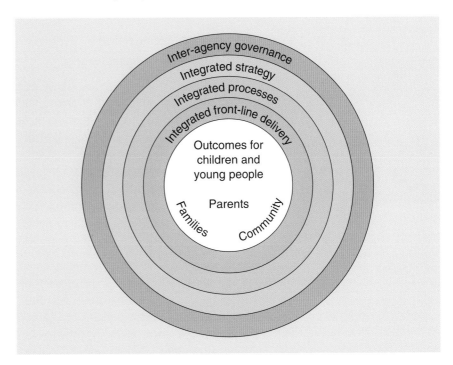

Integrated arrangements through a Children's Trust (DfES, 2005b, p. 7)

The Children Act 2004 introduced a duty for children's services to cooperate. Here, the key construct was that improved outcomes can be achieved and sustained only when agencies work together to design, deliver and evaluate integrated services around the needs of children. The Act required local authorities and their 'relevant partners' to cooperate to improve the wellbeing of children and young people and to safeguard and promote their welfare. 'Relevant partners' include:

- the district council – housing, leisure and recreation
- the Strategic Health Authority (SHA)

- Youth Offending Teams (YOTs)
- the police authority
- the Local Probation Board
- the Connexions Partnership
- the Learning and Skills Council (LSC).

However, cooperation arrangements were intended to operate not only at a strategic level but also at front-line level. Far from being limited to the local authority and relevant partners listed above, the Children Act 2004 stated that other agencies engaged in activities for or with children and young people should be involved, including:

- children and young people themselves
- voluntary and community sector agencies
- not-for-profit and private sector bodies – colleges, work-based learning providers, NHS trusts, GPs, Jobcentre Plus
- childcare, culture, sport and play organisations
- families, carers and communities.

Universal services such as schools and early years settings were also portrayed as central to the drive to improve outcomes and should be actively involved in helping reduce barriers to achievement which lie outside the school gate. Interestingly, unlike the 'relevant' partners, these 'other' partners were not statutorily obliged to cooperate. The statutory guidance suggested a 'strong case' for multi-agency working arrangements in and around places where children spend much of their time, such as schools or children's centres. Other settings might include village halls, sports centres, play schemes, libraries and health centres (DfES, 2005b).

As the next chapter will explore in some detail, it is widely accepted that more work is required to bridge the gap between the original policy intentions and working together in practice. Sloper (2004), in a review of relevant literature, concluded that there was little evidence of the effectiveness of multi-agency working in gaining improved outcomes for children and families. McConkey (2002), writing in relation to children with learning difficulties, also presents a somewhat negative picture:

> 'It truly has been a road "less travelled" as each service system has forged its own highway ... Worse still, at times they have worked competitively rather than cooperatively, blaming one another for perceived shortcomings. And perhaps most seriously of all, they have worked in ignorance of one another's values, priorities and achievements.'
>
> (McConkey, 2002, quoted in Wall, 2006, p. 158)

Despite this, numerous specific projects and initiatives continue to develop multi-agency work. For example, the Welsh Integrated Early Years Centres, the Scottish New Community Schools (now called Integrated Community Schools) and the English Early Excellence Centres have been influential in pushing forward the working together agenda, both as subjects for evidence-based practice and as exemplars of good practice. These are often described as 'beacons', 'trailblazers' and 'change agents', revealing a tendency amongst policy makers to promote multi-agency working as a pioneering and groundbreaking pursuit.

---

## Practice box 4.1

### Integrated Early Years Centres, Wales

Integrated Children's Centres have since 2002 been supported by the Welsh Assembly Government and the Big Lottery Fund. They are expected to provide Early Years Education, Childcare, Community/Parent Training and Open Access Play (Seaton, 2006). One of the first in Wales was the Ynyscynon Early Years Centre situated in a Communities First area in a location that has been used as a nursery since the 1930s (Rhondda Cynon Taf, 2006).

> The centre has a day nursery, nursery class, after school and breakfast club, toy library, forest school, parent and toddler group and a Sure Start Team.

> Key among the good practice at the centre is the good relationship with parents, the high levels of staff integration, the high levels of community involvement and the ethos of the centre. Challenges the centre has faced include, maintaining the forward momentum and changing the image of the centre.

> (Seaton, 2006, p. 8)

---

## Practice box 4.2

### Pen Green Early Excellence Centre, Corby, England

This Sure Start Trailblazer project is located in Corby, a town suffering from the loss of its steel mill, and comprises a new build extension and adaptation of existing school buildings to create new accommodation for a one-stop open access neighbourhood centre, operating since 1983.

It combines early years education, flexible day care for children in need and children with special educational needs, parent education and support, community health services, training and support for early years practitioners, and research and development.

(Commission for Architecture and the Built Environment, 2006, webpage)

In England, the government are committed to build on Sure Start and place a children's centre at the heart of every community. One of Pen Green's successes has been to share its practice with others and act as a model for the development of children's centres. It was also a partner in developing the National Professional Qualification in Integrated Centre Leadership (NPQICL).

## Practice box 4.3

Collaborative working between Integrated Community Schools (ICS) and Looked After children's teams in Scotland

'The development of Integrated Community Schools (ICS) in Scotland is a key element within the overall national strategy to raise young people's achievements and improve social inclusion in Scotland' (HM Inspectorate of Education (HMIE), 2004, Section 1.1).

HM Inspectorate of Education (2004) gives the following as an example of good practice.

The Looked After Children's Team in one authority had worked collaboratively with the ICS cluster. The team was innovative in the breadth of its approach and worked with children with home supervision requirements and with those whose families were homeless as well as those who were looked after and accommodated. Support was mainly provided for looked after children within their current school but there was a small unit for very disaffected young people. These young people were encouraged to undertake qualifications and were beginning to have some success. Overall, the attainment of looked after children in this authority was some of the best in Scotland and they had nearly three times the national average (90% rather than 31%) of their children on home supervision achieving some qualifications.

(HMIE, 2004, Section 5.2)

Thinking point 4.3   How far do these three projects interpret and recreate elements of their respective governments' policies?

## Key points

1   Although there are slight variations in the visions presented by different UK governments in relation to improving children's services, they are all committed to more integrated ways of working.

2   Policy implementation is not a simple linear process.

3   Policy is often presented in idealised terms yet its implementation requires complex interrelationships and actions.

4   Lessons learned from pioneering projects and initiatives can help others implement changes to services and improve outcomes for children.

## 2  The context of policy text production: a multi-agency approach to assessment

Governments translate their aims into guidelines and policy documents for practitioners and agencies to follow. This is particularly necessary where the focus is multi-agency working, to ensure a coordinated and consistent response. This section introduces and analyses aspects of implementation of one such policy known as the *Common Assessment Framework* (CAF) being gradually implemented in England since April 2006. (Common frameworks of different types are being introduced in the other UK nations.)

It was intended that once the CAF became embedded, the majority of common assessments would be carried out by schools, childcare providers, children's centres, other educational establishments, health services and the voluntary sector. The CAF would also sometimes be used by youth support, police and youth justice. The guide for managers suggested that every practitioner working with children, young people and families should know about the CAF (CWDC, 2007a). It was also seen as having the potential to 'drive multi-agency working by embedding a shared process, developing a shared language ... and improving the information flow between agencies' (DfES, 2005b, p. 15).

The rationale for introducing the CAF is to help practitioners develop a shared understanding of children, to avoid families having to repeat themselves to various agencies, and to develop common understandings of what needs to be done and how:

> 'Do not reassess when the information is already there'

> (Parents in consultation about assessment, in Scottish Executive, 2005b, p. 23)

It is intended to be an accurate, thoughtful process which acts as a basis for early intervention before problems can grow and become more harmful. Certainly the CAF is seen as a preventative measure as well as a tool to provide compensatory intervention before things reach crisis point (and to avoid more expensive intervention later on). It can be used by practitioners who have been trained, to assess the needs of unborn babies, infants, children and young people and their families.

The argument is simple and on the surface persuasive, the impetus based on helping individual children. But the relationship between assessment procedures, their purpose and their outcomes is rarely straightforward (Jones, 2004). Assessment is a lifelong process with social consequences and may be influenced by contextual factors and professional value positions. It is literally a point at which 'certain children are judged to be different' (Tomlinson, 1982, p. 82).

The statutory guidance accompanying the Children Act 2004 (DfES, 2005b) sets out the expectations of common assessment. It points to three key *interdependent* aspects of delivering better services. The first is the CAF process, the second is the role of a lead professional, and the third is legal and professional information sharing.

The common assessment was generic rather than specific. It was not concerned with measuring progress towards specific milestones or targets, and can be used earlier than specialist assessments. It was thought that the majority of children would not need a common assessment: 'Other assessments such as universal checks and targeted assessments (for children in need; those with special educational needs etc.) will remain in place' (CWDC, 2006, p. 8). Neither was it for children at risk of harm or neglect – local child protection procedures still need to be followed for this. It was not even for every child who has or may have additional needs, but only those for whom extra services may be needed.

> A common assessment is likely to be of most help when:
>
> - there is reason to think that a child is not making the progress they should be at their age but it is not clear what the underlying causes are or what would help;
> - the child is likely to need the support of another agency.
>
> (DfES, 2005c, p. 3)

Practitioners are left to decide which children are not making appropriate progress without support. Individual judgements are indispensable in this entire process, and decisions may be partly subjective and thereby arbitrary. Even when decisions are grounded in firm evidence, the formal and informal consequences for a child of being viewed as a potential failure need to be considered.

Welton et al. (1982) make the distinction between assessment as an ongoing 'professional' decision making process concerned with helping children progress, and assessment as an 'administrative' process relating to the allocation of resources. The CAF does not fall neatly into either of these categories, as although the basis for carrying out an assessment hinges largely on the need for extra services, it does not guarantee the provision of any services.

The CAF process was based on the idea of a continuum of needs and services. This idea was first introduced in the Warnock Report (DES, 1978) in relation to special educational needs.

As the diagram (overleaf) shows, children described as having 'additional' needs may require targeted support from either a single practitioner or a range of integrated services. However, children with complex needs (who are still part of the broad group with additional needs) require statutory or

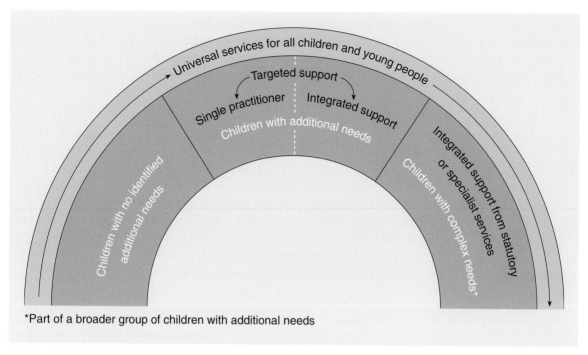

*Part of a broader group of children with additional needs

Continuum of needs and services (CWDC, 2007a, p. 8)

specialist services. These children may or may not have 'special educational needs' which are 'educational'.

Some commentators argue that the concept of 'need' and many of the decisions associated with that concept may be based on individual, often subjective judgements of professionals, based on the beliefs, interests and needs of those who have the power to make decisions which are then presented as objective (Vincent et al., 1996). 'Needs', in other words, are constructed rather than identified and sustain power because decisions about them take place in the interests of power. Armstrong (1995) contends that the construction of children's needs cannot be fully understood without recognising how the needs of professionals themselves are constructed by the state. He adds that for children and families the outcome of partnerships may amount to 'disempowerment by consensus' and that practitioners should 'go beyond the concept of needs to examine the use and legitimation of power in their practice' (Armstrong, 1995, p. 150). This process, he concludes, will lead some professionals to challenge their role within the state bureaucracy and 'forge genuine partnerships with children and their parents through which education becomes a true means of personal and social empowerment for those who today are disenfranchized by 'needs' (Armstrong, 1995, p. 150).

The CAF process consisted of three steps to be followed by the individual practitioner; the diagram below illustrates these steps. However, this simple

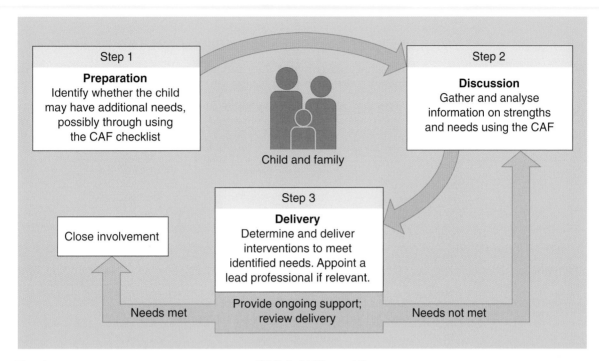

The three-step common assessment process (CWDC, 2007a, p. 18)

representation disguises the complexity of assessment. To begin with, a practitioner is meant to identify a child's additional or even 'potential' additional needs, without any clear definition or threshold explaining what the term 'additional needs' means, apart from possibly needing services additional to those already provided within the setting.

The practitioner needs to check if anyone else is working with the child. If the practitioner is not sure whether an assessment is needed, the CAF pre-assessment checklist (available electronically) can be used (CWDC, 2007b) to make a decision with the child and or the child's parent:

> 'I've spoken to mum. I now need to speak to the youngster in school. What I tend to do once I've spoken to parent and got permission to talk to other agencies I then send a copy of the assessment page to each of the professionals that know this child and ask them to fill in the relevant bits so whether it be like in this case the only other agency that was involved was school so I sent a copy to the year head who filled it out for me'
>
> (Education Welfare Officer's account of completing a CAF, in Dagley et al., 2007, p. 7)

The information is recorded during the discussion with child and family onto the CAF form. It is essential to ensure parents understand what information is being recorded, what will be done with it and when. Some parents when asked about assessment on their children show concern that their view is valued and considered alongside that of other professionals:

> 'Parents are expert ... they see the whole range of behaviour. They don't just come in and take a snapshot'

> 'Those who assess must know the child'

> 'Some professionals are prepared to give an opinion about a child's behaviour and its causes when they don't know the child'

(Parents in consultation about assessment, in Scottish Executive, 2005b, p. 19)

The CAF form has eight stages (CWDC, 2007b, pp. 16–19):

1  Explain the purpose of the assessment
2  Complete the basic identifying details
3  Assessment information
4  Details of the parents/carers
5  Current family and home situation
6  Details of services working with the child
7  Assessment summary
8  Conclusions, solutions and actions.

Stage 7 is the core basis of the discussion which was intended to be collaborative and based around the three domains shown in the figure above.

It may be that the child's needs are such that no additional action is needed. If action is needed, it could be by the family, within the service or setting carrying out the assessment, or there may be a need to try and access support from other agencies. Where it is agreed that the child has complex needs and integrated services are required, the practitioner will need to contact the relevant person in the local area.

Policy texts relating to the common assessment framework are still largely based on the vocabulary of caring and protection of children, or what some describe as 'benevolent humanitarianism' (Tomlinson, 1982): in other words, using the 'child's best interests' as a justification for increasing the amount of professional involvement in the care and control of children. Interventions at an early stage are seen as a legitimate solution to a given problem or even a potential problem. In this way, it could be argued that frameworks such as the CAF legitimate the continued labelling of problems and 'problem' groups, and leave in place a system of values and meanings which sustains and even creates divisions and inequalities.

The intense activity, record-keeping and assessment especially in the preschool period can result in vague descriptions and conflicting records. Important decisions are made at the discretion of practitioners operating within a context of resource constraints. Practitioner judgements are presented as scientific and objective yet they may be influenced by time, context, societal and political values and ideologies (Lindsay, 1995).

Allan (1996) points to the work of Foucault, where a central theme is the way in which constant surveillance, or 'gaze', shapes the experiences of children, who are subject to hierarchical observation, normalising judgements and formal assessment. All children are the objects of such scrutiny, but for certain groups, including those subject to common assessments, the 'gaze' penetrates even deeper. Many children are subjected to continuous monitoring, and their feelings about their parents, their self-worth, identities and experiences may be shaped by the formal assessment procedures and by informal daily interactions.

As discussed in Chapter 1, some parents' and children's views of their services have highlighted their wanting 'a coordinated service that is delivered through a single point of contact, a "key worker", "named person" or "link worker"' (Sloper, 2004, p. 572). A similar role has been created within the CAF. The *lead professional* (LP) takes responsibility for coordinating the action identified as a result of the CAF process and will support the child and their family as necessary. Where children have no additional needs or where their needs require support from just one practitioner, a lead professional is not required. If the common assessment identifies a number of practitioners who need to be involved, a lead professional will need to be selected. This idea has already been used in social work; however, in this context other professionals may be appropriate to take the lead for children receiving services from across agencies. As the following account shows, the LP may well be someone such as a teacher who knows the child well:

> 'At the first one I actually called the meeting, I had the concern I called the meeting, the second one was the same the school had the concern and we called the meeting there was just two of us in school that could've taken LP but I knew the child the best so I took the role'

> (Teacher/lead professional quoted in Dagley et al., 2007, p. 8)

School staff are considered to be in a strong position to take on the role of LP because '[s]eeing the children daily allows frequent monitoring and support' (Dagley et al., 2007, p. 9). However, the role does take up a lot of time in terms of maintaining contact with other agencies and may become a barrier for some teachers who lack time or do not see children's wider social needs as part of their role.

> 'The CAF itself is brilliant but it's the fact that we don't have time in education to do it properly, it's squeezed in amongst other jobs and that's when it becomes not satisfying because you want to spend some more time to make sure and it just feels like it's being

squeezed in amongst loads of other work and no one's actually recognising the importance of it'

(Teacher quoted in Dagley et al., 2007, p. 8)

'... it's more to do with the time it's taking to write the form, to complete the forms, to call together multi-agency meetings because in education we don't have secretaries so it's that sort of time that it's taking up that social services were doing beforehand and then sort of the minutes from the meetings and then posting the minutes'

(Teacher quoted in Dagley et al., 2007, p. 8)

'Ah, the workload, that's a nightmare. I'm involved – although I've done three, we have six running at the moment in our school, and I've actually hiked three of those off to different EWOs, saying OK we need to do this, but I can't – I just physically don't have the time! Otherwise you're just running meetings and you're not teaching!'

(School inclusion manager quoted in Dagley et al., 2007, p. 8)

In some cases where the child's needs are more complex and they receive a specialist assessment there should already be a single point of contact who will assume the role of lead professional, for example a named social worker or key worker. The lead professional has potential, however, as some research indicates that families with key worker type relationships 'report improved quality of life, better relationships with services, better and quicker access to services and reduced levels of stress' (Sloper, 2004, p. 575). Research into the Scottish Assessment Framework (Gibson et al., 2006) suggests that a close relationship between a key worker and parents is beneficial for the child being assessed. The effectiveness of lead professionals is discussed further in Chapter 5.

Thinking point 4.4    What are the advantages and disadvantages of information sharing amongst different agencies and practitioners?

One of the key intended purposes of the CAF is to support better information sharing between services. The non-statutory guidance on information sharing intended for everyone working with children or young people, in the public, private and voluntary sectors, suggests that improving information sharing is a 'cornerstone' of the government strategy to improve outcomes for children (DfES, 2006).

It was claimed that sharing information is essential to enable early intervention to help those who need additional services, thus reducing inequalities between disadvantaged children and others. The guidance set out six key points:

1    Practitioners should explain to children, young people and families, from the beginning of the process, which information will be shared, and the reasons why and how it

will be shared. An exception is if an open explanation would put the child or others at risk of significant harm.

2   The safety and welfare of the child is paramount and must be an overriding consideration.

3   Whenever possible, if the child or family do not consent to have information shared, their wishes should be respected.

4   You should seek advice especially if you have concerns about a child's safety or welfare.

5   It is essential to check that information is accurate, up to date, necessary for the purpose, and shared securely with only those who need to see it.

6   Record decisions, whether you decide to share information or not to share it.

(DfES, 2006, p. 5)

One daunting factor is the sheer number of professionals with whom practitioners may have to work in education, health and social services as well as the many voluntary organisations. The information hub illustrated below shows key agencies working with children or young people.

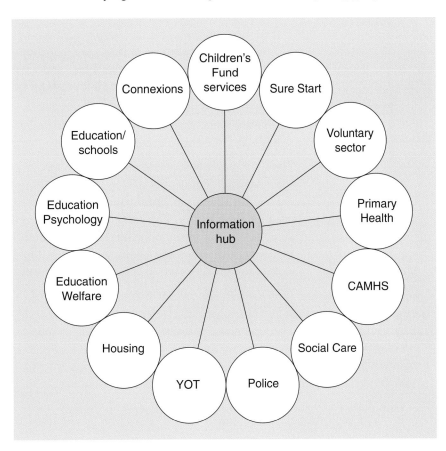

The information hub
(DfES, 2003, p. 54)

This hub has thirteen sectors, and each sector has its own internal communication network. It can be a huge task for settings to find out who the support services and agencies are and how to contact them. Despite this, there are some early signs from evaluations of the CAF that it is overcoming some of the tensions previously encountered around sharing information:

> 'I just hope that it's successful to be honest with you because I find it so helpful for me at the moment and just the speed that things go through because so often you don't know what anyone else is doing, you get sort of bits and bobs of information which isn't very clear, I just feel that this is like singing from the same hymn sheet so I do hope it's successful and I do hope it's the way forward.'
>
> (Learning mentor quoted in Dagley et al., 2007, p. 7)
>
> 'You've got a bigger network now; you're actually meeting people that previously you just phoned.'
>
> (Education Welfare Officer quoted in Dagley et al., 2007, p. 7)

Strategies to enable more successful interagency work also give rise to other concerns and possible unintended consequences. Information sharing, for example, can increase the level of paperwork and therefore time spent away from direct work with children:

> 'I felt that I was a very highly paid photocopying person, because I spent an awful lot of time photocopying bits of paper for the classteacher, for the child's file, and for the educational psychologist file. I felt I spent an awful lot of time doing that type of thing but I don't enjoy that at all.'
>
> (Primary school Special Educational Needs Coordinator quoted in Jones, 2000, p. 120)

The CAF process depends on parental cooperation and raises issues of a sensitive and confidential nature. The Data Protection Act 1998 does not prevent the sharing of information but sets parameters for sharing information lawfully. The practitioner would need to record and update the parental consent to share the information with others, preferably in writing. In some cases this could undermine trust with parents, particularly those identified by Dagley et al. (2007, p. 10) who prefer working with schools because they lack 'the stigma that can be attached to the involvement of social services'.

## Key points

1   The Common Assessment Framework is a shared generic assessment tool to be used in England across all settings and services; other nations have developed their own assessment frameworks.

2   The three interdependent elements of the CAF (process, lead professional and information sharing) require practitioners to work with each other in new, sometimes unfamiliar, ways.

3   The term 'additional needs' is ill-defined and could have a negative impact on how children view themselves and are viewed by others.

4   As an example of policy text production, the CAF illustrates some of the general tensions and issues involved in developing multi-agency working, in particular the influence of practitioners' judgement, power and ability to access appropriate resources.

# 3 From rhetoric to reality: the context of practice

This section considers multi-agency working as a practical evolving process of negotiation and communication between groups of professionals, occupations, sectors, agencies and disciplines. The previous discussion around the CAF revealed some of the issues encountered by practitioners attempting to work towards the vision presented within a policy text. In particular it identified possible sources of tension relating to differences in professional cultures including resources, attitudes, values, beliefs and working practices. Similar tensions are evident in the following practice box.

---

**Practice box 4.4**

Jack, a four-year old boy with Down's Syndrome, is quite small compared to his peers. He has spent a year in a private nursery (on the school site) which is well known locally for inclusive practice. With the support of a key worker, Jack has been fully included in the life of the nursery, without any adaptations. His parents and the nursery manager assumed that transition to reception class would be smooth. The school, who wanted to admit Jack, were concerned that the chairs were too big for Jack and his feet would not touch the floor. The occupational therapist came in several times, and Jack was taken over to the school to be measured and fitted into a special wooden chair, with straps to prevent him falling out. The nursery manager was furious that this chair would segregate Jack, reduce his independence (which the nursery staff had worked hard to promote) by confining him, and make him stand out as different, undoing all the work the nursery had done to ensure that Jack was valued and included. She suggested that a more inclusive approach would be to buy a few small nursery-sized chairs for Jack and the other small pupils, and a lower table. Jack was distressed by the interventions and cried every time he went to the reception classroom.

---

Thinking point 4.5    What does this fictional example highlight with regard to multi-agency working in children's services?

This example shows that multi-agency working involves a complex process of negotiation between individuals and that engagement with the child's standpoint is an essential ingredient. It highlights a situation where a simple visit to the nursery beforehand, observing Jack, seeking his view and that of his parents, and a discussion with the nursery manager, might have avoided embarrassing professional conflict and distress to the child and his parents.

It illustrates the potential negative impact of leaving individual practitioners who are not, strictly speaking, part of any 'agency' out of the loop.

By contrast, the following comment from a school special educational needs coordinator shows that where particularly positive relationships with the individuals visiting schools exist, the situation becomes very productive.

> I'm very impressed with the people that we see, the Educational Psychologists, and the special needs advisors. The people are very keen to help and support. The Advisory teacher from Learning Support Services sat with me and helped me with Individual Education Plans for children that she sees. I had help from a member of the Pupil Support service. She's given me worksheets and talked about what she's doing. The Ed. Psychologist is just a mine of information really to me, on what to do next and where to go next.
>
> (Personal communication)

In a review of the work of Early Excellence Centres, Anning (2001) notes that teams of professionals from different agencies are appointed with the brief to work in 'joined-up' ways although scant attention has been given to the challenge this creates for workers in creating new professional identities. The challenge is for workers to articulate and share their personal and professional knowledge for new ways of working. Effective communication and reflection are therefore at the heart of developing good collaborative relationships (Rodd, 2006). Research highlights the importance of professional and agency cultures facilitating joint working through valuing and supporting joint training (Sloper, 2004). 'There is now some evidence that shared learning and interagency/interprofessional training, especially as part of continuing professional education, is one way of promoting better multi-agency collaboration' (Sloper, 2004, p. 578). (This is discussed further in Chapter 6.)

A survey conducted as part of an evaluation of a local Sure Start Initiative confirmed that multi-agency working could disrupt existing professional and agency cultures and lead to conflict. The establishment of a common vision or aims across agencies was regarded as essential but less straightforward to establish in practice (Aubrey and Dahl, 2006). Garrett (2006) suggests that:

> the emphasis on the 'common' can be interpreted as a censoring mechanism which seeks to render other dissenting visions, skills, and vocabularies marginal or even subversive of the 'common' endeavour: perhaps, for example, vocabularies which include *uncommon* words which, nonetheless, reflect people's experiences (for example, 'exploitation', 'capital', 'power', 'inequality' and so on).
>
> (Garrett, 2006, p. 13)

This points to one of the dangers of imposing a top-down model of multi-agency working and instead suggests that true collaboration is only possible through shared ownership of both the problems to be addressed and the solutions to be attempted to address them. As we have discussed in this chapter, an alternative model accepts that practitioners will reinterpret the government's vision (Bowe et al., 1992) based on their knowledge of both policy texts and their awareness of local conditions. This could potentially be enhanced through locally-based evaluations involving all stakeholders, including parents and children (Sloper, 2004), to ensure that multi-agency working does not become another policy initiative which further marginalises the most vulnerable groups and causes more problems than it solves.

## Key points

1   There are a number of clearly defined characteristics that enable or prevent multi-agency working.

2   A clear understanding of roles, responsibilities and identities can assist multi-agency working.

3   Multi-agency working is a continual process of communication, evaluation and negotiation involving individual practitioners, policy makers and other stakeholders.

# 4 Evaluation of multi-agency working

Evaluation is often distinguished from other forms of social research in terms of its usefulness, its application to particular areas of policy or practice, and its orientation towards action (Taylor, 2006). The process of evaluating attempts to judge or make recommendations that in turn can help sustain or improve the quality of a service or practice intervention. Evaluation can focus on both the process and the outcome, and can be either an ongoing process or a one-off event. Different types of evaluation can be identified: a distinction, for example, exists between internal evaluation (undertaken by the practitioners or policy makers) and external evaluation (undertaken by independent professional researchers, inspectors or peers), and between summative evaluation (measuring the effects or outcomes of a service or intervention) and formative evaluation (an ongoing process of gathering evidence to make improvements while a service or intervention is still developing or forming).

As the following table illustrates, periodic reviews and regular and consistent data gathering can be attempted to inform different levels of both strategic and operational evaluation, which in turn influence planning. Anyone involved in designing or delivering children's services can be expected to both evaluate and be evaluated.

| Planning levels | Examples | People involved in evaluation |
| --- | --- | --- |
| Government level | *Building on Progress* – in 2007 the government produced the findings from a review into several areas of policy including public sector services and support for families (HM Government, 2007). | Cabinet ministers<br>Regional forums with random members of the public |
| Local authority level | Joint Area Review. | Statutory inspectorates<br>Service providers<br>Service users (children and parents) |
| Level of agency or service | Statutory inspection or self-evaluation, e.g. school inspection. | Statutory inspectorates and commissions<br>Service providers<br>Service users |
| Level of practitioner or service user | Periodic case review to ensure that a care plan or intervention is working, e.g. statutory review for a Looked After child. | Service providers<br>Service users<br>Other practitioners and people who know the child well |

Thinking point 4.6   To what extent are the above examples either internal or external evaluation and/or summative or formative evaluation?

Evaluation serves a number of different purposes that in turn are linked to the wider context in which a particular service or practice approach is placed. People involved in designing, delivering or receiving children's services are generally funded by (and therefore accountable to) the public purse or other funding bodies. Evaluation can be used as evidence of accountability and value for money. Work with children is subject to political and media scrutiny and debate which itself feeds on anecdotal evidence and ideology. Evaluations of practice are therefore useful for providing feedback to support or challenge the different views within these debates. As highlighted in the previous section, evaluation can also contribute to the process of reinterpreting the government's policy vision. As discussed in Chapter 1, the trend towards interagency working for many practitioners and service providers has resulted in new relationships, environments and methods of working. Evaluation provides an opportunity to bring together people with different standpoints to learn and reflect on these changes and develop new ways of working.

As with the policy trajectory highlighted earlier in this chapter, the process of feeding back evaluation findings to policy makers can also be shaped and distorted by external influences (Bate and Robert, 2003). A particular problem arises where the evaluation findings contrast with or demonstrate a failure to achieve the intended outcomes and their underlying values.

Kelly (2002) identifies the role that values play in the presentation of outcome studies related to foster care. Most research that has looked at outcomes in adults who were fostered as children has reported positive results, yet much of this receives adverse commentary. Kelly suggests that this is because the dominant values that favour permanence and adoption within social policy have been applied to evaluations of foster care, which has the 'effect of making its successes almost look like failures' (Kelly, 2002, p. 63). Bate and Robert (2003) highlight how evaluation findings are sometimes ignored by policy makers, with little evidence of them having any impact on practice. This is particularly true of evaluations of flagship modernisation policies and pilot projects.

Evaluators can take on different roles depending on whether summative or formative evaluation is being undertaken. First, they could evaluate whether something worked and whether it was good value for money. Second, they could present insights or make suggestions as to how a particular service or method of practice could be improved. They could also do a combination of these. Bate and Robert (2003) express the view that evaluation cannot be separated from practice and is in itself a form of intervention. Consequently, during the process of finding out whether something works, ideas concerning new ways of approaching the problem under scrutiny often emerge (perhaps reflecting the subjective opinions of practitioners and service users).

One of the difficulties with summative evaluations is that they encourage dualistic thinking, that is, something either works or does not work. An outcome or performance target that has not been met does not necessarily indicate that a policy or practice approach is not working. Such approaches to evaluation can sometimes obscure contextual issues or hidden and unforeseen gains or losses separate from the intended outcome. Formative evaluation that is part of an ongoing process of dialogue and reflection between practitioners, service users and evaluators can potentially avoid this dualism.

Identifying to what extent children's services can be held accountable for particular outcomes being met is not easy to achieve. 'Purely summative evaluations often do not help with explaining whether the recorded outcomes were determined by the method or programme itself or the way the programme was managed, and/or the resources and context within which it was managed' (Bate and Robert, 2003, p. 256). Within a multi-agency context, conflict may develop in relation to which agency contributed more or less to a particular outcome being achieved or unmet. A failure to achieve a particular outcome may also be affected by wider circumstances. Hudson (2005) reflects on the government's own identification of factors associated with poor outcomes highlighted in *Every Child Matters*:

> 'We have a good idea of the factors associated with poor outcomes – low income and parental unemployment; homelessness; poor parenting; poor schooling; post-natal depression among mothers; low birth weight; substance misuse; individual characteristics such as intelligence; community factors such as living in deprived neighbourhoods.'
>
> (Chief Secretary to the Treasury, 2003, para 1.10, reproduced in Hudson, 2005, p. 521)

Thinking point 4.7   To what extent can children's services individually or collectively be held accountable for the factors associated with poor outcomes highlighted above?

Hudson (2005) queries how many of these 'factors affecting achievement of the five outcomes lie well beyond the scope of the new children's services authorities'. It could be argued that the responsibility for many of these factors 'lies with people and organizations over whom the children's services authorities will have little or no control, such as parents and carers, schools, general practitioners, and the voluntary and private sectors' (Hudson, 2005, p. 521).

Such constraints have led to suggestions that the impact of summative evaluations on the policy-making process is only marginal at best (Pawson and Tilley, 1997, cited in Bate and Robert, 2003, p. 251). Instead, it has been suggested that evaluation should be a formative process (Bate and Robert, 2003) in which the boundary between practitioner and evaluator is less defined, 'co-creating a peer community of inquiry, one that offers a developmental learning process for all those involved' (Bate and Robert, 2003, p. 259). This idea of learning together through communities of practice is explored further in Chapter 6.

The reform of children's services in the early twenty-first century coincided with new ways of evaluating multi-agency working including more formative approaches engaged with practitioners and service users. This in part reflected the growing demands of service users to be more involved, as well as resistance from practitioners themselves to the traditional external inspection model of evaluation.

The national and devolved UK governments all had their own statutory inspection systems which contributed to the evaluation of how well children's services were performing. As an example, we concentrate here on the role in England played by an extended Ofsted (Office for Standards in Education, Children's Services and Skills). Different data-gathering methods and sources were used to examine both the process and outcomes of multi-agency working. The inspectors provided feedback directly to the service providers, and produced publicly available summaries and reports linked to the strategic vision or outcomes produced at the government level.

Thinking point 4.8    What are the benefits and potential drawbacks of using external inspectors to evaluate children's services?

The usefulness of external inspections has been hotly debated, particularly within schools. According to Ehren and Visscher (2006), more research is needed into the effectiveness or otherwise of school inspections. A mixed picture exists from research, indicating in some cases improvements, in other cases no improvements (or even declines) to student learning or attainment. Significantly, a number of unintended negative effects have been attributed to inspections. Some studies 'show that inspections can lead to stress and to a higher workload for school staff, window dressing, and being afraid to innovate because they fear that this will conflict with the school inspection criteria' (Ehren and Visscher, 2006, p. 53). The following quotes highlight the uneasy relationship that in the past has been generated between some inspectors and practitioners. One teacher found her inspection:

> 'a very negative experience, even after the nice bloke who watched the PE lesson was quite complimentary about it. He said, "You've got some lively children in your class, haven't you, but you've got some pretty good strategies for dealing with them". At first I

was quite pleased, and then later I thought: "why on earth should I be pleased with him telling me that I know how to deal with some naughty children?" If I didn't know by now, I bloody well need shooting after 25 years! ... I know whether I'm a good teacher or not – I don't need him to tell me.'

(Teacher quoted in Jeffrey and Woods, 1998, p. 74)

'It's the system that imparts this view of what an Ofsted inspector is and can be. You're perceived as the enemy. You're made very welcome when you come into schools. They're very polite and they're as helpful as they can be, but they don't want you there.'

(Inspector quoted in Jeffrey and Woods, 1998, p. 45)

Criticisms of independent inspections led to changes in the way they were undertaken. One significant development was self-evaluation. This generally placed the onus on individual agencies or services to conduct their own review of their performance. This in theory can help install an ethos of service improvement within the agency and improve management systems. It can also become part of the formal external inspection process. Ofsted encouraged schools through self-evaluation to ask the questions 'How well are we doing?' and 'How can we do better?' (Ofsted, 2004). Schools were expected to fill in a self-evaluation form to be used as a starting point when the school was inspected by Ofsted.

Ofsted became the primary organisation for inspecting a range of service areas including early years education and children's social care provision in England. It had responsibility for inspecting the development of multi-agency working within local authority children's services. It involved two complementary processes: an Annual Performance Assessment (APA) and a Joint Area Review (JAR). Three 'inspecting principles' were identified by Hudson (2005) within the process.

*The coordinating principle*: The APA effectively brought together the existing procedures previously carried out separately by both Ofsted and the Commission for Social Care Inspection (CSCI) into one coordinated process overseen by an enlarged Ofsted (Hudson, 2005). All council-run children's services were evaluated against the five outcomes for children and given an overall graded rating. It did not involve investigative fieldwork, although inspectors could meet with service managers. The grades were published on Ofsted's website each November (Ofsted, 2007c).

Joint Area Reviews (JARs) reported on how far services were working together to secure positive outcomes for children and young people. Each local authority would have one JAR within a three-year period and include on-site investigative fieldwork. The reviews involved nine inspectorates and commissions in assessing how social, health, education and criminal justice services and systems *taken together* contributed to improved outcomes for children. Fieldwork focused on the most vulnerable children and could follow up areas of weakness highlighted in the APA. Progress was monitored against priority national targets and other indicators, and a report was published, including both graded and non-graded judgements, on the Ofsted website (Ofsted, 2007c).

*The proportionate inspecting principle*: This reflected an attempt to cut down on the bureaucracy involved in inspection. This was in part achieved by cutting down on the number of inspections of individual services. Inspections were proportionate to the strengths and weaknesses identified in the APA, and no additional fieldwork was necessary if judgements could be made based on existing evidence (Hudson, 2005). Inspectors were required to 'scrutinise a number of randomly selected case files relating to some of the most vulnerable children and young people in the area to examine how far services work together to address the specific needs of these children and young people and promote their well-being' (Ofsted, 2007c). Interestingly, consultations about the new inspection system revealed that children 'wanted inspectors to check up just as often whether they know there are problems, or whether they know things have been going well in the past' (Morgan, 2005b, pp. 7–8). Children expressed concern that 'places can change, and new problems can happen even if things were good in the past' (Morgan, 2005b, p. 8):

> 'because things may change, you regularly have to check up on things.'
>
> (Child quoted in Morgan, 2005b, p. 8)

*The engagement and involvement principle*: The on-site fieldwork investigations for the JAR included gathering evidence directly from children, young people, their parents and carers, front-line workers, senior managers, elected council members and the council's partner agencies and organisations. Such inclusive methods are better placed to identify issues that are largely hidden from view. This was illustrated in an evaluation of healthy schools projects where a number of stakeholders including parents, teachers and school students were consulted. However, each group appeared to have a slightly different view of what constituted a health issue in the school. Students, for example (consistent with many similar evaluations elsewhere in the UK), but not teachers, appeared troubled by the lack of access to clean and hygienic toilets:

> 'You can't go to the toilet when you want to go ... Toilets aren't clean and have tissues stuck on the ceiling.'
>
> (Primary school student quoted in Warwick et al., 2005, p. 704)

This not only indicates one of the benefits of consulting widely with service users but also raises the possibility that service users themselves could be involved in setting outcomes against which services can be evaluated. In Wales, the Children's Commissioner suggested that in the light of consistent children's concerns, 'the role of Estyn [Inspector of Education and Training in Wales] and the Framework for Inspection in Schools needs to be reviewed ... to clarify their role in the inspection of school toilets' (Children's Commissioner for Wales, 2004, p. 16).

Of course, children's views are only one of several perspectives on what should be inspected. 'The need here is to strike a balance between national priorities and pupils' own concerns' (Warwick et al., 2005, p. 706). The *Every Child Matters* Green Paper (DfES, 2003, p. 6) indicated that the government 'consulted children, young people and families' about its vision and outcomes for children (see Practice box 4.5). It is claimed that the five eventual outcomes chosen by the government in its strategic vision were the ones that 'mattered most to children and young people' (DfES, 2003, p. 6). Subsequent consultations have been undertaken by the government with children about the outcomes (see Practice box 4.5).

Increasingly, government and other agencies are consulting with children about the services they provide

## Practice box 4.5

Consultation with children and young people across England was carried out by the Children and Young People's Unit (CYPU, 2001), designed to help develop the Unit's future strategy. This targeted specific groups of children, including 6- to 8-year-olds, toddlers with parents, children from rural and coastal areas, disabled children, children from black and ethnic minority backgrounds, boys and girls. During the consultation, children were presented with a number of outcomes that are not dissimilar from those eventually included in *Every Child Matters*: health and wellbeing, achievement and enjoyment, participation and citizenship, protection, responsibility, and inclusion. The children were then consulted using the following questions:

Do you share these goals for monitoring outcomes for children and young people?

Do you think the proposed outcomes could be improved?

Who should be responsible for delivering improved outcomes in communities?

(CYPU, 2001, p. 24)

Thinking point 4.9    To what extent is the government approach highlighted in the practice box above involving children in deciding the outcomes for services?

## Practice box 4.6

A consultation with a group of 700 children aged under 12, subsequent to the implementation of *Every Child Matters*, asked them about the government's five outcomes (these were rewritten in language that was understandable to children). 99% of these children said they did agree that all these five things are important to children, and they ranked them in the following order: staying safe, being healthy, enjoying life and learning, helping others, and having enough money. However, some children had their own ideas about further outcomes:

'I think all of the five things are correct. They have made good choices, but there are a few more things we care about'

Seven further outcomes were added by children to the original five: family, friends, food and drink, fun, love, respect and being happy, collectively making a 'children's dozen' outcomes.

(Morgan, 2005a, p. 10)

Regardless of the extent to which children contributed to the creation of the original outcomes, there has been significant activity designed to involve them in evaluating service delivery. Some commentators have suggested that the reform of children's services presented itself as an ideal opportunity and 'local government structures ... the most appropriate context ... for child participation' (Aubrey and Dahl, 2006, p. 23). In primary schools, Ofsted inspectors judged the extent to which the education in the school met the needs of the range of pupils, and the contribution made by the school to the wellbeing of those pupils. Inspectors assessed the overall effectiveness of the school including how far the curriculum was responsive to external requirements and local circumstances. This includes any extended services, and the effectiveness of links with other providers and services so as to enhance learning and promote wellbeing.

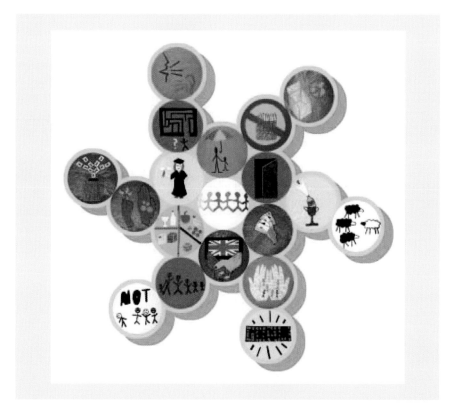

Participatory approaches can be used to enable children to contribute to evaluation. The diagram is a visual representation of how the government's outcomes fit together, made during a CYPU strategy consultation workshop with children and young people in Derby, September 2001 (CYPU, 2001, p. 24).

As Taylor (2006, p. 264) argues, the 'choice of method' needed to involve children and other service users in evaluation is 'value-driven' particularly where the intent is to ensure inclusive and representative participation. Attempts to move beyond tokenism or manipulation (Hart, 1992) require varied and imaginative methods. O'Kane (2000) suggests that participatory approaches, including activities familiar to children such as drawing, drama, play and games, are the most effective. Ofsted's decision to apply a web-based survey (named Tellus) to a random sample of children (along with case-tracking interviews) was arguably an effective way of seeking evaluative information (Aubrey and Dhal, 2006), although it assumed that all children were comfortable with this medium. A more enhanced version (known as Tellus2) aimed to gather together a wide range of data to be held nationally and used as a benchmark for all local authorities. The Tellus2 survey asked 'children and young people questions about their satisfaction with services (including aspects of their school life) and questions relating to the five Every Child Matters outcomes, including issues like healthy eating, participation in positive activities and bullying' (Ofsted, 2007b).

There are advantages to asking children questions about their wider experiences and networks. Primarily it acknowledges the reality of children's lives where issues and experiences overlap and interrelate between the different relationships that they hold. Furthermore, it provides holistic data for policy makers and practitioners around children's lives enabling them to identify the most effective places to locate services and encourage multi-agency working. The following, for example, could be used to justify more cooperation between schools and health agencies. In its 2005/6 Report, Ofsted was able to use the Tellus data to evaluate the outcome of being healthy from the perspective of 19,000 children and young people involved in the JARs:

> Of the children and young people who completed the survey, 94% saw themselves as healthy or very healthy; 5% of boys and 7% of girls felt they were unhealthy ... Of those who felt they were not very healthy, the availability of healthier food, more sport or exercise at school and being happier and having less stress in their lives were their priorities for improving their health.
>
> (Ofsted, 2006, p. 38)

Local services were effective in working together to promote the health of children and young people. No local area inspected was judged to provide an inadequate contribution to healthy outcomes.

(Ofsted, 2006, p. 37)

**33. Do you receive extra help at school with your learning or behaviour from someone other than your teacher?** (e.g. a learning mentor or learning support assistant).
This might be in your main lessons, or in one-to-one lessons separate from the rest of your class.

PLEASE TICK ONE BOX ONLY
O Yes
O No
O Don't know

**34. How often, if at all, have you been bullied in school in the last four weeks?**
Bullying is when someone makes you unhappy by being nasty on purpose (for example by teasing or hurting you, by taking or breaking your things, or by leaving you out).

PLEASE TICK THE ONE BOX THAT BEST FITS YOU
O Never
O A couple of times in the last four weeks
O About once a week
O Two or three times a week
O Most days

**35. How well does your school deal with bullying?**

PLEASE TICK ONE BOX ONLY
O Very well
O Quite well
O Not very well
O Not at all well
O Bullying is not a problem in my school
O Don't know

**36. Which of these have you done in the last year?**

PLEASE TICK ALL THAT YOU HAVE DONE
O Voted in a school, class or year group election at school
O Been on a school council or parliament
O None of the above
O Don't know

**37. What do you hope to do when you leave school?**

PLEASE TICK ONE BOX ONLY
O Get a job at 16
O Study then get a job at 18

Examples of questions included in the Tellus2 questionnaire designed to survey primary children's views

**Key points**

1 Evaluation can be conducted externally or internally and be either formative or summative in design.

2 Attempts are being made to ensure that external inspections of children's services become less intrusive, better coordinated and complementary to methods of self-evaluation.

3 Inclusive methods designed to access the views of all stakeholders (including children) can be used as a basis for designing outcomes for children and useful feedback on whether these outcomes have been met.

4 Evaluations of children's services should be considered in relation to the wider social and economic context.

# Conclusion

The ideal of multi-agency working is present in the vision for children's services across the UK. However, the process of turning policy on multi-agency working into practice is far from being a simple top-down approach and instead involves multiple perspectives and inputs. Policies such as the Common Assessment Framework in England require practitioners to work with each other in new, sometimes unfamiliar, ways. Despite having benign intentions, policies can inadvertently expose or even perpetuate existing power relationships between practitioners and lead to the disempowerment of service users. Reflective skilled practitioners who can evaluate policy and practice with service users, both internally and in partnership with external inspectors, are necessary to ensure that policies do lead to positive outcomes for children and their families. Service users can also potentially help governments construct the appropriate vision from which polices are developed. A formative approach to evaluation that encourages dialogue and ongoing improvements to both policy and practice would appear to offer a positive way forward. However, this is not without its challenges and there are still issues to be addressed, not least training and clarification of roles and responsibilities. It is up to individual practitioners to promote an inclusive approach to professional difference and to develop a range of different models enabling collaboration, respect, reciprocity, realism and risk-taking.

# References

Allan, J. (1996) 'Foucault and Special Educational Needs: a "box of tools" for analysing children's experiences of mainstreaming', *Disability & Society*, vol. 11, no. 2, pp. 219–233.

Anning, A. (2001) *Knowing Who I Am and What I Know: Developing New Versions of Professional Knowledge in Integrated Service Settings*, Paper presented to the BERA Annual Conference, University of Leeds, 13–15 September.

Armstrong, D. (1995) *Power and Partnership in Education*, London, Routledge.

Aubrey, C. and Dahl, S. (2006) 'Children's voices: the views of vulnerable children on their service providers and the relevance of services they receive', *British Journal of Social Work,* vol. 36, no. 1, pp. 21–39.

Axford, N., Berry, V., Little, M. and Morpeth, L. (2006) 'Developing a common language in children's services through research-based inter-disciplinary training', *Social Work Education*, vol. 25, no. 2, pp. 161–176.

Ball, S.J. (1994) *Education Reform: A Critical and Post-structural Approach*, Buckingham, Open University Press.

Bate, P. and Robert, G. (2003) 'Where next for policy evaluation? Insights from researching National Health Service modernisation', *Policy & Politics*, vol. 31, no. 2, pp. 249–262.

Bowe, R., Ball, S. and Gold, A. (1992) *Reforming Education and Changing Schools: Case Studies in Policy Sociology*, London, Routledge.

Chief Secretary to the Treasury (2003) *Every Child Matters*, Cm 5860, London, The Stationery Office.

Children and Young People's Unit (CYPU) (2001) *Building a Strategy for Children and Young People: Consultation Document*, available online at <http://www.dfes.gov.uk/consultations/downloadableDocs/140_1.pdf>, accessed 11 September 2007.

Children's Commissioner for Wales (2004) *Lifting the Lid on the Nation's School Toilets*, Cardiff, Children's Commissioner for Wales.

Children's Workforce Development Council (CWDC) (2006) *Common Assessment Framework for Children and Young People: Frequently Asked Questions*, available online at <http://www.everychildmatters.gov.uk/_files/FAQCommonAssessmentFramework0907.pdf>, accessed 20 January 2008.

Children's Workforce Development Council (CWDC) (2007a) *Common Assessment Framework for Children and Young People: Managers' Guide*, available online at <http://www.everychildmatters.gov.uk/_files/C90390EA0078D3E9721C7C1A8F04DDBE.pdf>, accessed 20 January 2008.

Children's Workforce Development Council (CWDC) (2007b) *The Common Assessment Framework for Children and Young People: Practitioners' Guide*, available online at <http://www.everychildmatters.gov.uk/_files/0C734C7BC2984FA94F5ED0D500B7EF02.pdf>, accessed 20 January 2008.

Commission for Architecture and the Built Environment (2006) *Case Studies: Pen Green Early Excellence Centre*, available online at <http://www.cabe.org.uk/default.aspx?contentitemid=345>, accessed 11 September 2007.

Dagley, V., Howe, A., Salter, C., Brandon, M., Warren, C. and Black, J. (2007) 'Implications of the new Common Assessment Framework and lead professional working for pastoral care staff in schools', *Pastoral Care in Education*, vol. 25, no. 1, pp. 4–10.

Department for Education and Skills (DfES) (2001) *Special Educational Needs: Code of Practice*, Nottingham, DfES.

Department for Education and Skills (DfES) (2003) *Every Child Matters,* London, The Stationery Office.

Department for Education and Skills (DfES) (2005a) *Common Core of Skills and Knowledge for the Children's Workforce*, Nottingham, DfES.

Department for Education and Skills (DfES) (2005b) *Statutory Guidance on Inter-agency Co-operation to Improve the Wellbeing of Children: Children's Trusts*, Nottingham, DfES.

Department for Education and Skills (DfES) (2005c) *Common Assessment Framework for Children and Young People: Guide for Service Managers and Practitioners*, London, The Stationery Office, also available online at <http://www.everychildmatters.gov.uk/_files/A89032796BB8E09711ADA7129A42B8E8.doc>, accessed 11 September 2007.

Department for Education and Skills (DfES) (2006) *Information Sharing: Practitioners' Guide*, available online at <http://www.everychildmatters.gov.uk/_files/ACB1BA35C20D4C42A1FE6F9133A7C614.pdf >, accessed 11 September 2007.

Department of Education and Science (DES) (1978) *Special Educational Needs: Report of the Committee of Enquiry into the Education of Handicapped Children and Young People (The Warnock Report)*, London, HMSO.

Ehren, M.C.M. and Visscher, A.J. (2006) 'Towards a theory on the impact of school inspections', *British Journal of Educational Studies*, vol. 54, no. 1, pp. 51–72.

Garrett, P.M. (2006) 'How to be modern: New Labour's neoliberal modernity and the *Change for Children* programme', *British Journal of Social Work*, available online at <http://bjsw.oxfordjournals.org/cgi/reprint/bcl345v1>, accessed 10 September 2007.

Gibson, P., Baldwin, N. and Daniel, B. (2006) *Ayrshire and West Lothian Pilot Projects Assessing Children in Need*, Research Findings No.15, Scottish Executive, available online at <http://www.scottishexecutive.gov.uk/Resource/Doc/90597/0021795.pdf>, accessed 11 September 2007.

Goacher, B., Evans, J., Welton, J. and Wedell, K. (1988) *Policy and Provision for Special Educational Needs: Implementing the 1981 Education Act*, London, Cassell.

Hart, R. (1992) *Children's Participation: from Tokenism to Citizenship, Innocenti Essays no. 4*, Florence, UNICEF.

HM Government (2004) *The Children Act 2004*, London, The Stationery Office.

HM Government (2006) *Working Together to Safeguard Children: A Guide to Inter-agency Working to Safeguard and Promote the Welfare of Children*, London, The Stationery Office.

HM Government (2007) *Policy Review: Building on Progress*, available online at <http://archive.cabinetoffice.gov.uk/policy_review>, accessed 20 January 2008.

HM Inspectorate of Education (2004) *The Sum of its Parts? The Development of Integrated Community Schools in Scotland*, available online at <http://www.hmie.gov.uk/documents/publication/dicss.html>, accessed 19 September 2007.

Hudson, B. (2005) '"Not a cigarette paper between us": integrated inspection of children's services in England', *Social Policy & Administration*, vol. 39, no. 5, pp. 513–527.

Jeffrey, B. and Woods, P. (1998) *Testing Teachers: The Effect of School Inspections on Primary Teachers*, London, Falmer Press.

Jones, C. (2000) *Special Educational Needs: Identification and Assessment in the Early Years*, PhD thesis, University of Warwick.

Jones, C. (2004) *Supporting Inclusion in the Early Years*, Maidenhead, Open University Press.

Kelly, G. (2002) 'Outcome studies of foster care' in Kelly, G. and Gilligan, R. (eds) *Issues in Foster Care: Policy Practice and Research*, London, Jessica Kingsley, pp. 59–84.

Lindsay, G. (1995) 'Early identification of special educational needs' in Lunt, I., Norwich, B. and Varma, V. (eds) *Psychology and Education for Special Needs*, London, Arena, pp. 7–24.

McConkey, R. (2002) 'Reciprocal working by education, health and social services: lessons for a less-travelled road', *British Journal of Special Education*, vol. 29, no. 1, pp. 3–8.

Morgan, R. (2005a) *Younger Children's Views on 'Every Child Matters'*, Newcastle, Commission for Social Care Inspection.

Morgan, R. (2005b) *Sorting Out Inspection: Views from Children and Young People on the Government's Proposals about the Future of Inspection for Children and Learners*, Newcastle, Commission for Social Care Inspection.

NI Children and Young People's Unit (NICYPU) (2006) *Super Six Cartoon Strip*, available online at <http://www.allchildrenni.gov.uk/the_super_six.pdf>, accessed 11 September 2007.

O'Brien, S., Hammond, H. and McKinnon, M. (2003) *Report of the Caleb Ness Inquiry: Executive Summary and Recommendations*, available online at <http://www.edinburgh. gov.uk/internet/Attachments/Internet/Social_care/About_Social_Care_and_Health/ Monitoring_performance/Special_enquiries_and_reports/O_Brien_Report/ Caleb_Ness_Report_Summary_and_Recommendations.pdf>, accessed 11 September 2007.

Office of the First Minister and Deputy First Minister of Northern Ireland (2006) *Our Children and Young People – Our Pledge. A Ten Year Strategy for Children and Young People in Northern Ireland 2006–2016*, available online at <http://www. allchildrenni.gov.uk/tenyearstrategychildren1.pdf>, accessed 19 September 2007.

Ofsted (2004) *A New Relationship with Schools: Improving Performance through School Self-Evaluation*, available online at <http://www.ofsted.gov.uk/assets/3862.pdf>, accessed 11 September 2007.

Ofsted (2006) *The Annual Report of Her Majesty's Chief Inspector of Schools 2005/06*, Norwich, The Stationery Office.

Ofsted (2007a) *TELLUS2 Questionnaire aimed at primary school age children*, available online at <http://www.ofsted.gov.uk/assets/Internet_Content/Shared_Content/ Childrens/files/Tellus2Questionnaire_primary.pdf>, accessed 11 September 2007.

Ofsted (2007b) *TELLUS2 Factsheet: Gathering the views of children and young people: Information for local areas*, available online at <http://www.ofsted.gov.uk/assets/ Internet_Content/CSID/files/Tellus2FactSheet.doc>, accessed 11 September 2007.

Ofsted (2007c) *Joint Area Review*, available online at <http://www.ofsted.gov.uk/portal/site/ Internet/menuitem.455968b0530071c4828a0d8308c08a0c/? vgnextoid=c049b018b5631110VgnVCM1000003507640aRCRD>, accessed 11 September 2007.

O'Kane, C. (2000) 'The development of participatory techniques; facilitating children's views about decisions which affect them' in Christensen, P. and James, A. (eds) *Research with Children: Perspectives and Practices*, London, Falmer Press, pp. 136–159.

Pawson, R. and Tilley, N. (1997) *Realistic Evaluation*, London, Sage Publications.

Power, S. (2001) '"Joined-up thinking?" Inter-agency partnerships in Education Action Zones' in Riddell, S. and Tett, L. (eds) *Education, Social Justice and Inter-agency Working: Joined-up or Fractured Policy?*, London, Routledge.

Rhondda Cynon Taf (2006) *Ynyscynon Early Years Centre*, available online at <http://www.rctearlyyears.org.uk/eYears/ynyscynon.html>, accessed 11 September 2007.

Rodd, J. (2006) *Leadership in Early Childhood*, Maidenhead, Open University Press.

Scottish Executive (2005a) *Getting it Right for Every Child: Proposals for Action*, Edinburgh, Astron, also available online at <www.scotland.gov.uk/Publications/2005/06/20135608/56098>, accessed 11 September 2007.

Scottish Executive (2005b) *Getting it right for every child: Proposals For Action. Section 3: Integrated Assessment, Planning and Recording Framework. Supporting Paper 1: The Process and Content of an Integrated Framework and the Implications for Implementation*, Edinburgh, Scottish Executive.

Seaton, N. (2006) *Development and Implementation of Integrated Centres in Wales*, PowerPoint Presentation, Institute for Wales Integrated Centres Conference, 13 March, available online at <http://www.iwa.org.uk/publications/NSeaton.ppt>, accessed 11 September 2007.

Sloper, P. (2004) 'Facilitators and barriers for co-ordinated multi-agency services', *Child Care, Health and Development*, vol. 30, no. 6, pp. 571–580.

Social Services Inspectorate for Wales (2004) *The Report of the Chief Inspector 2003–4*, Cardiff, Social Services Inspectorate for Wales.

Taylor, D. (2006) 'Critical policy evaluation and the question of values: a psychosocial approach', *Critical Social Policy*, vol. 26, no. 1, pp. 243–267.

Tomlinson, S. (1982) *A Sociology of Special Education*, London, Routledge and Kegan Paul.

Troyna, B. (1993) 'Critical social research and education policy', paper presented to the Conference on New Directions in Education Policy Sociology, 30–31 March 1993.

Vincent, C., Evans, J., Lunt, I. and Young, P. (1996) 'Professionals under pressure: the administration of special education in a changing context', *British Educational Research Journal*, vol. 22, no. 4, pp. 475–491.

Wall, K. (2006) *Special Needs and Early Years*, London, Paul Chapman.

Warwick, I., Aggleton, P., Chase, E., Schagen, S., Blenkinsop, S., Schagen, I., Scott, E. and Eggers, M. (2005) 'Evaluating healthy schools: perceptions of impact among school-based respondents', *Health Education Research*, vol. 20, no. 6, pp. 697–708.

Welsh Assembly Government (2004) *Children and Young People: Rights to Action*, available online at <http://www.assemblywales.org/N0000000000000000000000000016990.pdf>, accessed 19 September 2007.

Welton, J., Wedell, K. and Vorhaus, G. (1982) *Meeting Special Needs: The 1981 Education Act and its Implications*, Bedford Way Papers 12, London, Institute of Education, University of London.

# Chapter 5

## Working together for children?

Bill Stone and Andy Rixon

## Introduction

Having explored the rationale for interagency working in earlier chapters (the 'what' and the 'why'), this chapter focuses on the questions of 'whether' and 'how' it is working in practice. Are the barriers to interagency working being overcome? Has the drive towards closer relationships between agencies and professionals produced more integrated services? And, in the end, are children and their families receiving a better service as a result? Evaluations in a number of areas of children's services, in particular the Sure Start initiative, provide the opportunity to attempt to answer some of these questions and identify some potential indications of the way forward. This exploration will also include a more critical look at 'working together' for children and the consequences of this approach.

### Core questions

- How is the effectiveness of more integrated ways of working to be evaluated?
- What evidence is there concerning the outcomes of interagency work for children?
- What are the consequences of the drive towards more integrated working?
- What positive indicators are there of the way forward in successful 'working together'?

# 1  Is it working? How would we know?

Thinking point 5.1    How would you evaluate whether or not interagency working was successful?

How is the success of more integrated ways of working to be judged? One element of evaluation might be to consider to what extent integrated teams or new initiatives or structures have overcome obstacles and enabled more positive ways of working. What learning has come out of these experiences for other such projects? Even if the successful recipe for practitioners working together were to be discovered, would this automatically improve services for children? As we have discussed, government policy and the literature on children's services all emphasise the importance of agencies working together and the value of partnership structures, yet:

> Despite such exhortations, there appears to be a dearth of evidence to support the notion that multi-agency working in practice brings about actual benefits for children and families.
>
> (Townsley et al., 2004, p. 6)

The same message echoes in numerous other research studies. A systematic review of joint working (Cameron and Lart, 2003) found that:

> Disappointingly, the vast majority of the studies in the review focused their attention on the process of joint working and the perceptions of those involved as to its success. Very few of the studies looked at either the prior question of why joint working should be seen as a 'good thing' and therefore why it should be done, or at the subsequent question of what difference joint working made. This makes the literature somewhat circular, and almost silent on the question of effectiveness.
>
> (Cameron and Lart, 2003, p. 15)

Similarly, research on one of the key mechanisms for the delivery of joined-up services – partnerships – is heavily weighted towards process rather than outcomes (Percy-Smith, 2006).

The evaluation of any service for children and families raises a number of interrelated questions. Increasingly, new projects and initiatives have been set clear targets against which performance can be measured. This is partly a reflection of the preference for 'evidence-based' interventions and partly concerned with issues of value for money and accountability. The importance of targets inevitably raises the question of how they are set and whether they are the right ones. Practitioners recognise that targets can enable clarity and equity, and focus attention on important areas of practice (Banks, 2004). Critics of this outcome-led trend have often pointed to targets necessarily being linked to outcomes that can be measured. These outcomes may not be able to take into account 'softer' measures about relational elements of work with children and families – engagement and relationship-building – or important achievements that are not in the list of selected targets. In deciding whether a service has been a success or not, the chosen measures of success always need to be carefully examined. Parents and children may have their own perspectives on targets appropriate to their own lives (Morgan, 2005).

Townsley et al. (2004) review a number of studies that reveal little evidence of improved outcomes of multi-agency working across a range of services and settings. Their review also makes clear that the task of evaluation itself is a complex one. Inherent problems include:

> difficulties in generalising from individual case studies; diverse views of different stakeholders as to what counts as success; the length of time needed to evaluate change; and causality and attribution.
>
> (Glendinning, 2002, cited in Townsley, 2004, p. 6)

Certainly interagency working is only one variable amongst many. How do we know which of these improvements, if any, are due to more effective interagency working and which are due to other factors which may or may not be anything to do with this style of working, or even to other children's services?

In evaluating the impact of Sure Start programmes, Tunstill et al. agree that evaluating large-scale community interventions is highly complex and argue for less reliance on the 'sometimes simplistic rhetoric around "evidence based policy and practice", to a stress on building knowledge over time' (Tunstill et al., 2005, p. 169). This would allow for a broader, more inclusive range of evidence to count towards evaluation.

One specific element we will focus on is also the extent to which families were included in decisions that were made about the shape of services. Both children and parents have come to be considered important partners in 'working together' and were to be empowered to participate in service developments – have they been? And if they were, what impact did this have?

## 1.1  A 'Sure Start'?

The UK Sure Start programme launched in the late 1990s embodied the philosophy behind the drive towards interagency working and, as such, was an important example of an attempt to achieve 'joined-up' thinking and working. It was always envisaged that the gains from such an early years initiative would be long term; however, sufficient time has elapsed for aspects of this programme to have been evaluated and so offer some insight into how successful this approach has been. It provides a case example to enable some disentangling of reality from the rhetoric.

The Sure Start programme was announced in July 1998 and the first 'trailblazer' areas launched in early 1999. The Labour government saw the programme as a key policy initiative. It was proof of their social justice aspirations and a prime example of the government's ambition to place children at the heart of its social policy agenda, as evidenced by David Blunkett's and Yvette Cooper's then enthusiastic endorsement:

> In January 1999, we launched the first 60 Sure Start programmes. Just as we asked, they have blazed a trail. We are seeking and seeing a step-change: better services, more holistic services and – perhaps most important of all – services designed around the child and the family. This is an enormous breakthrough. Those trailblazers have shown us the change we need in this country can be achieved. Sure Start does bring people together. It will deliver improvements in children's health, it will deliver improvements in children's well-being, children will be ready to thrive when they start school, Sure Start does help families and communities become stronger and more cohesive.
>
> Sure Start is at the centre of our commitment to eradicate child poverty within 20 years, by helping to break the inter-generational cycle of poor children's under-achievement and poverty of aspiration.
>
> This is a prize worth working hard for. It's clear what needs to be done. The challenge now is to make it happen.
>
> David Blunkett, Secretary of State for Education and Employment
> Yvette Cooper, Parliamentary Under-Secretary of State for Public Health
>
> (Quote from the foreword of Sure Start, 2000)

The programme was backed by substantial funding, and over 500 Sure Start programmes were established in England by 2004. Sure Start was also frequently referred to by the government as the exemplar 'par excellence' of multi-agency approaches to working with young children. Norman Glass, a senior civil servant from the Treasury, was a key influence in the development of the programme. He describes the philosophy of Sure Start as follows:

> In many ways it is a prime example of 'joined-up government' and evidence-based policy making ...
>
> Sure Start is a radical cross-departmental strategy to raise the physical, social, emotional and intellectual status of young children through

improved services. It is targeted at children under four and their families in areas of need. It is part of the Government's policy to prevent social exclusion and aims to improve the life chances of younger children through better access to early education and play, health services for children and parents, family support and advice on nurturing.

(Glass, 1999, p. 257)

The quote above offers a number of important points about the thinking behind this initiative. First, although other government departments, such as Education, the Home Office and Health, subsequently adopted this thinking, the initiative originated in the Treasury with a concern about spending taxpayers' money on public services. Shortly after being elected in 1997, the Labour government had set up a number of cross-cutting reviews, chaired by the Treasury, one of which looked at services for children under eight years old. This review concluded, rather gloomily, that £10 billion was being spent by thirteen different government departments, with no shared purpose and little coordination. In spite of all this money being spent on children and their families, child poverty was, in fact, increasing to such an extent that significant discrepancies were being noted in the life chances of children as young as 22 months (for analysis of this see Feinstein, 2003).

Secondly, central to the Sure Start philosophy is the belief that comprehensive, sustained early intervention makes a significant difference to children's lives. Policy makers were impressed with evidence of programmes in America such as 'Head Start' that purported to demonstrate that one dollar spent on the early years can save seven or eight dollars in later life (Glass, 1999). These savings were achieved through reductions in offending, conduct disorders, family breakdown, school avoidance, teenage pregnancy and a host of other adverse outcomes that had become central

Sure Start – 'a radical cross-departmental strategy'

concerns of UK government policy. It supported the idea that evidence-based interventions were not only desirable but achievable (France and Utting, 2005). The original Sure Start programme, launched with the 'trailblazers' and followed by successive waves of new local partnerships, was aimed at only the most deprived areas of the country. Sure Start covered local authority wards deemed to be among the 20 per cent most disadvantaged in England. This reflected another feature of policy at the time of identifying and targeting communities most in need of intervention.

Thirdly, all these social problems were bigger than any one agency or government department and so needed a coordinated response that would bring a subsequent payoff to the whole range of agencies. Unlike previous approaches to working with children that offered no incentives for a corporate approach, Sure Start would build into the programme a robust, multi-agency framework. It was an explicit and concerted attempt to overcome the fragmentation of services:

> At a policy level [Sure Start] represents a commitment to investing in our children for a long-term future and a commitment to the belief that statutory and voluntary agencies working together with a common goal can achieve more than the sum of the individual parts.
>
> (Glass, 1999, p. 264)

This idea that value is added by coordinating and streamlining services was central to the Sure Start strategy. Instead of separate agency 'silos', the vision was of a seamless service, accessible to all. It meant that: 'Preschool teachers, health visitors, social workers and community development workers had an unprecedented opportunity to work together' (Hannon and Fox, 2005, p. 7).

## Sure Start

Objectives

Improving social and emotional development

Improving health

Improving learning

Strengthening families and communities

(Sure Start, 2002, webpage)

Principles

1 Working with parents and children

2 Services for everyone

3 Flexible at the point of delivery

4 Starting very early

5 Respectful and transparent

6 Community driven and professionally coordinated

7 Outcome driven

(Sure Start, 2002, webpage)

The services provided by local Sure Start programmes had a great deal in common with pre-existing community-based provision such as neighbourhood nurseries and family centres, but what was distinctive about them was not so much the range of provision as the joined-up way in which that provision was to be delivered. There were a number of central objectives (see the box above) with a range of related and detailed targets (Sure Start, 2002). Certain core services were expected to be delivered in all communities where local Sure Start programmes existed. However, while this common core was target led, there was flexibility for local programmes to plan and provide services tailored to the needs of their particular community. A typical model of a Sure Start programme might include the following.

- A children's centre – the hub of local support providing early education integrated with childcare for children aged 0–4, child and family health services, employment and training advice for parents, toy library, breastfeeding support, and 'bookstart' schemes. The centre is also the base for outreach work and coordinators for a childminders' network and children with special educational needs.

- Education and social services teams based at the local authority headquarters identifying children's needs and sustaining a local children's information service.

- Health visitors based in a GP surgery and health centre running a drop-in baby clinic: weighing, advice on feeding, immunisation and health issues. Sure Start health visitors, where employed, would also work from here.

- A nursery school for free part-time education for all three- and four-year-olds.

- Jobcentre Plus for help into employment and advice over tax credits and child benefit.

- Library and mobile playbus facilities taking immunisation services, fresh food stalls and toys into the community. It might also run holiday playschemes and a fathers group.

A wide range of practitioners would be responsible for developing and delivering these services, along with local people, parents in particular, who were seen as important members of the partnership boards. Working in accordance with community development principles, parent participation workers aimed to recruit and train local parents to play an active role, as employed or volunteer workers, on the programme. The practitioners working in Sure Start might be employed by the local Sure Start partnership or they might be seconded from their original agency. In terms of their professional background the Sure Start workforce was very diverse, including early years workers, nursery teachers, social workers, health visitors, occupational therapists, speech therapists, psychologists and community workers. In the early days of Sure Start there was a great deal of emphasis on the local programmes being administered by local partnerships between the statutory authorities and the voluntary and independent sectors.

Funding for Sure Start was set at a relatively generous level and was originally to last for 10 years although, in the event, the programme was overtaken by national policy changes. In 2003, before the original Sure Start programme had completed its implementation stage, there were some major developments at the level of national policy. In summary, the intention expressed in government guidance was to move towards integrated children's centres that would eventually cover all areas (DfES, 2003). Children's centres were to share much of the Sure Start thinking in terms of multi-agency working, but local authorities were envisaged as taking a lead role. It might be argued that this was simply part of the process of 'mainstreaming' Sure Start principles, although there are significant differences of emphasis, particularly with respect to the involvement of local parents and communities in the planning process.

## 1.2 Evaluating the impact

Sure Start: aiming to improve children's health, learning and social and emotional development

> Perhaps unsurprisingly ... government policy in respect of children and families has continued to develop, in advance of conclusive research findings to emanate from NESS [the National Evaluation of Sure Start].
>
> (Tunstill et al., 2005, p. 166)

The 'mainstreaming' of Sure Start was a source of exasperation for some, confirming that government policy has a tendency to move on without the lessons of the previous policy initiatives having been learnt. The political urgency felt by government to demonstrate to the electorate that it has fulfilled its mandate and delivered the changes it promised, clashes strongly with the slower and more measured process of doing research and gathering evidence.

Extensive evaluation, at both local and national level, had been built into the Sure Start programme from the start and so there is a growing body of evidence about the difference that Sure Start is making to children and communities (see, for example, National Evaluation of Sure Start (NESS), 2004). Early findings on the overall impact of Sure Start local programmes (SSLPs) on child development and family functioning were, however, disappointing in that the measurable positive effects had been modest and only observable in the less disadvantaged families. This was analysed in terms of forms of capital available to families, as discussed in Chapter 2:

> Findings of the Impact Study were that among the disadvantaged families living in SSLP areas, parents/families with greater human capital were better able to take advantage of SSLP services than those with less human capital (i.e. teen parents, lone parents, parents in workless households).
>
> (NESS, 2007, p. 81)

Early indications were that Sure Start projects had found it difficult to engage with 'hard to reach' groups. This is hardly surprising as all the mainstream agencies have struggled with this too. Interestingly, this national evaluation found that health-led programmes had slightly more success with the hard to reach groups and this may well be related to health professionals' practice of visiting parents with young babies and children in their own homes. Certainly the importance of outreach work was found to be crucial to successful engagement (Tunstill et al., 2005).

Within the overall evaluation of the impact on families, the more detailed experiences of some can be lost. The degree to which programmes engaged fathers, for example, was found to be variable, success depending on the degree to which individual programmes had a worker dedicated to this role (Lloyd et al., 2003). Tunstill et al. (2005) noted the challenges of Sure Start programmes meeting the needs of ethnically diverse communities. There is insufficient knowledge of why certain ethnic groups are significantly less likely than others to engage with family support services in general, and this was again reflected in Sure Start programmes. There were also some examples of difficulties in providing a culturally sensitive service:

> There were obvious challenges in recruiting an appropriate workforce, and the failure of staff to understand the culture within

which families are operating, could lead to inappropriate and counter-productive interventions.

(Tunstill et al., 2005, p. 162)

This evaluation also reinforces the importance of the 'personal characteristics' of individual practitioners, a theme which emerges repeatedly in evaluations of interagency working as in every other mode of working with children and their families.

A detailed study of one programme – Foxhill and Parson Cross Sure Start (Weinberger et al., 2005) – reveals some of the tensions and contradictions in achieving success in interagency and partnership work. Within the objective of 'improving health', Sure Start programmes attempted to increase the rate of breastfeeding in their area. This project reported a significant rise in the numbers of women breastfeeding over a three-year period. The success of starting to change the culture around breastfeeding appeared to be primarily due to a group of paid peer support workers (Battersby, 2005). This success, however, perhaps masked the relationships between agencies in the area as there was little success in engaging health professionals in the breastfeeding programme. The same project reviewed the impact of Sure Start on local health visitors and reported that collaborative working was difficult to establish. Role confusion, overlapping boundaries, conflicting priorities and different management structures all contributed to the problem:

> 'they [health visitors] want us to mop up the things that really they feel aren't that important for them to do ... and some of the things that we're more capable of doing, they want to keep hold of'.

(Sure Start worker quoted in Rowe, 2005, p. 105)

However, some health visitors felt that Sure Start had the money and took all the credit:

> 'Well it's us and them, it means they start and develop all their whatever they're going to do, but we've done the groundwork and then the other thing is ... all the work we are doing, where is that shown because every figure is Sure Start'.

(Health visitor quoted in Rowe, 2005, p. 104)

Effective services were therefore delivered via the partnership structure of Sure Start but not necessarily reflecting interagency working on the ground. In fact there were many positive examples of working practices, but this evaluation emphasises that easy assumptions by policy makers about how practitioners will work together in new structures are misplaced. The complex nature of interagency relationships needs to be recognised and given specific attention otherwise families will not 'experience the high quality co-ordinated care that they are entitled to receive' (Rowe, 2005, p. 112).

This evaluation concludes that the service Sure Start offered was ultimately more than the sum of its parts, illustrated by evidence of the cross-fertilisation and added value that results from professionals from different service backgrounds working together for children and families in a holistic way:

> There is some evidence that offering a combination of services within one programme has added to the value of all the services. There have been links between them. Parents using one service can be referred on to, or encouraged to take up, other services, for example, from the breastfeeding support scheme to baby massage or, for a parent with a sensory disability, from a language check to support to attend a mother and toddler group ... Every service has the potential to support every other service.
>
> (Hannon et al., 2005, p. 254)

As discussed in Chapter 3, 'partnerships' have increasingly meant the involvement of families as well as statutory and voluntary agencies. This was reflected in the requirement to have parental involvement in all Sure Start boards as part of objective 4 – 'strengthening families and communities'. One other measure of success might be the extent to which this partnership was achieved. Foxhill and Parson Cross Sure Start again

Promoting breastfeeding through peer support

shows a mixed picture, particularly in relation to the low rates of involvement of fathers, but illustrates the progress that has been made through a number of personal stories:

> 'The meeting was quite daunting at first. My doctor was at the meeting, which felt strange ... I had a great time meeting new parents in the Parson Cross area and professionals who were there. Before I knew it I was questioning people, putting my views forward and those views of people too shy to speak up too!'

> (Excerpt from Cheryl's story in Lomas and Hannon, 2005, p. 201)

The experience of this particular programme is supported by the national evaluation of Sure Start. The same picture emerged of working in partnership – from encouraging, with positive results for parents:

> There is widespread enthusiasm from front-line staff and managers for working in multi-disciplinary teams. Positive aspects of multi-disciplinary working have been identified as greater flexibility, opportunities to work beyond rigid professional boundaries, sharing good practice and being better able to inform parents about the range of support available to them.

> (NESS, 2004, p. 3)

to recognising the problems:

> SSLP's have made some good progress in working in partnership at both strategic and operational levels. However joint working is challenging and time consuming and there is still some way to go.

> (NESS, 2004, p. 3)

The National Audit Office evaluation of Sure Start children's centres takes this theme further and emphasises how having people from different organisations working together in an integrated way is both essential and very challenging. The report concludes:

> Children's centres provide an opportunity for effective joint working for the benefit of families, but there is a risk of confusion and disenchantment with collaboration because in many centres the expectations and responsibilities of the various partners are unclear.

> (National Audit Office, 2006, p. 9)

These problems were not just at the point of the individual practitioner but were experienced at the highest levels. Measuring the success of a programme is complicated if the aims are not clear. Sure Start was a victim to some extent of the impact of government shifting priorities and changing lines of responsibility:

> The 'joining up' also turned out to be problematical – at least at a national level; it often worked very well locally. At first, the programme was a joint programme between health and education, with the health minister in the day-to-day lead. But after Jowell and Yvette Cooper had played this role successfully, departmental inertia began to exert itself. The programme reverted solely to DfES control and, ominously, was run by a joint DfES/Department for Work and Pensions minister. This reflected its capture by the 'employability' agenda.
>
> For poor mothers, work was the answer, and Sure Start was to play its role as a sort of New Deal for Toddlers. The Department of Health, never Sure Start's most devoted fan, faded even further into the background. So Sure Start, originally a child-centred programme, became embroiled in the childcare agenda and the need to roll out as many childcare places as possible to support maternal employment.
>
> (Glass, 2005, webpage)

## Key points

1 Whether interagency work is more successful than traditional service delivery needs to take account of the views of practitioners, children and their families. The basis on which success is measured needs to be viewed critically.

2 Sure Start provides an example of a major attempt to promote interagency working for children. The idea of partnerships between agencies and including families was built into the programme from the outset.

3 Evaluations of the impact of Sure Start on children and families have shown a mixed picture of success, although longer-term evaluations will need to be undertaken.

4 The centrality of interagency working has enabled some positive examples of working practice but has reinforced the need for specific attention needing to be given to this style of working to maximise outcomes for children and families.

# 2 Learning from practice

While Sure Start provides a useful case study, evidence of the impact of working together in different configurations can be seen in a range of other settings and areas of work. This section will look at a number of other examples where there has been some evidence of whether they work but also emerging evidence about what helps make things work.

## 2.1 Services for disabled children

Disabled children are likely to experience higher levels of disadvantage and social exclusion (Beresford, 2002). Parents of disabled children have been an important influence in the demands for better multi-agency working, and many services have moved towards more coordinated delivery. There have, however, been few evaluations of whether services have become more coordinated as a result. Townsley et al. (2004) undertook research in six multi-agency services across the UK, interviewing professionals, parents and children (aged 0–15) with complex healthcare needs, to assess the impact on each. Within these six sites, the services involved had different funding arrangements, staffing mixes and management arrangements, underlining the complicated nature of services, the variety of configurations, and therefore the ability to compare evaluations.

The practitioners involved in the six projects identified the variation that might be expected given the range of issues involved in this style of working. However, while many outstanding problems were identified, they generally reported positive improvements in issues such as communication as people were easier to access and information easier to share:

> 'It cuts down a huge amount of duplication when other professionals are there. Sometimes we can short-cut outpatients – go straight to the consultant for an opinion. Cuts down on phone calls. Makes things more efficient and easier.'
>
> (Practitioner quoted in Townsley et al., 2004, p. 29)

It was reported that this had an impact on working relationships and shifting the 'blame culture'. This seemed particularly the case where teams were co-located, balancing some of the concerns about the assumptions behind co-location discussed in Chapter 3. There was, however, less evidence that new structures had enabled better relationships between practitioners and families even when key working relationships were established; time pressures and communication difficulties remained disappointingly familiar barriers:

> 'It's a bit of a luxury now to think about having meaningful individual relationships with children.'
>
> (Practitioner quoted in Townsley et al., 2004, p. 35)

Across all the sites, the practitioners believed that the multi-agency services were improving the quality of the lives of families. Much of this assessment revolved around more support at home (rather than being delivered in hospital) and families having to deal with less people; practitioners were, however, less sure how significant positive change had been. Practitioners' reflections also tended to focus on the wellbeing of the 'family' rather than specifically any of the children or young people within them:

> 'It's not a significant difference to quality of life. More co-ordination of what is already happening. Families are not getting things they weren't getting before. It's just better co-ordinated now. It pulls things together and makes them more effective.'
>
> (Practitioner quoted in Townsley et al., 2004, p. 36)

Thinking point 5.2   How might families define whether they are benefiting from an interagency service?

What, then, were the families' perspectives on their wellbeing and the impact of multi-agency working? Townsley et al. (2004) considered quality of life across seven key indicators – daily family life, physical environment, financial wellbeing, social wellbeing, emotional wellbeing, skills and learning, and contact with services and professionals. Experiences were extremely variable. In relation to family life there was little evidence of support with the major difficulties of travel and transport, while there was positive evidence of families being supported to care for their children's complex needs at home. Financial, social and emotional wellbeing all raised difficult issues. The social exclusion of disabled children proved a huge barrier to overcome. Lower levels of income and employment have long been recognised as issues in families where there are disabled children, but these projects made little difference to that core problem.

Interagency disagreements were another source of stress. This was often linked to lack of resources available to the teams, although sometimes it did seem to be an issue of coordination:

> 'It was all about money and not how we were suffering as a family. I don't need to know the details of how budgets work, or to get involved in writing to different people. I don't care who pays so long as they pay.'
>
> (Family member quoted in Townsley et al., 2004, p. 46)

There was, it was felt, a lack of a 'whole family' approach to wellbeing:

> 'They all get together to discuss [child]. They don't talk about the rest of us much.'
>
> (Family member quoted in Townsley et al., 2004, p. 45)

Enabling children to participate in activities and families to go on holiday together or have support services available out of normal hours remained a huge problem. When this approach was in evidence, for example enabling the family to do something together, or making a real effort to get to know the child and family, families felt the impact was substantial.

Emotional support did seem to be more available where a key worker was available:

> 'She's a friendly face to talk to. I mean perhaps she doesn't know what its like to have a disabled child, I don't know, but she's very supportive and I feel that I can actually open up to her quite easily so yes, she is very supportive.'
>
> (Family member quoted in Townsley et al., 2004, p. 48)

This issue of key working was explored in the study in more detail – this has become a crucial aspect of policy developments for children and young people generally. Increasingly, this key worker/link worker/lead professional/etc. has been advocated as a key element in ensuring better coordination of practitioners and better interface between the services and children and families (DfES, 2004). There were other positive examples of this:

> 'I was spending so much time on the 'phone, I would be chasing up changed appointments ... so yes, that's cut down on oodles of 'phone calls.'
>
> (Family member quoted in Townsley et al., 2004, p. 54)

However, many families did not seem to know if they had a key worker or exactly what their role was, and experienced difficulties with staff turnover. Neither did the presence of a key worker necessarily cut down on the numbers of assessments and reviews that were involved.

Ascertaining the views of children with complex health needs on a topic such as multi-agency working proved challenging; however, the children were able to express opinions on what they liked or didn't like and on adults who were involved in their lives. Most children were accepting of the need for such a wide variety of people in their lives (although one child was clear that it was 'silly' and 'boring to have to see so many different people'). This study illustrated the view that despite the good intentions of the agencies, children still experienced multiple barriers to exercising some basic human rights such as the rights to communication, to independence, and to be consulted and informed about their care. While the key worker role could in theory enable communication and consultation, there was little evidence of key workers having significant contact with children.

The overriding message was less about the way multi-agency working was

Evaluation of key worker services for disabled children has revealed a mixed picture of success

organised and more about the interpersonal skills of individual practitioners:

> there was little real evidence of effective consultation between the multi-agency services and disabled children with complex health care needs about their care and support. Even where families had access to a keyworker, we did not get a strong sense that there were strong relationships between this person and the children themselves. Some children were unaware of the identity of their keyworker even when named and described. A close relationship with a keyworker could give an opportunity for young people to be more involved with their care and allow them to have a voice.
>
> (Townsley et al., 2004, p. 68)

Sloper et al. (2006) have explored different models of key working with disabled children to identify which elements of it have the best outcomes for families. Their analysis is in relation to four areas – quality of life, satisfaction with key worker service, parental unmet need and child unmet need. Findings identified that key workers who were most involved and who performed the many different elements of their role had the biggest impact on the first two outcomes. Levels of unmet need, however, were related to the time that key workers were able to spend with families. Factors such as training and supervision were also influential. However, child unmet need seemed to be mainly influenced by other factors:

> Factors such as the general amount of resources for children, children's access to play and leisure facilities and their

relationships with friends and peers, may be stronger influences on disabled children's unmet needs. There is also a possibility that key worker services may be mainly focussing on supporting parents.

(Sloper et al., 2006, p. 156)

## 2.2 Changing schools

Behaviour and Education Support Teams (BESTs) brought together a range of professionals working together to support schools, families and children who present, or are at risk of developing emotional, behavioural and/or attendance problems. BESTs have been operating in England for several years in some areas and, as such, are another useful source of information about interprofessional working. An evaluation of BESTs, conducted by Karen Halsey and colleagues (2006), found that BESTs had a positive impact on children and young people in the areas of attainment, attendance, behaviour and wellbeing. One of the key factors behind this success emerged as being multi-agency working:

> Fundamental to the concept of BEST was the multi-agency composition of teams, including representation from the three main statutory services of education, (mental) health and social care. Several of the BESTs in the case-study sample had extended this brief to include, for example, professionals from youth or play work backgrounds. The inclusion of staff with varying professional backgrounds and specialisms was seen as a key factor in the effectiveness of BESTs, with key benefits of this multi-agency approach being: the ability to take a holistic approach to the educational, health and social needs of children and families; the collaborative pooling of skills and exchange of expertise around casework and interventions; and the opportunities for professional development this presented.

(Halsley et al., 2006, p. iv)

This represents the project meeting its target aims, no doubt being beneficial to the children and young people involved, although not necessarily targets negotiated with them.

In a study of the early development of extended schools commissioned by DfES (Wilkin et al., 2003), information was collected, in 2002/3, from some 160 schools across England that were beginning to operate some form of 'extended' service. There was a wide diversity of types of service provision, and extended school delivery was said to impact positively on pupil attainment, attendance and behaviour. Facilities were offered to increase engagement and motivation, and learning was thought to be enhanced as the school was regarded as a site of resources for the community. Multi-agency input on-site was also felt to meet a range of pupil and family needs more readily.

Initiatives based around schools had already been developing in Scotland since 1999. The New Community Schools (NCSs) programme represented another attempt to tackle social exclusion in a fundamentally interagency way, initially targeted at the most disadvantaged areas although later rolled out across all schools.

In recognition of the relationships between educational achievement, health and socio-economic factors, NCSs were charged with expanding and integrating the range of services offered to young people in disadvantaged areas, with the intention of both raising attainment and promoting social inclusion (Scottish Executive, 2003, p. 1).

Community schools: an interagency approach to raising educational attainment and promoting social inclusion

Early evaluation of the programme was conducted through a mixture of methods – surveys, interviews, observation and school-related statistical information – revealing an emerging patchy but encouraging picture.

Despite early start-up problems, the development of multi-agency and multi-disciplinary approaches was seen as one of the key areas of success. Funding was drawn from Education, Social Services and Health, stimulating the expansion of existing provision and the development of some new projects. Provision featured out-of-hours provision, breakfast clubs and support programmes for children with specific difficulties, although there were varying perceptions of how successful this provision had been in supporting vulnerable children (Scottish Executive, 2003). Given the importance of how interagency initiatives are managed, it was notable that most schools had appointed an 'integration manager' to enable the development of the pilot projects. Educational attainment was again initially a mixed picture as the improvements over the evaluation period were seen in Scotland's schools as a whole. Taking account of young people's views was also a feature of developments in New Community Schools, with a rapid growth in the number of school councils (Scottish Executive, 2003).

Although such evaluation can shed light on which aspects of community-oriented schooling are most successful, it does not necessarily demonstrate that this particular interagency strategy is the most effective solution to the problems raised by social exclusion. Dyson and Raffo (2007) question both the existing evidence for the success of community schooling and also the ability of this strategy to tackle the wider issues of disadvantage within which schools are located. The promotion of this way of delivering services makes a number of assumptions that need to be questioned – 'assumptions about the processes whereby socio-economic disadvantage arises and is translated into educational disadvantage, and about how community-oriented schools can intervene in these processes' (Dyson and Raffo, 2007, p. 300). It is unlikely that schools will be able to challenge socio-economic issues or even the education system in which they operate.

## 2.3  Having a say – the Children's Fund

> The Children's Fund was set up, in part, as a catalyst to move forward interagency co-operation and child and family-led preventative services in local authorities. It is, therefore, part of a long-term strategy aimed at strengthening communities and families as places where children and young people can develop as healthy, responsible and engaged citizens.
>
> (National Evaluation of the Children's Fund (NECF), 2004a, p. i)

Like Sure Start, the Children's Fund was established as a fundamentally interagency enterprise with the intention of creating partnerships involving statutory and voluntary agencies, children and families. Alongside its key targets, three guiding principles of the Children's Fund were *prevention*, *partnership*, and ensuring children and young people's *participation* in the design, delivery and evaluation of preventative services (NECF, 2004a). In terms of whether such interagency initiatives 'work', the extent to which such participation happened in practice can provide another measure of evaluation.

The extent to which the Children's Fund was evaluated was unusual in its breadth (for a discussion about the theoretical perspectives used in the evaluation, see Chapter 6), and how the different partnership boards managed this participatory aspect of the Children's Fund was one of a range of areas that were analysed. The evaluation found that the models of participation had not been prescriptive so different projects used different

Children and young people chair a conference (Swindon Children's Fund)

methods as a result of different understandings of participation and its purposes. This had a major impact on the outcomes since those seeing the primary purpose as 'informing' service development focused on consultation with children, while projects who saw it as 'engagement' and 'enabling children's rights' saw more involvement in partnership boards, commissioning and even recruitment. 'This represents moving towards the goal of what is often termed *co-configuration*, where children, young people and parents/carers are involved as equal partners in developing responsive services according to their needs and aspirations' (NECF, 2004b, p. 18).

Some partnerships even saw building resilience and reducing social exclusion as key aims in involving children in participation which seemed to chime with children's own perspectives on the meaning of participation:

> 'It really has made my confidence. It has brought more people into my life and made more friends and I feel more happy going places instead of being stuck in or say it is like a cold day or something ... and instead of going out playing I can go and do something else, like go to [the participation officer's] office and write a newsletter.'
>
> (Young person quoted in NECF, 2004b, p. 19)

Practice box 5.1

### Enabling participative practice

A notable example is the children's management committee of a project working with children of multiple heritage that organised a conference for 150 other children of multiple heritage from schools across the local authority. When they were allocated a sum of money to spend as they chose, the children's management committee had the idea of a conference to give children of multiple heritage the space to discuss issues of concern to them as well as have fun meeting other children of multiple heritage backgrounds. Project workers supported them in planning and delivering the conference, with additional support from the Children's Fund core team.

(NECF, 2004b, p. 18)

Despite the challenges, the evaluation of the Children's Fund identified many examples of participatory practice where children were involved in decision making and exerted influence on the activities developed by the projects. In terms of interagency working it is notable that having a specific participation officer enabled participation but also resulted in less understanding about participation across the other stakeholders.

Practice box 5.2

### The problems of involving children in partnership board meetings

A case study partnership employed child-friendly and jargon-free language in order to overcome the potential for meetings to be uninteresting to children, young people and parents/carers. To enforce this, a system was applied whereby any board member, including children, young people and families, could hold up a *yellow card* if they felt inappropriate language was being used. The participation officer facilitated children and young people and families' participation by ensuring that they were actively drawn into discussions in ways that they could relate to. Considerable use was made of flip charts to simplify, clarify and summarise issues and concepts and ensure that children, young people and families understood the implications of certain decisions for potential service users.

(NECF, 2004b, p. 28)

Evaluation of other aspects of the impact of the Children's Fund in relation to preventative services and social exclusion were undertaken across a range of groups. Work with Black and Asian families was explored in two sites, and its impact was broadly found to be positive.

> The data gathered indicates that those children and families that used the Children's Fund Black and ethnic minority provision experienced the services as helpful and useful. The gains described by those providing the services and those using the services suggested that the services have supported children to learn and to take up new opportunities and experiences. There is also evidence that families have seen a change in their children's behaviour and that the services have encouraged the take-up of productive, less disruptive activities by children.
>
> (NECF, 2006, p. iv)

> The intended outcomes for children as a result of supporting the valuing of their heritage and the promotion of skills for coping with racism are very difficult to measure. Children, families and service providers talked about increased confidence and self-respect as well as cultural knowledge and appreciation.
>
> (NECF, 2006, p. v)

At the same time, the question of what is evaluated and how was clearly an issue; the evaluators noted the lack of data beyond the descriptive, making the impact of these services difficult to track.

## 2.4  Co-located services – Coram Campus

Some services have been working in a co-located environment for many years. Services on the same site, in the same office or in integrated teams may have been rapidly developing but are not a new concept. One model of co-location was attempted on the 'Coram Campus' starting in 1998. This project brought a range of voluntary and statutory agencies together on the same site, including an early years excellence centre, a project for working with disabled children, and services for homeless families, as well as representation from health, education and social services. A key feature of this model was the coordination and facilitation role played by a voluntary organisation, the Coram Family.

From the array of terminology in this area, the Campus was aiming to achieve not integration but a multi-agency 'network'. Networks vary in nature but essentially describe a collaborative arrangement between services that have some 'shared or overlapping interests' and can work towards common goals (see Chapter 3). The evaluation attempted to go beyond the delivery of services from each agency to the Campus 'itself' and the network of relationships within it to answer the question of whether the service provided could be more than the sum of its individual parts (Wigfall and Moss, 2001).

Although, as discussed in earlier chapters, it cannot be assumed that co-location will significantly improve interagency or interprofessional relationships, early evaluation of the Coram experience did suggest that being part of the campus did have an effect on its participants:

> 'You are part of something called the Campus. There is an expectation that we will all work together, which is not to say that if we were simply round the corner we wouldn't. It sort of puts an onus on you to work together rather than not.'

> (Practitioner from the Early Childhood Centre quoted in Wigfall and Moss, 2001, p. 26)

This process was not just a product of being on the same site but was reinforced by trying to create a shared vision, consolidated by a negotiated set of aims and objectives. Other strategies such as joint training, open days and seminars attempted to build on this – with varying degrees of success. The evaluation noted the value of the aims and objectives but also that awareness had not filtered down to all levels of staff within the organisation (Wigfall and Moss, 2001).

Inevitably the campus experienced many of the same problems and barriers that we have already explored, for example, communication difficulties both on the ground and at a strategic level. A particular concern was the pressure on each individual agency in terms of time and targets that left less energy and resources to put into working across the agency boundaries:

> 'by the time you include inspections and filling in things for the Government Office of London and so on , monitor, monitor, monitor ... people are really overburdened.'

> (Worker from Coram Family quoted in Wigfall and Moss, 2001, p. 40)

Families do not always experience the multi-agency nature of a service, and this can add to the difficulties of evaluation. Parents' broader knowledge of the Campus was found to be limited but there were many examples of the one-stop shop having been successful as families drew on the services of other agencies on-site. Some of the services provided – for example, parent support courses, shared outreach workers – were also cross-agency initiatives. This initial evaluation recognised the need for more work to be done to advance interagency practice but argued that this structure was adding value to the experience of families that could be replicated elsewhere:

> Our findings suggest that the strong links between the services and their proximity can ease the passage of families between them.

Families, in turn, acquire trust in individual services from which they gain confidence to move around services, deriving added benefits that might not have been possible without the Campus structure. The examples where this is happening, though relatively few in number, indicate how effective it can be.

(Wigfall and Moss, 2001, p. 73)

## Key points

1  Evaluations of the practice of interagency and interprofessional working are far from conclusive. It has brought some positive benefits for children and families but its success cannot be assumed. Attention needs to be paid to the detail of why some examples of practice are more successful.

2  Working together in partnerships that include children and their families is a major challenge but there are indications of how this could be achieved.

3  Co-locating services can enable closer working together but this needs to be supported by other strategies to enable services to deliver more than the sum of their combined parts.

# 3 Information overload: sharing information about children

Public policy, whatever its stated aims, often has unintended consequences. These unintended consequences may be the opposite of what was hoped for. For example, when the Sure Start programme was first brought to the notice of hard-pressed social services departments, they welcomed the initiative eagerly, thinking that it would reduce the number of referrals to their front-line duty and assessment teams. In fact, what often happened was that Sure Start projects, based in the most disadvantaged communities, actually generated more referrals for social services because they uncovered previously unmet need. Information sharing is recognised as a critical part of interagency working. Removing barriers to sharing information became an important part of government strategy in trying to ensure that no child slipped through the net and to enable greater interagency working (DfES, 2003). While strategies are being put in place to achieve this, concerns have also been expressed about other consequences of this trend.

Sharing information has had a particularly high profile in the area of safeguarding children. Children who may be experiencing neglect, for example, can come to the attention of workers in a wide variety of settings. Nurseries, playgroups and children's centres may be the first to notice a child who looks rather forlorn, lonely, unkempt and hungry, whose carer is frequently late and always seems to avoid contact with staff. A health visitor may pick up concerns about possible neglect on a routine home visit, or a social worker may be aware of a family history of childcare concerns. It might be the police who first get contacted by worried neighbours because a child has been left alone. Or it might be a professional who works with adults, such as an adult mental health worker or a housing support worker, a community worker or a substance misuse project worker, who is aware of parenting difficulties. Any or all of these workers may be the first point of contact for a vulnerable child or their struggling parent.

Thinking point 5.3    What action should any of these workers take if they have concerns? What might prevent them from taking such action?

Whether the child gets support and help at an early stage can depend on sharing information as the first stage in working together. If the front-line worker who first encounters the child does not discuss their concerns with someone else, then the opportunity for early and effective intervention is likely to be lost. Practitioners often report higher levels of confidence about positive outcomes for children in cases where there was early interagency involvement (Stone, 1998). In more serious cases where the child is at risk of significant harm, any one worker in any particular setting will be unlikely to have a very full and complete picture of the child's circumstances. A proper assessment is impossible without information from other practitioners who have observed the child in different settings and who, crucially, are aware of the family circumstances and family history. This can be particularly valuable in cases of neglect.

Different professions, because of their training and experience, are more attuned to some areas of a child's experience than others. These differences in perspective and attention are not only inevitable, they are also very helpful in building up a picture of the child in the round. Any assessment of need for a child requires information from a number of professionals involved with that child and his or her family. In practice deciding to contact another agency is not necessarily straightforward; there are many long-standing problems. Practitioners and managers of all children's services need to develop confidence to act and see safeguarding as their responsibility rather than that of other people. Training may also be needed to help them understand and recognise issues like neglect amongst the children they work with, as well as the legal framework around confidentiality within which practitioners operate. On top of these issues this are also the problems of communication and understanding between practitioners that we discussed in Chapter 3.

It is sometimes asserted that, in the absence of the parent's or carer's explicit consent, professionals should not share information about particular children with others because that would be to breach their duty of confidence – except, of course, when there is a specific child protection issue. This is a view that has been somewhat against the prevailing tide in the attempt to develop common systems and a common 'language' between practitioners. Along with common frameworks and core knowledge and skills, one of the central recommendations made in the Inquiry into Victoria Climbié's death (Laming, 2003) was the establishment of a national database to include information on every child under the age of 16. Along with this national Index (Contact Point), Laming also recommended that the government issue guidance on how data protection law and confidentiality protocols may impact on the sharing of information between professionals in cases where they have concerns about a child's welfare. Across the UK, policy changes have been made to enable the easier flow of information.

However, while this is seen as a key solution to enabling agencies to work more closely together, it has also raised a number of questions and issues. There has been a great deal of debate about precisely what information should be stored on such databases and who should have access to it. Given the problems associated with other ambitious government information technology projects, the technical challenges associated with the creation and operation of such giant databases should not be underestimated. The Children Act 2004 requires children's services authorities in England and

Wales to establish and operate information databases and allows for the establishment of regional or national databases. Information to be contained on these databases is strictly limited, but aspects of their operation were not clear:

> The only information that the databases will contain will be: the child's name, address, gender, date of birth, a unique identifying number, name and contact details of any person with parental responsibility or day-to-day care of the child, education provider (whether at home, school, or children's centre) and primary care provider (such as, doctor or health visitor). The data record should also include a flag to indicate that a professional working with the child has a 'cause for concern', but what constitutes a cause for concern is left undefined. The government suggests that any decision about whether or not a concern exists should remain one for professional judgment. All children and young people up to the age of 19 who reside in that area will be included in the database.
>
> (Payne, 2004, p. 384)

On the one hand this could lead to minor issues being flagged (possibly due to anxiety and defensiveness) leading to the databases being overloaded with irrelevant concerns. As Payne (2004, p. 386) stresses, such a system is also 'simply a technical tool' and the importance of professionals' judgement remains. As Dow (2005) argues, it is important to maintain as far as possible a consent-based approach to information sharing.

Communication and information sharing between professionals working with children are not ends in themselves. The sharing of information should be purposeful and should lead to better outcomes for the children concerned. However these policies and databases work in practice, the

Databases and information sharing can be valuable tools but also a source of concern

issues of confidentiality remain. Work with children by the Children's Commissioner for England made clear that children have particular anxieties about who has information about them and why (Morgan, 2005).

The issue of information sharing can also be seen in the context of escalating centralisation, surveillance and government control. The logic of joining up could seem to be the state and its agencies needing to be able to '"see everything", "know everything" and "do anything", and thus they produce a "holistic power" to discipline and control every aspect of welfare recipients' lives' (Allen, 2003, cited in Frost, 2005). Combined with the drive towards early identification and intervention, Parton (2006) argues that while preventive policies appear to be benign, they add to the potential for growing surveillance in all aspects of society.

> Partly because of the growing reliance on new information and communication technologies, we are now witnessing a convergence of what were once discreet surveillance systems to the point where we can now speak of an emerging 'surveillant assemblage' (Haggerty and Ericson, 2000).
>
> (Parton, 2006, p. 173)

Specific issues about the flow of information in children's services are set within a broader social context. The role of Information Commissioner was created by the government to promote good information handling practice and enforce data protection and freedom of information legislation. In January 2005 Richard Thomas, then Information Commissioner, was interviewed by *childRIGHT* magazine. At the close of this interview, he issued a challenge and a warning:

> 'The Select Committee report which looked at ID cards quite rightly observed that there is a proliferation of databases being set up by Government. We are at risk of sleepwalking into a surveillance society with the Government holding more information about us than people feel comfortable with.'
>
> (Richard Thomas quoted in Wadsworth, 2005, p. 8)

To use an analogy: if the welfare state is thought of as a safety net to catch those in danger of falling into adversity, then what appears to be happening is that the mesh used for the net is being progressively refined. The spaces between the overlapping cords are ever more restricted, with the result that more and more people are caught up in the state's embrace. The intention of the state may be benevolent but the result for children and families is increasing intrusion by the state into areas that have previously been thought of as 'private'.

## Key points

1 Information sharing is important to the success of multi-agency working in contributing to safeguarding children, and government policy is enabling a greater flow of information about children.

2 There is an inevitable tension between information sharing and confidentiality. Some of these concerns are to do with increasing surveillance by the government and the loss of individual freedoms.

# 4  Making it work

Thinking point 5.4   Reviewing the material in the preceding chapters, what do you think are the main messages about what works in relation to interagency working that have come out of the discussion?

Writing in the context of child protection work, Murphy concludes:

> Some of the most important factors in achieving good interagency work do not involve highly technical, complicated issues of interagency coordination, but rather are to do with the people skills that staff bring to the child protection process. When practitioners are asked about the factors that they value about good interagency cooperation, it is these human inclusive skills that they value most highly.
>
> (Murphy, 2004, p. 131)

There are numerous lists in many publications about the key features of successful interagency and interprofessional working; some of the most important factors, however, are related to very individual issues. Anecdotally, many practitioners comment that communication is problematic not because of the complexity of the system but because one person in the network is 'difficult'. The role of individuals and personalities in the success or failure of wider systems cannot be ignored. While Murphy warns against blaming individuals for breakdowns in communication, the value of interpersonal skills is a recurrent theme in interpractitioner relationships just as in practitioners' relationships with children and their families (Murphy, 2004). An overview of research in this area (Cameron and Lart, 2003) also found indications of the importance of involving 'the right people' (p. 12) in terms of skills and experience to act as link workers between agencies, and involving the key agencies in recruitment in order to reinforce the position of the people in these central roles.

These ideas emphasise the essentially relational nature of this work. The Coram Campus experience discussed above emphasised the value of shared aims and values and the need to invest time in developing relationships. Percy-Smith (2006), in her analysis of what works in strategic partnerships for children, reinforces this point: building trust and respect is key and this requires time to establish the process of team building.

Raising the educational attainment of children who are Looked After by the local authority is a key target for children's services and one that requires significant interagency collaboration. A study by the National Children's Bureau (Harker et al., 2004) into three local authorities' responses to this

Research is identifying some of the key themes that can contribute to successful integrated working

challenge found that some of the key factors that related to effective multi-agency working were:

● commitment by all parties to joint working

● structures to support joint working (partnership agreements and clear accountability with defined roles and responsibilities)

● effective working relationships

● clarity about information sharing

● strong leadership

● adequate resources.

> In both education and social services departments, personnel reported that there were limits on the time available to move beyond core roles to focus on joint work.

> (Harker et al., 2004, p. 190)

Frost (2005) draws, from extensive research in integrated teams, perhaps the most comprehensive conclusions about the key themes which include:

● Effective leadership – Leaders of multi-agency teams need flexibility and entrepreneurial skills to operate across traditional boundaries and create new solutions.

● Role clarity – Roles and responsibilities within multi-agency working can easily become blurred.

● 'Clear lines of accountability' – Multi-agency organisations tend to be complex and multi-layered; clear lines of accountability, support and supervision are essential.

● Addressing pay, conditions, issues of hierarchy and professional diversity.

- Joint procedures and inclusive planning – Front-line staff from different professional backgrounds need to be jointly engaged in the process of devising and implementing procedures. Frost also stresses the need to allow time for working relationships to develop.

- Strategic objectives and core aims – Multi-agency working can be effective only if there are shared aims to which each team member is fully committed.

- Pooled budgets and transparent governance structures – Pooled budgets have the potential to minimise interagency conflicts over priorities.

- Relationship to partner agencies – Multi-agency teams need to relate well and communicate efficiently with agencies that fund, second, host or manage joined-up teams. Structures and funding need to be as clear and coherent as possible.

- Interagency agreement over thresholds for service – This is one of the most problematic areas for multi-agency working, particularly within a climate of funding shortfall.

- Co-location – This is not sufficient, on its own, to ensure effective working together but it can enhance communication, learning and understanding of roles.

- Joint working with children and their families – Best multi-agency practice emerges from doing the work together. A common culture is developed through partnership both with other professionals and with service users.

- Active involvement of service users – Having this in planning and delivery helps keep a focus on the impact of change on children and families.

- A 'communication mindset' – It is fundamental that different professionals and their host agencies encourage open communication and sharing of information including talk about the emotional consequences of the work.

- Opportunities for reflection and professional development – Staff need time to reflect and learn from each other. Support and training, especially in the early stages of a new multi-agency project, are essential.

- Shared tools and protocols – These can help to standardise practice and create a culture of working together, for example, the Common Assessment Framework and lead professional protocols and agreements about sharing information.

- Interprofessional respect and trust – This is perhaps the most fundamental requirement for effective multi-agency working. This mutual respect does not come at the cost of individual assertiveness, as specialist skills and expertise are still necessary. Working together for children is not about 'lowest common denominator' practice.

Katz and Hetherington (2006) have taken a European perspective on integrating services for children. While we stress in Chapters 3 and 7 that there can be much to be learnt from alternative approaches and structures, some of the core features of successful integrated working seemed to be common:

> The factors that facilitated good interdisciplinary and interagency work point to the centrality of a professional and managerial culture that values the development of good working relationships both with families and with other professionals. Conflictual and defensive inter-professional relationships created problems, however well organized the system.
>
> (Katz and Hetherington, 2006, p. 429)

## Key points

1   A number of research studies are now helping to develop an understanding of what factors enable successful interagency and interprofessional working in terms of both process and what produces improved outcomes for children and families.

2   One of the many recurring themes is the need for individual practitioners to have the interpersonal skills to work across boundaries and roles.

# Conclusion

Evaluation of the impact of interagency working (and other configurations of practitioners working more closely together) has not been conducted extensively, so a critical view can be maintained of the seemingly unassailable assumptions behind the continuing drive in this direction. Some major initiatives like Sure Start and the Children's Fund were established with built-in evaluation and have provided some evidence of improving the wellbeing of children, although direct connections between what services deliver and their interagency nature are not always clear. They have certainly provided evidence that partnership working is possible, in an inclusive way, with children and parents even if this experience is variable and complicated by issues such as resource shortages, changing funding streams, and shifting government policy. Other initiatives such as New Community Schools are also providing valuable insights into new ways of working. Aspects of 'what works' are emerging and providing lessons for enabling the closer integration of services; however, in terms of improving the wellbeing of children, we also need to be clear about who is deciding the measure of what it is that is working. Learning from these lessons may enable more integrated ways of working to contribute to delivering government policy for children; improving the wellbeing of children will also depend on which policies are pursued and recognising the limitations of reconfiguring the workforce.

# References

Allen, C. (2003) 'Desperately seeking fusion: on "joined-up thinking", "holistic practice" and the *new* economy of welfare professional power', *British Journal of Sociology*, vol. 54, no. 2, pp. 287–386.

Banks, S. (2004) *Ethics, Accountability and the Social Professions*, Basingstoke, Palgrave Macmillan.

Battersby, S. (2005) 'Supporting breastfeeding mothers' in Weinberger, J., Pickstone, C. and Hannon, P. (eds) *Learning from Sure Start: Working with Young Children and Their Families*, Maidenhead, Open University Press, pp. 86–101.

Beresford, B. (2002) 'Preventing the social exclusion of disabled children' in McNeish, D., Newman, T. and Roberts, H. (eds) *What Works for Children?*, Buckingham, Open University Press, pp. 147–164.

Cameron, A. and Lart, R. (2003) 'Factors promoting and obstacles hindering joint working: a systematic review of the research evidence', *Journal of Integrated Care*, vol. 11, no. 2, pp. 9–17.

Department for Education and Skills (DfES) (2003) *Every Child Matters*, London, The Stationery Office.

Department for Education and Skills (DfES) (2004) *Every Child Matters: Change for Children*, London, The Stationery Office.

Dow, D. (2005) 'Information-sharing databases under the Children Act 2004', *Journal of Integrated Care*, vol. 13, no. 5, pp. 31–34.

Dyson, A. and Raffo, C. (2007) 'Education and disadvantage: the role of community-oriented schools', *Oxford Review of Education*, vol. 33, no. 3, pp. 297–314.

Feinstein, L. (2003) 'Inequality in the early cognitive development of British children in the 1970 cohort', *Economica*, vol. 70, no. 1, pp. 73–97.

France, A. and Utting, D. (2005) 'The paradigm of "risk and protection-focused prevention" and its impact on services for children and families', *Children & Society*, vol. 19, no. 2, pp. 77–90.

Frost, N. (2005) *Professionalism, Partnership and Joined-up Thinking*, Dartington, Research in Practice.

Glass, N. (1999) 'Sure Start: the development of an early intervention programme for young children in the United Kingdom', *Children & Society*, vol. 13, no. 4, pp. 257–264.

Glass, N. (2005) 'Surely some mistake?', *Guardian*, 5 January, available online at <http://education.guardian.co.uk/earlyyears/story/0,,1383617,00.html>, accessed 11 October 2007.

Glendinning, C. (2002) 'Partnerships between health and social services: developing a framework for evaluation', *Policy & Politics*, vol. 30, no. 1, pp. 115–127.

Haggerty, K.D. and Ericson, R.V. (2000) 'The surveillant assemblage', *British Journal of Sociology*, vol. 51, no. 4, pp. 605–622.

Halsey, K., Gulliver, C., Johnson, A., Martin, K. and Kinder, K. (2006) *Evaluation of Behaviour and Education Support Teams*, London, DfES.

Hannon, P. and Fox, L. (2005) 'Why we should learn from Sure Start' in Weinberger, J., Pickstone, C. and Hannon, P. (eds) *Learning from Sure Start: Working with Young Children and Their Families*, Maidenhead, Open University Press, pp. 3–12.

Hannon, P., Pickstone, C., Weinberger, J. and Fox, L. (2005) 'Looking to the future' in Weinberger, J., Pickstone, C. and Hannon, P. (eds) *Learning from Sure Start: Working with Young Children and Their Families*, Maidenhead, Open University Press, pp. 248–262.

Harker, R., Dobel-Ober, D., Berridge, D. and Sinclair, R. (2004) 'More than the sum of its parts? Inter-professional working in the education of looked after children', *Children & Society*, vol. 18, no. 3, pp. 179–193.

Katz, I. and Hetherington, R. (2006) 'Co-operating and communicating: a European perspective on integrating services for children', *Child Abuse Review*, vol. 15, no. 6, pp. 429–439.

Laming, Lord (2003) *The Victoria Climbié Inquiry*, London, The Stationery Office.

Lloyd, D., O'Brien, M. and Lewis, C. (2003) *National evaluation summary: Fathers in Sure Start local programmes*, London, DfES.

Lomas, H. and Hannon, P. (2005) 'Community involvement' in Weinberger, J., Pickstone, C. and Hannon, P. (eds) *Learning from Sure Start: Working with Young Children and Their Families*, Maidenhead, Open University Press, pp. 193–204.

Morgan, R. (2005) *Younger Children's Views on 'Every Child Matters'*, Newcastle, Commission for Social Care Inspection, also available online at <http://www.rights4me.org/content/beheardreports/14/young_views_on_everychildmatters_report.pdf>, accessed 19 September 2007.

Murphy, M. (2004) *Developing Collaborative Relationships in Interagency Child Protection Work*, Lyme Regis, Russell House Publishing.

National Audit Office (2006) *Sure Start Children's Centres*, London, The Stationery Office.

National Evaluation of the Children's Fund (NECF) (2004a) *Collaborating for the Social Inclusion of Children and Young People: Emerging Lessons from the First Round of Case Studies*, Research Report No. 596, London, DfES.

National Evaluation of the Children's Fund (NECF) (2004b) *Children, Young People, Parents and Carers' Participation in Children's Fund Case Study Partnerships*, Research Report No. 602, London, DfES.

National Evaluation of the Children's Fund (NECF) (2006) *Preventative Services for Black and Minority Ethnic Children*, Research Report No. 778, London, DfES.

National Evaluation of Sure Start (NESS) (2004) *Towards Understanding Sure Start Local Programmes: Summary of Findings from the National Evaluation*, Nottingham, DfES.

National Evaluation of Sure Start (NESS) (2007) *National Evaluation Report: Understanding Variations in Effectiveness Amongst Sure Start Local Programmes*, Nottingham, DfES.

Parton, N. (2006) *Safeguarding Childhood: Early Intervention and Surveillance in a Late Modern Society*, Basingstoke, Palgrave Macmillan.

Payne, L. (2004) 'Information sharing and assessment (ISA): can data management reduce risk?', *Children & Society*, vol. 18, no. 5, pp. 383–386.

Percy-Smith, J. (2006) 'What works in strategic partnerships for children: a research review', *Children & Society*, vol. 20, no. 4, pp. 313–323.

Rowe, A. (2005) 'The impact of Sure Start on health visiting' in Weinberger, J., Pickstone, C. and Hannon, P. (eds) *Learning from Sure Start: Working with Young Children and Their Families*, Maidenhead, Open University Press, pp. 102–114.

Scottish Executive (2003) *Insight 7: Key Findings from the National Evaluation of the New Community Schools Pilot Programme in Scotland*, available online at <http://www.scotland.gov.uk/Publications/2003/08/17925/24651>, accessed 19 September 2007.

Sloper, P., Greco, V., Beecham, J. and Webb, R. (2006) 'Key worker services for disabled children: what characteristics of services lead to better outcomes for children and families?', *Child: Care, Health and Development*, vol. 32, no. 2, pp. 147–157.

Stone, B. (1998) *Child Neglect: Practitioners' Perspectives*, NSPCC, available online at <http://www.nspcc.org.uk/Inform/publications/Downloads/childneglectpractitionersperspectives_wdf48097.pdf>, accessed 19 September 2007.

Sure Start (2000) *Our Principles*, publicity booklet produced by the DfEE on behalf of the government.

Sure Start (2002) *PSA Targets 2003–06*, available online at <http://www.surestart.gov.uk/improvingquality/targets/psatargets200306>, accessed 3 January 2008.

Townsley, R., Abbott, D. and Watson, D. (2004) *Making a Difference?*, Bristol, The Policy Press.

Tunstill, J., Allnock, D., Akhurst, S. and Garbers, C. (2005) 'Sure Start local programmes: implications of case study data from the National Evaluation of Sure Start, *Children & Society*, vol. 19, no. 2, pp. 158–171.

Wadsworth, N. (2005) 'Richard Thomas – Information Commissioner', interview in *childRIGHT*, no. 214 (March), pp. 6–8.

Weinberger, J., Pickstone, C. and Hannon, P. (eds) (2005) *Learning from Sure Start: Working with Young Children and Their Families*, Maidenhead, Open University Press.

Wigfall, V. and Moss, P. (2001) *More Than the Sum of its Parts? A Study of a Multi-agency Child Care Network*, York, National Children's Bureau/Joseph Rowntree Foundation.

Wilkin, A., Kinder, K., White, R., Atkinson, M. and Doherty, P. (2003) *Towards the Development of Extended Schools*, London, DfES.

# Chapter 6

## Learning together

Andy Rixon

## Introduction

Improving the level of skills and qualifications across the workforce has been a central part of the drive to change and modernise children's services. There has been much activity in revising the required knowledge and skills for specific roles as well as defining areas that are essential to be shared by all practitioners. As the composition of the workforce changes and new practice roles emerge, so key knowledge bases are woven together in new ways. The emphasis on learning, not just for a particular role but as a continuous, 'lifelong' activity, has probably never been stronger.

Previous chapters have examined the increasingly integrated ways in which practitioners are expected to work, and many of the potentially problematic elements – agency structures, practitioner identities, power and hierarchy, divergent knowledge bases, cultures and values. The arena of learning holds the potential for at least some of these issues to be addressed. Opportunities for practitioners to come together, share their knowledge, and gain insight into the world of other practitioners can contribute to overcoming barriers and blocks. This sharing can also give rise to new understandings, solutions and ways of working – learning how to work together.

As we will discuss, this learning does not necessarily have to take place in formal teaching or training situations but can also happen in the workplace both formally and informally. Practitioners should also recognise other sources of knowledge including that which children, parents and carers have and can contribute. It is these sources of knowledge, theories of learning, and experiences of practitioners that this chapter intends to explore.

## Core questions

- What models are available to analyse the ways practitioners can learn, particularly across agency and professional boundaries?

- What role can children and families play in enhancing the learning of practitioners?

- What can the theory of 'communities of practice' and other theories of social learning contribute to our understanding of how professionals learn?

- What is the role of reflection in learning?

# 1 Learning

Any separation between what constitutes formal learning and that which occurs in more informal or social ways, is ultimately artificial. Different elements have been separated out in this chapter for the sake of simplifying analysis and evaluation, but in the end practitioners have to bring them back together again to apply within their work. The experience of most practitioners will be of learning new things in the workplace from trial and error and interactions with children, their families, and other colleagues. This learning is likely to build on some initial qualifying course and be supplemented by subsequent opportunities to undertake courses or attend training days. Practitioners have to blend together what they learn from 'theory' and 'practice' in the workplace and perhaps different forms of knowledge, what Eraut (1994) has described as 'codified' knowledge (for example, theory derived from textbooks) and 'personal' knowledge (for example, what is learning from the workplace and what they themselves bring to practice). It has been increasingly argued in training and qualifying training across most groups of practitioners that reflective practice is a key mechanism through which practitioners can synthesise these different elements of their learning: the opportunity to stand back and review critically how their learning has been applied *to* practice and what in turn they have learnt *from* practice. There are different variations and degrees of complexity on this basic principle, and after exploring different elements of learning we will return to reflection in the final section.

With the growing expectations of 'continual professional development', these 'subsequent opportunities' may be both required and substantial. Many practitioners – for example, nurses, midwives, social workers – have to demonstrate that they are keeping themselves up to date with new developments in their field. This is an issue for all staff but has particular resonance with the discussion in earlier chapters on the meaning of being a professional in an era when professional status is under attack. The pace of change ensures that initial training that was received five or more years ago can no longer be seen as current. If the status of professionals in the eyes of the public is maintained by expert knowledge, then they also need to constantly renew these claims for expertise by the acquisition of new knowledge (Frost, 2001).

This section examines some examples of more formal approaches to learning. Although the importance of more informal learning is recognised, it is also important to stress the value of formal qualifications, and not just in terms of knowledge and skills. Research by Davies and Bynner (1999) found that the certification of learning had an important impact on individuals, increasing their sense of achievement and their belief that it improved the quality of their work. It also has an important role to play in

Recognising the value of
formal learning

providing career opportunities and providing further opportunities for
learning even if career pathways are less than clear in the constantly
changing structure of the children's workforce.

Much of the move to modernise local government and the health services
can be viewed in the wider context of an emphasis on the increasing
importance of knowledge in a global society.

> To continue to compete, we must equip ourselves to cope with the
> enormous economic and social change we face, to make sense of the
> rapid transformation of the world, and to encourage imagination and
> innovation. We will succeed by transforming inventions into new
> wealth, just as we did a hundred years ago. But unlike then, *everyone*
> must have the opportunity to innovate and to gain reward – not just
> in research laboratories, but on the production line, in design
> studios, in retail outlets, and in providing services.
>
> (*The Learning Age: A Renaissance for a New Britain*, DfEE, 1998, webpage)

'Continuous improvement', discussed in Chapter 1, is therefore seen to be
underpinned by the continued integration of new knowledge. Jarvis (2007)
argues that while lifelong learning and the learning society are important for
a wide range of reasons such as 'citizenship', 'social inclusion' and
'personal fulfilment', the needs of advanced capitalism are actually the
driving force behind their development (Jarvis, 2007, p. 195).

The chapter does not set out to tackle the complex issue of the nature of
knowledge, although the importance of this debate is highlighted at various
points. Similarly, while 'training' and 'education' are often seen as very
different forms of learning, here it is argued that training does not
necessarily equate to the acquisition of 'technical' knowledge but can equip
practitioners with the skills of critical thinking and reflection, just as
'education' does not need to be abstract theory unrelated to practice.

Thinking point 6.1    Thinking back to when you last attended a work-related course, can you identify some examples of things you learnt that were useful when back in work? What were they – a new way of doing things, a piece of research, a new contact? How do you think you learnt them – through a talk/lecture, a group discussion, chatting in the coffee break, or perhaps just thinking about it later?

## 1.1 Training together to safeguard children

In the search for successful interagency working, the importance of practitioners training together is one of the most frequently cited key contributory factors. Staff with a mixture of disciplinary backgrounds within evolving settings such as children's centres reinforce the view that joint training is invaluable (McInnes, 2007). However, just as the view that working together is inevitably the solution to a range of social issues, so the reality of learning together needs to be explored in more detail.

One particularly high profile area of interagency working has been that required for protecting or safeguarding children. The success, or otherwise, of these working relationships has always been a subject of close scrutiny when there have been instances of children being seriously harmed. Over many years nearly all inquiries and reviews of serious cases have recommended to some degree the need for improvement in communication or working practices between the range of agencies involved, citing interagency training as one key way of achieving them.

> Joint training will assist in the development of nationally recognised procedures and enhance the relationship between the agencies when they require to work together.
>
> (Clyde, 1992, p. 337)

> Almost all of the professional witnesses identified child protection training as a major requirement before services could be improved. Many expressed the view that it will have to be mandatory at all levels.
>
> (*Report of the Caleb Ness Inquiry*, O'Brien, 2003, p. 8)

These conclusions were reflected in policy terms by interagency training becoming a cornerstone of government guidance for improving 'Working Together' between practitioners in the area of child protection (HM Government, 2006; Scottish Executive, 2002; Welsh Assembly Government, 2004).

> Training delivered on an inter-agency basis is a highly effective way of promoting a common and shared understanding of the

respective roles and responsibilities of different professionals, and contributes to effective working relationships.

(HM Government, 2006, p. 91)

More specifically such training is claimed to promote 'improved communication', 'sound decision-making' and 'more effective and integrated services'; in addition, it will enable 'an ability to work in multi-agency groups or teams' (HM Government, 2006, pp. 91–92).

Following the Laming Report (Laming, 2003) on the circumstances leading to the death of Victoria Climbié, the nature of education and training for interagency work was again the subject of investigation. An audit of existing training in England was undertaken by Salford University; it noted the lack of, and recommended the establishment of, a set of common standards for health staff, police, teachers and social workers:

a It is clear from our review that no agency or practitioner group, in their vocational or ongoing training, uses specific standards for inter-agency training.

b Where standards exist, there are very few that refer specifically to inter-agency work issues in relation to safeguarding children.

c Standards are not held in common between occupational/ professional groups.

d Some standards for inter-agency training are embedded and implicit in some existing training.

(Salford Centre for Social Work Research (SCSWR), 2004, p. 7)

The problems with having a children's workforce inadequately trained in protecting children has a long history. A major government research programme in the mid-1990s (Birchall and Hallett, 1995) into the working of the child protection 'system' included a review of practitioners' experiences of this type of training. One striking finding was just how many workers had not had any child protection training at all even within their own agencies 'despite the apparently endless round of training events and professional conferences' (Birchall and Hallett, 1995). While 90 per cent of social workers and health visitors had received training, many other groups such as teachers and junior doctors had received very little: the figure was only 20 per cent for GPs. Of other 'relevant' staff, 40 per cent had received no training at all. These figures were even lower for training that involved a range of agencies even though the importance of training with other agencies had been constantly stressed. A key conclusion here related to the sense of responsibility that agencies and individuals took in relation to training. 'It seems that different professions invest interdisciplinary training on this topic with varying degrees of priority' (Birchall and Hallett, 1995, p. 8).

Actual responses to the value of training in Birchall and Hallett's research were generally favourable, practitioners from all settings describing a range of gains. The most frequently cited value was that of 'understanding diverse roles and skills', suggesting that one of the basic aims of bringing different professionals together, to help them see beyond their own work 'silos', can be achieved through this type of training. However, the second most common value was 'personal contacts', which might tend to reinforce the view that one of the keys to interagency and interprofessional working is the ability to form and sustain working relationships. The success of local working arrangements may depend ultimately on interpersonal skill as much as interprofessional understanding. The more informal gains of these training events, such as the development of personal contacts, should not be underestimated. As we will discuss later, these can provide a valuable contribution to groups of workers developing shared aims and continuing to develop their knowledge once they have returned to their day-to-day practice.

The most significant element of training that could succeed in improving practice is a matter of debate. The communication issues highlighted in Chapter 3 and the need for practitioners to focus on communication skills could be addressed:

> interagency communication would improve if *all* professionals concerned acquired a 'communication mindset' as part of their core skills. It is, admittedly, a well-rehearsed recommendation that training is the key to such improvements: but it is true.
>
> (Reder and Duncan, 2003, p. 96)

Reder and Duncan (2003) argue that this emphasis should be in pre- and post-qualifying training as well as being addressed in an interprofessional learning environment.

Most interagency training is designed to enable practitioners from different agencies and disciplines to work more closely together. However, as discussed in Chapter 1, there was also an interesting emphasis in the Laming (2003) inquiry on the role of training in enabling practitioners to challenge each other's views, such as in this recommendation to the police:

> Training for child protection officers must equip them with the confidence to question the views of professionals in other agencies, including doctors, no matter how eminent those professionals appear to be.
>
> (Laming, 2003, p. 321)

Interagency training, then, is an opportunity not just to help to develop a common knowledge base but also to consider, question and address other important dimensions to interagency working – such as power and hierarchy.

The variation in training between professionals identified by Birchall and Hallett (1995) seems not to have improved significantly in subsequent years (SCSWR, 2004). A Department of Health report on learning from serious case reviews noted the need for better training for 'professionals perceived as difficult to reach' (DH, 2002, p. 61). Of course, one element of the apparent reluctance of different staff groups to undertake courses relating to child protection relates to whether they see this as a core part of their role. Re-emphasising that safeguarding children is everyone's responsibility sits alongside other changes such as early identification and prevention, where all practitioners have been expected to become more involved in work with families and the wider community.

Interagency training repeatedly stresses the value of helping different practitioners to develop a shared understanding of practice and procedure in child protection work. The Laming Report suggested that increased commonality was the answer proposing the possibility of a 'common language', common assessment, common referral forms, and 'common elements' in training (Laming, 2003, p. 352). This trend is reflected elsewhere in the development of common qualification frameworks across practice groups.

Training across agencies was also recognised as a key element in the introduction of a framework for assessing children in need and their families in England (DH et al., 2000). Two of the fundamental principles of this framework were that assessments should be 'inter-agency' and 'ecological' in their approach (DH et al., 2000, p. 10). This acknowledged different specialisms and knowledge bases but provided a theoretical framework for bringing them together. While this provided an important step forward in having a common framework for practitioners, follow-up evaluation suggested that the inability of agencies to sustain training meant that its potential impact was not fully realised (Cleaver et al., 2004), raising questions for the implementation of any other common frameworks as they are introduced.

## 1.2  What works?

Thinking point 6.2    To what extent is practice in children's services informed by research?

Another fundamental principle of this framework for assessing children in need and their families (DH et al., 2000) was that assessment should be 'grounded in evidence'. Its introduction was supported by training materials and underpinning research and theory (Horwath, 2001). This touches on the question of what exactly it is that those working with children should be learning and on the contested nature of evidence and of knowledge itself. Macdonald (2001), while recognising the importance of the law, policy, values and 'practice wisdom' in shaping what it is that practitioners do, asserts that they also have 'an ethical responsibility', when making decisions to intervene in the lives of children, to also be informed by the best available research evidence; research which itself should be conducted to explicit standards.

> Evidence-based practice indicates an approach to decision-making which is transparent, accountable, and based on a careful consideration of the most compelling evidence we have about the effects of particular interventions on the welfare of individuals, groups and communities.
>
> (Macdonald, 2001, p. xviii)

Consequently, training for practitioners related to, for example, safeguarding children should make them aware of not just their responsibilities and procedures, but also what works in relation to contributing to a protective environment for children and when assessing and intervening in the lives of families. Macdonald reviews what we know of the consequences of child abuse and which interventions are most successful both at the level of broader primary prevention as well as secondary and tertiary work (Macdonald, 2001). Central to this 'knowing' is applying a rigorous approach to research evidence – systematically reviewing it, making explicit the methodology used, and placing more weight on the outcomes of those with experimental designs using, for example, control groups. This in turn focuses attention on the need for practitioners to be able to interpret and evaluate research and use it to inform their practice.

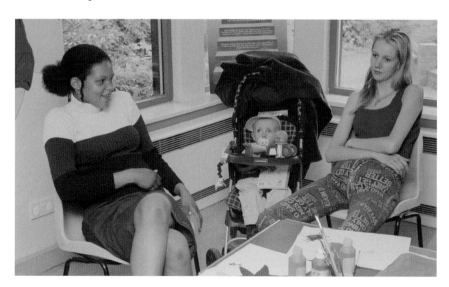

Is good practice with families shaped by knowledge of 'what works'?

The importance of utilising strategies that are shown to be successful has become a major strand in government thinking as confidence has grown in identifying risk factors in families and communities which can be linked to later problems (France and Utting, 2005). This has underpinned the agenda of early intervention, as discussed in Chapter 3, and helped shape the nature of outcome targets that children's services are set to achieve.

Already well-established in the education and professional development of health practitioners, there has been an attempt to establish evidence-based practice more firmly within social care, for example with the development of the Social Care Institute for Excellence (SCIE). The audit of child protection by the Scottish Executive was typical in its emphasis on wanting to identify 'links between research and knowledge and staff education and training and how this can be consolidated' (Scottish Executive, 2002, p. 14). There is little clear evidence of how much research is used overall by practitioners, especially those without professional qualifications (SCIE, 2004). One questionnaire survey of 1226 social care professionals (Sheldon and Chilvers, 2000) revealed the use of research evidence to be very limited. Fifty-seven per cent had never read any evaluative research (or were not sure), and twenty per cent had not read anything related to work in the last six months. Various strategies have been employed by social care organisations to address this, for example investment in resources like Research in Practice (see Practice box 6.1). Certainly there is a debate as to the extent that agencies need to facilitate access to research and the responsibility of practitioners to become 'research minded'.

## Practice box 6.1

### Research in Practice (RiP)

Research in Practice, whose focus is on children and families, has grown as a developmental network that works closely with a small number of agencies, experimenting and evaluating with them a range of approaches to integrating research and practice. It is based on a partnership of agencies, for which RiP staff view themselves as a resource rather than as the organisation itself. RiP aims to build the capacity of service organisations to develop a research and evaluative culture. The focus is on local adaptation of research, and RiP supports a range of development groups working towards strategic and practice advancements. RiP's work is more concerned with changing culture than structure, supporting organisations to become open to new thinking and able to promote and respond positively to change.

(SCIE, 2004, p. 24)

The increasing focus on evidence-based practice is not without its critics. It has been seen as overemphasising positivistic approaches above other sorts of knowledge and as minimising the complexity of engagements with families. The rise of evidence-based practice has also been linked to our increasing preoccupation with risk (Trinder, 2000) and the search for 'a level of certainty in highly uncertain times' (Turney, 2007, p. 58). However, it is clearly an important element in the debate about the nature of education, knowledge and, given the interdisciplinary nature of our discussion here, what it is that we should be 'learning together'.

## 1.3 Structured learning in the workplace

Learning within the workplace can be a complex process with a variety of different elements, some of which will be explored in more detail later. It is worth noting, however, that formal, more structured mechanisms can provide a valuable starting point for promoting continued sharing of knowledge and enhancing interprofessional understanding.

Thinking point 6.3   What strategies could teams in the same workplace use to encourage learning from each other?

Anning et al. (2006), in their research with a number of integrated teams, found that a range of mechanisms for learning and exchange of knowledge, often based around the team meeting structure, were being employed. This could involve using team meetings as points for discussion of particular cases or inviting experts to give presentations to the team. Learning also emerged from undertaking joint activities:

> 'If you do it together, you get it together. And so actually going on home visits and doing things in people's front rooms with colleagues is what really binds the system. Because you're actually trusting each other and you're seeing each other doing it.'
>
> (Psychologist quoted in Anning et al., 2006, p. 81)

In some teams these mechanisms were well developed. A child development team had used video to enable reflective discussions about specific sessions that had been undertaken with a family – professional exposure requiring a high degree of trust, and, as practitioners reported, humour. (The importance of being able to build in structured opportunities for reflection is discussed further below.) Similarly, a consultant observing a physiotherapist and occupational therapist working with a child provided a shared picture of the treatment required. Another example was the use of the key worker role to pull together information on and advocate for a particular child or client group – acting as a particular source of knowledge for the team (Anning et al., 2006).

However, the research also noted that while these positive strategies for sharing knowledge were valued by the teams, part-time members, who were not always able to attend team meetings, were inevitably not benefiting from the learning to the same extent. This was important in terms of some practitioners potentially feeling excluded from the shared understandings emerging in the team.

Team meetings can play an important role in developing learning

One conclusion that Anning et al. (2006) draw from their research is the potential value of structured discussions within teams that reflect on the very nature of the team itself and directly confront some of the well-known issues and barriers to integrated working. They propose a series of checklists that practitioners complete individually and which are then used as the basis of team discussion. These checklists range across structural, ideological and procedural, and interprofessional issues – see one example in Practice box 6.2.

Although co-location has been identified as a potentially important contribution to interagency working, it is likely that even some highly integrated teams will be dispersed geographically. While not replacing the value of face-to-face meetings, other communication technologies – conferencing, email discussion mechanisms, websites – may play a key role in supporting teams in a virtual environment and supplement more traditional ways of structuring learning.

**Practice box 6.2**

**Multi-Agency team checklist**

| Domain 2: Ideological – sharing and redistributing knowledge/ skills/beliefs | Strongly disagree/ never | Disagree/ sometimes | Agree/ often | Strongly agree/ always |
|---|---|---|---|---|
| Different theoretical models are respected within the team | | | | |
| Different professional groups are accorded equal respect within the team | | | | |
| Supervision of work is attuned to the needs of the individuals within the team and their various professional backgrounds | | | | |
| The team encourages members to share skills and ideas with each other | | | | |
| The team has an awareness of the potential impact of multi-agency working on both professional identity and service users | | | | |

(Anning et al., 2006, p. 131)

## 1.4 Interprofessional education

Practitioners, perhaps particularly those with established 'professional' training, tend to be socialised into a particular worldview with an established frame of reference. A key task, and a key difficulty, for interagency training is to try to enable practitioners to question these perspectives, consider the way that knowledge is socially constructed, and understand the worldviews of others. Interprofessional Education (IPE) – bringing students from different disciplines together during their qualifying training – would seem therefore to provide the ideal opportunity to establish this way of thinking at the outset of practitioners' careers. Clark (2006) suggests that students must be empowered to ask 'who am I ... and what do I know?', 'who are the others ... and what do they know?' and finally 'who are we collectively ... and what do we know?' (Clark, 2006, p. 585).

Many professional courses now include at least some element of interprofessional learning yet while interprofessional education is frequently cited as a vital feature of the future success of working together, there has been a lack of any conclusive research evidence of its effectiveness (Zwarenstein et al., 2001). Clark (2006) similarly argues that its success is anecdotal and remains poorly theorised and poorly evaluated. He proposes several models or theoretical approaches to learning that could enable a more critical discussion of IPE. While some of these models overlap, each emphasises the importance of a different aspect of learning that will help inform some of the discussion later in the chapter.

Practitioners as students learn with, from and about each other

### Cooperative, collaborative and social learning

IPE's essence is the knowledge students learn 'with, from, and about' each other in interdependent work groups. Indeed, observers have noted that the skills needed to function in interprofessional teams are most often those that are gained by using problem- or case-based educational methods.

(Clark, 2006, p. 579)

Through these methods (rather than the more individualised approaches common in education) students learn about each other and also teamwork skills such as 'leadership, communication, and conflict management that are critical for collaborative practice' (Clark, 2006, p. 580).

For students this also partly follows the real world models of informal knowledge acquisition. The idea of how this social learning occurs in 'communities of practice' will be explored later in the chapter.

## Experiential learning

Experiential learning is closely related to the idea of social learning in that it too emphasises the importance of collaborative learning. Learning together should be in a real environment or on realistic case studies. The emphasis here is that the learning is *the process* rather than the outcomes, and students need to be enabled to reflect on the process of this learning to integrate their learning into new situations.

## Cognitive and normative maps

Understanding where other professionals are coming from is an important element of any interagency education. IPE provides the opportunity to explore this in a more fundamental way. The emphasis in this approach is to examine the roots of the core knowledge and values of professional groups. Clark (2006) draws on the idea that these core features can be characterised as 'maps', thus a 'cognitive' map:

> represents the entire paradigmatic and conceptual apparatus used by a profession and includes its basic concepts, modes of inquiry, problem definitions, observational categories, representational techniques, standards of proof, types of explanation, and general ideas of what represents a discipline.
>
> (Clark, 2006, p. 582)

A 'normative' map charts the areas of values, beliefs, moral reasoning and ethics. Enabling students to understand the cognitive and normative maps of other professions is essential because 'they may *look* at the same thing but not *see* the same thing' (Clark, 2006, p. 582). In day-to-day practice, practitioners need to be able to reach a common understanding of the problems and issues they are confronted with before being able to move on to finding effective solutions. The previous chapter noted how some integrated teams were able to work collaboratively once a shared theoretical perspective had emerged.

Ultimately, the process can also advance interprofessional knowledge and practice by enabling professionals to 'borrow' the 'tools' of another discipline once they have gained an understanding of them (Lattuca, 2002).

Thinking point 6.4    Can you think of an experience when you and a colleague from your own or another group of practitioners were looking at the same thing but clearly not seeing the same thing?

## Cognitive and ethical development

This perspective suggests that understanding the developmental process that students go through during education can give IPE insights into how transformations can occur in their thinking about other professionals and knowledge bases. The theory argues that students move from a belief that knowledge is an accumulation of facts, to accepting that ambiguities exist, to 'relativism' – accepting that knowledge is constructed. Only at this stage can students make informed choices about which knowledge and values they will commit to in relation to other professional knowledge and value bases.

One implication of structuring learning based on this theory is the recognition of the time required for students to go through these stages. Clark stresses that the social and experiential approaches need to take this into consideration to be effective.

## Reflective practice

As noted above, effective experiential learning relies on students being able to 'reflect' on the process of their learning. Schön (1987), a key figure in the development of reflective theory, argues that reflection is a mechanism for enabling practitioners to integrate both the knowledge and values bases of their practice. A reflective practitioner is also able to manage the uncertainties beyond the technical knowledge of the profession. Reflection is discussed in more detail in a later section and in the next chapter.

Many of the same issues relate equally to post-qualifying education and training. The example of training in relation to safeguarding illustrated both the strengths and limitations of bringing professionals together, and even more highly structured qualifying courses cannot guarantee that merely by bringing people together they will understand each other's worldviews. The methods and models employed need careful consideration.

## Key points

1   Interagency training has been a long-standing strategy in protecting and safeguarding children to enhance closer working together, yet the prioritisation of this training has remained variable between agencies and practitioners.

2   Evidence-based practice provides an important benchmark for the content of learning, one increasingly stressed in policy and practice.

3   A range of formal learning mechanisms can also be used in the workplace although they overlap with more informal learning; making clear distinctions between them can be artificial.

4   There is limited evidence of the effectiveness of interagency training and education, but there are many theoretical approaches that might help its development.

# 2  Learning together with children and families

In her work on participation, Braye (2000) has categorised a whole range of areas where 'service users', including children and families, can participate:

- participation in his/her own use of a service
- participation in strategic planning for service provision and development
- participation through the development of user-led services
- participation in research into social care provision
- participation in the education and training of staff
- participation in the community as citizens rather than service users.

(Braye, 2000, cited in Taylor, 2004, p. 78)

Just as children and their families have a contribution to make to shape the services they receive through the various forms of partnership discussed in previous chapters, so they can contribute to the development of practice and practitioners. This can happen at many levels through evaluation, feedback, consultation and research, as well as direct involvement in training. Practitioners and the organisations they work for need to recognise that children and their families have specific knowledge that cannot be 'learnt' from anywhere else:

> Children are party to the subculture of childhood which gives them a unique 'insider' perspective that is critical to our understanding of children's worlds.
>
> (Kellett, 2005, p. 4)

This in turn raises further questions about knowledge and knowing – recognising that versions of knowledge are not value free, and questioning the difference between 'lay' and 'expert' knowledge (Brechin and Siddell, 2000). Frost (2001, p. 14) argues that lifelong learning can be seen as a way of 'deconstructing the professional elitist model of training by having direct input into that training from lay people'.

Taylor (2004) suggests that despite an increasing acceptance that service users are part of the network of relations within which practitioners operate, there is little research focusing on their involvement or the impact of it on practitioners, practice or themselves. While arguing for the importance of the involvement of children and families in practitioner learning, Taylor questions whether in expecting the greater involvement of service users the issues of power, trust and communication have been sufficiently addressed.

Only through participatory ways of working and being open to learning can this knowledge be accessed. It is likely that strategies for empowerment will need to be integral to our expectations of family involvement.

Thinking point 6.5  How are children and families involved in the learning of practitioners? In what other ways might they be involved?

Some qualifying training courses now require the involvement of service users in course development. The Scottish Institute for Excellence in Social Work Education (SiSWE) developed good practice guidelines to promote the involvement of service users and carers in the education of social work students (SiSWE, 2005). This recognises the need for involvement to be properly enabled and that for it to be more than tokenistic will require addressing existing structures:

> Building new systems and structures *and* changing systems and structures within universities is needed to empower and enable service users and carers to participate in a meaningful way.
>
> (SiSWE, 2005, p. 4)

It also highlights the range of areas of learning that service users can contribute to: case studies, curriculum design, large and small group teaching, role play, and evaluation. Many universities were also developing ways in which service users could contribute directly to the assessment of students' practice (see Practice box 6.3) and indeed the initial selection of students.

## Practice box 6.3

'Service User Conversations', a method used at the University of Plymouth to assess readiness to practice, provides feedback on communication skills, links between theory and practice, writing reports, exploration of assumptions and values, time management, self assessment skills. The process includes a conversation with a service user or carer, followed by the student's self-assessment and the service user's or carer's feedback. A report of the conversation is written by the student and verified by the service user or carer.

(SiSWE, 2005, p. 6)

Cooper and Spencer-Dawe (2006) looked at user involvement in interprofessional education with students from a range of settings (drawn from medical students, nurses, social workers, occupational therapists and physiotherapists). Their study concluded that involvement of service users particularly enabled a bridging of the theory/practice 'gap' and reinforced for students the principles of 'service user-centred' care. They argue that 'when learning addresses complex issues, such as interprofessional team working, it has to be amenable to new and creative ways of teaching' (Cooper and Spencer-Dawe, 2006, p. 616). At the same time service users also felt they had made a contribution to breaking down barriers not only between service users and professionals but also between the different professional groups.

### 'Total Respect'

In 1999 the Department of Health (England) commissioned a training course to promote the participation of children looked after by the local authority (Children's Rights Officers and Advocates (CROA), 2000). This recognised, from the research and conclusions of inquiry reports, that the voices of Looked After children and young people had long been insufficiently heard (Utting, 1991; Waterhouse, 2000). The aim of the training was to focus on:

- children and young people's participation in individual care planning
- making sure children and young people are taken seriously when they make complaints or allegations of abuse or poor practice
- children and young people's participation in local authority policy and service development.

(CROA, 2000, p. 2)

Children and young people evaluating a conference activity with practitioners (Swindon Children's Fund)

A training pack was produced after extensive consultation with Looked After children and young people to ensure that the material reflected their priorities. The training itself was designed to be delivered to practitioners with the children and young people's direct involvement, as reflected in the work within one local authority which has continued to develop the training:

> 'The training has brought together young people and staff in workshops over 2 days. The emphasis is on listening and understanding each other and practical exercises in body language, listening skills and jargon busting proved a real winner. During training, young people suggested ways care reviews could be less boring, meetings less intimidating and social workers more approachable.'

(Children's Participation Officer quoted in Funkee Munkee, 2007, webpage)

Emphasising these messages from children and young people about how they feel about their reviews – crucial meetings for agreeing their future care – can provide valuable learning for all practitioners who are involved in these meetings (see Practice box 6.4). The training also promoted the sharing of good practice from other agencies or local authorities who had developed information packs, or systems of advocacy or other mechanisms for enabling the participation of children of all ages and abilities.

---

**Practice box 6.4**

Spotlight on reviews

Many children and young people find review meetings difficult because:

- They feel uncomfortable when there is conflict between adults
- There are too many people at the meeting who know all about them but they know nothing about the adults
- They do not feel able to say what they want in front of carers or parents
- They do not want a particular adult to attend or to have access to minutes (such as a parent or teacher)
- They prefer a neutral venue
- Adults in the meeting often focus on their 'difficult behaviour', and forget to celebrate their achievements.

(CROA, 2000, p. 43)

> '[Review meetings are] boring and they can be embarrassing.
> Jargon – don't understand half of it.'
>
> (Young person quoted in CROA, 2000, p. 42)

As well as adding to the value of the training that staff receive, such initiatives can enhance the skills and self-esteem of those involved:

> The young people are now becoming trainers and will be passing on the skills they've learned to other adults and young people. So the programme is set to grow and grow.
>
> (Children's Participation Officer quoted in Funkee Munkee, 2007, webpage)

This view was also voiced by the young people themselves, some of whom reported that they had 'Gained confidence in communicating' and 'Enjoyed busting social work jargon' (Funkee Munkee, 2007):

> 'When I went on total respect, it really influenced me to join the team and to work with young people, even though I am a young person myself, I would still like to work with others and to get involved.'
>
> (Young person quoted in RAW, 2007, p. 1)

The Total Respect training was also an opportunity for practitioners to learn about additional issues for children who are Black and from minority ethnic groups, such as the limited investigation of racial abuse, dealing with cultural needs and lack of placement choice (CROA, 2000).

## Children's contribution to learning

It has been increasingly recognised that children are social actors in their own right and can make a contribution to the shape of services that they receive and the environments in which they live (James and Prout, 1997). Government policy acknowledges the importance of children's views, and most new policy and practice initiatives require elements of consultation or the participation of children and young people. This principle extends to the learning that practitioners can derive from listening to children's views more broadly, as was emphasised by the Children's Rights Director for England:

> Like many who regularly consult children and young people, we find that their views are always serious, concise, thoughtful and highly relevant – and cut through the pre-existing agendas and diplomatic avoidances that beset many consultations with 'professional' adults. We find that even very young children are more than able to analyse and give clear views on many issues within their experience.
>
> (Morgan, 2005, pp. 181–182)

Enabling children to participate: voting at a school council

The potential mechanisms for learning can be diverse. There are direct contributions to training as in the case of the 'Total Respect' initiative, but more likely the voices of children will emerge through consultation, research, and other forms of participation.

Kellett (2005) advocates the value of research not just on children but by and with children themselves. Adults can no longer access the perspective of a child without filtering it through the adult perspective they have acquired since their own childhood. Adult researchers still retain the power and the framing of the questions, and so need to work alongside children to enable them to develop their own questions, ways of collecting data and evaluating outcomes.

> Children observe with different eyes, ask different questions – they ask questions that adults do not even think of – have different concerns and have immediate access to peer culture where adults are outsiders. The research agendas children prioritise, the research questions they frame and the way in which they collect data are substantially different from adults and all of this can offer valuable insights and original contributions to knowledge.
>
> (Kellett, 2005, p. 8)

The views of young children have been more difficult to access because of uncertainty about the methods of ascertaining them. However, approaches such as 'Mosaic' have attempted to use mixed methods (for example, observation, children's photographs, map making) to compile an overall children's perspective (Clark and Moss, 2001). This approach has demonstrated how the views of young children can be valuable learning for practitioners. Clark and Statham (2005) discuss how the method can be used both in broader discussions such as redesigning a play space and in individual cases enabling children to contribute to decision making in fostering and adoption situations.

Research techniques have also been developed in work with disabled children. Watson et al. (2007) illustrate how children with complex healthcare needs can contribute their views to inform service developments when methods are adapted (for example, photos, drawing, choosing faces with a range of expressions). Similarly, Rabiee et al. (2005) describe other visual methods developed for work with children who do not communicate through speech. Computer-assisted questionnaires have also been used to facilitate consultation and participation with disabled young people (Davies and Morgan, 2005).

## Key points

1   Children, parents and carers have unique knowledge about their own lives and can make valuable contributions to practitioners' learning.

2   Children, young people and adults can be enabled to make direct contributions to the education and training of students and practitioners in all areas of children's services.

3   Research by and with even very young children can ascertain their views and support practitioners in making decisions with them about their lives, both day-to-day decisions and in more difficult circumstances.

# 3  Learning as social activity

While there is clearly an important role for formal training and formal structures, there is an increasing recognition that 'social' learning also occurs in a more informal and unstructured way. This has been theorised in different ways but perhaps most significantly by Etienne Wenger (Lave and Wenger, 1991; Wenger, 1998) in the concept of 'communities of practice'.

Communities of practice are not just descriptions or models of what happens in the workplace. Wenger stresses that 'communities of practice are everywhere', in social settings – families, churches, online – as well as in offices and institutions; they are an experience common to us all. In the work context a community of practice is not synonymous with a team; a community of practice can be much broader or smaller than the formal parameters of a single team. Similarly, just because a team is created does not mean a community of practice is instantly formed (it could even potentially survive after a team is dissolved); such communities are organic in nature. However, the theory of learning contained within this idea has a potentially valuable application to our discussion and in particular to interagency working and integrated teams. It also provides another perspective on how practitioner identities are shaped through participation in such a community.

A community of practice is defined through three key dimensions which we can think about in relation to both single agency and multi-agency groups and teams in children's services:

- **Mutual engagement** – all of its members are engaged in a specific activity.

- **Joint enterprise** – the collective process of negotiation as people are jointly finding some way of managing the tasks they need to perform. This process also creates a mutual accountability between those involved.

- **A shared repertoire** – this represents a common set of shared resources – for example, routines, tools, concepts – and structures that members of the community have developed over time.

Thinking point 6.6   From Wenger's definition, can you identify a community of practice that you belong to outside of work? What is its 'shared repertoire'?

Wenger argues that there are processes within communities of practice that generate new knowledge through the daily interaction of members of that community. This knowledge is created by two different, but complementary, processes which he describes as *participation* and *reification*.

*Participation* is the 'active involvement in social enterprises' (Wenger, 1998, p. 55). Essentially this involves the daily interactions and shared experiences of members of the community. These individual activities combine to generate new, shared forms of knowledge and practice that are greater than the sum of their parts. This participation shapes practitioners' individual identities, but equally individuals contribute to the identity of the community. This does not mean that it is a process which is necessarily harmonious or free from power dynamics.

*Reification* refers to the process whereby abstract knowledge is made into more solid form in the shape of law, procedures, schemes of work, assessment tools, etc. This includes not just objects; it also includes a wide range of processes – common ways of naming, describing and encoding. In the context of a multi-disciplinary team, effective working will depend to some extent on reification, the creation of new shared procedures and policies.

> However, procedures are simply pieces of paper until they are enacted through practice by the front-line professional staff involved in building the actuality of joined-up working.
>
> (Frost and Lloyd, 2006, p. 12)

Wenger suggests that 'communities of practice can be thought of as shared histories of learning' (Wenger, 1998, p. 86). Learning is not always explicitly identified as such by the practitioners involved as it is not static or discrete but occurs in their very participation in developing practice. A community of practice is a place for the *acquisition* of knowledge,

Informal learning at work

for example from colleagues, but can also become 'a locus for the creation of knowledge' (Wenger, 1998, p. 214).

Research by Anning et al. (2006) within five integrated teams, attempted to specifically explore the applicability of this concept in practice. They assessed that all these teams to varying degrees were operating as communities of practice. The example of integrated teams being able to develop a shared theoretical perspective (Anning et al., 2006) could be seen as part of the process of building such a community. This process is not straightforward, as different practitioners will join a team with different theoretical perspectives, knowledge bases and views on childhood. However, common dominant models and ways of working did emerge which helped draw teams together.

This process is not without its tensions. Frost et al. (2005) explored the position of social workers in a range of multi-agency teams and found examples of conflicts between different theory bases and models of practice (for example between medical and social models of disability). The successful development of a community of practice depends in part on the ability of workers to learn from each other and move on from fixed positions:

> Underlying these variations a common theme is the challenge for professionals in multiprofessional, multi-agency teams to contain and embrace diversity while not sacrificing those beliefs which underpin their commitment. Professionals are challenged to reflect on which beliefs about practice are imbued with core values, and which can be modified through the development of new forms of knowledge within the team, which form the basis of a 'shared repertoire' (Wenger, 1998).
>
> (Frost et al., 2005, p. 191)

So professionals will argue and defend their value bases, but will also review their assumptions in the light of these discussions. The role of learning through working together mirrors a key theme in the previous chapters of practitioners retaining specialist knowledge and core values while accommodating new knowledge and values through the process of working with others. Clark (2006), in his analysis of interprofessional learning, suggests that practitioners can have two communities of practice – the professional one and the interprofessional one; practitioners need to be able to operate in both, acquiring two sets of skills.

As in all communities of practice, in interagency or integrated teams the level of engagement may vary between workers, which can affect the degree to which they are 'signed up' to the shared core values. Minority members, seconded workers, part-time staff, and practitioners who feel that their status is not as high or as valued as others, can all experience a lack of inclusion:

> 'all the core members have a voice and I think we do it together. But some of the people who only come in for two sessions a week may not feel like that because they're much more on the periphery.'

> (Psychologist quoted in Frost et al., 2005, p. 192)

Understanding the roles and valuing the contributions of all members, including those who are peripheral or marginal, is important to maximise the sharing of knowledge.

If communities of practice and the learning within them occur regardless of organisational structures, this raises the question of whether organisations can enable this form of learning. Wenger argues that this is possible if the structures of learning and education are examined in order to facilitate and support communities of practice. Organisations need to be able to strike the balance between being institutional but flexible enough to enable practice development. Policies and procedures are important but should not result in practice 'serving the institutional apparatus, rather than the other way around' (Wenger, 1998, p. 244). Organisations can facilitate communication, encourage learning to be seen as a participative activity and provide support in terms of communal space and finance. This could involve negotiation with communities themselves about how learning can be enhanced. However, beyond this, the role of the agency in developing communities of practice may be limited:

> That is not to say that they do not require energy, commitment, work, or financial wherewithal to pursue their enterprise; nor is it to say that they are best ignored or left to themselves. But it is to say that they are driven by doing and learning rather than by institutional politics.

> (Wenger, 1998, p. 251)

Wenger reinforces the idea that formal and informal training are not mutually exclusive and can overlap, and training can supplement learning in practice. Smith (2003) argues that these ideas have implications for educators as they refocus attention on learning occurring between people, which can be lost in the emphasis on individual accreditation. This in turn can also lead to reflection on the nature of knowledge and practice. Like organisations as a whole, educators need to explore how communities can be engaged with to enable everyone to participate. This model is also potentially transferable to work within children's services, for example, in schools where 'learning activities are planned by children as well as adults, and where parents and teachers not only foster children's learning but also learn from their own involvement with children' (Rogoff et al., 2001, quoted in Smith, 2003).

Can the principles of 'communities of practice' be transferred to schools?

Other theories place more emphasis on the conflictual nature of knowledge creation:

> Wenger argues that communities of practice are not necessarily harmonious and co-operative but essentially his model is about working steadily towards agreement and stability in work-based learning.

(Anning et al., 2006, p. 83)

Activity theory (Engeström, 2001) argues for the need for conflict within teams in order to generate new learning. This theory also takes place within a community, but one 'of multiple points of view, traditions and interests', which are 'a source of trouble and a source of innovation' (Engeström, 2001, p. 136). It proposes that 'contradictions' are the catalyst for change, development and learning beyond that which can be taught. Engeström used the example of a children's hospital to explore how traditional ways of working come under question (experience 'disturbances and contradictions') when confronted by evidence that they do not work that well. In this instance current practice in the hospital showed a lack of coordination and communication between the different care providers in the area, excessive numbers of visits, unclear lines of responsibility, and failure to inform other involved care providers (including the patient's family) of the practitioner's diagnoses, actions and plans. Engeström describes how new innovations resulted from the network of practitioners involved, from a range of professional backgrounds, focusing on these core problems. But innovations emerged only after the collision of new and old ideas (Engeström, 2000). In a stable network, it is suggested that learning is likely to be limited

(National Evaluation of the Children's Fund (NECF), 2004), which may run counter to what many interagency contexts are aiming to achieve. Identifying difficult issues as barriers to interagency working which must always be overcome might be ignoring the creativity of working and learning in unstable environments (Warmington et al., 2004).

This theory has been used in relation to developing children's services. When the Children's Fund was being evaluated, the researchers used activity theory as a way of analysing the working of partnership boards and promoting further learning. For example, in a series of workshops, evidence was presented to the partnership boards of individual local Children's Fund programmes of the differences in understanding between its members that the researchers had observed. Similarly, 'contradictions' were pointed out between what people said they want to develop and how they were going about achieving it:

> An example of difference might be two descriptions of the purpose of participation which reveal different ambitions for the participation of children and families in the programme. A contradiction might be that Board members argue that they are aiming at interagency service provision, but are not using a commissioning process that encourages it. We show the evidence as quotations or video clips at the workshop and so create an opportunity for participants to discuss quite fundamental matters in a safe environment.
>
> Differences and contradictions are not seen as weaknesses, but as points from which individuals and organisations learn and move on.
>
> (NECF, 2004, p. 17)

Ultimately, none of our approaches to understanding these mechanisms are context-free; they too are shaped by the broader social environment and its dominant political and economic ideologies (Jarvis, 2007). No one theory is complete in being able to account for the complexity of informal learning.

## Key points

1   There is a range of theories about knowledge creation, which stress that it occurs in an unstructured way in the workplace as well as in formal settings.

2   The theories of 'communities of practice' and 'activity theory' illustrate in different ways how teams can be challenging but also create new ways of working together. This can be particularly relevant to the development of interagency and increasingly integrated teams.

3   Organisations can recognise the value of communities of practice and, to a certain extent, support their development.

# 4 Reflecting and learning

Reflective practice has emerged as a key approach to learning at the heart of much practitioner training and professional development, with its own substantial and complex literature. The principle has even been adopted by government guidance to all practitioners working with children in that they should '[k]now how to use theory and experience to reflect upon, think about and improve [their] practice' (DfES, 2005, p. 12). Reflective practice stresses that learning can be a perpetual process and that for practitioners in areas such as health, education and social care, knowledge based on 'technical rationality' will take you only so far (Payne, 2002). Practitioners need skills to develop theory and knowledge in new and complex situations. Reflection is also seen as a cornerstone of 'relationship-based' approaches to practice in social work (Ruch, 2005), in the classroom (Pollard, 2002), and in health care (Taylor, 2000) where knowledge of and use of self is emphasised as a vital element.

Reflection is usually portrayed as a cyclical process: current practice experiences can be reviewed – 'reflected' upon – and new ideas and strategies can be formulated and then tested out again in practice (Kolb, 1984; Schön, 1987). From this reflective cycle and its consideration of alternative approaches, new learning will emerge to support the improvement of future practice. Idealistically this has been portrayed as an upward spiral where continual reflection on current practice will consistently enhance professional competence (Pollard, 2002). This circular reflective process can be carried out when looking back on the event (reflection-on-action), but also can occur simultaneously with practice (reflection-in-action) (Schön, 1987). Given that practitioners do not always see theory as related to real-life experience (Eraut, 1994), reflection can also provide the opportunity for them to integrate theory into their practice. The literature is full of circles and spirals illustrating variations on this theme, each model attempting to take account of different dimensions of the complexity of day-to-day practice. That proposed by Kolb (1984) is often seen as a starting point (see figure).

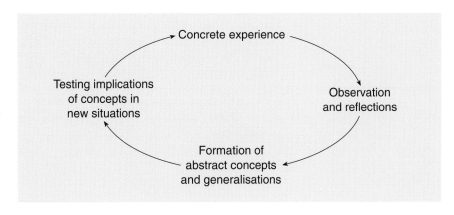

A model of experiential learning (Kolb, 1984, p. 21). 'Learning is the process whereby knowledge is created through the transformation of experience' (Kolb, 1984, p. 38).

Eby (2000) argues that successful reflective practice is much more than being able to reflect back thoughtfully on an incident, but requires the synthesis of the skills of reflection with those of 'self-awareness' and 'critical thinking' (Eby, 2000, p. 52).

Self-awareness requires the recognition that much practice is intuitive. The stress on self-awareness is crucial in encouraging practitioners to understand their own impact on the situation. We all bring our own histories, cultural frames of reference, beliefs, values and experience to any interpersonal interaction. Practitioners need to be 'self-aware' if they are to be able to understand the process and outcomes of their practice.

Concerns that reflection can be a very individualised process – one practitioner reflecting on one interaction – have led to an emphasis on the need for the 'critical' aspect of reflection. Practice continually takes place within a changing social, political and cultural environment, and is affected by a whole range of other issues such as those relating to resources or staffing levels. Critical thinking emphasises the importance of questioning in this broader context in which practice takes place, including power relations between workers and those they are working with. This can be a key part of the process of challenging some of the roots of oppression and issues often taken 'as a given' in practice, establishing reflection as part of an empowering process (Eby, 2000).

Thomas (2004) draws on a model proposed by Taylor (2000) in a health context which brings together some of the strands discussed above. This suggests that there are three elements that reflective practitioners can focus on: technical, practical and 'emancipatory'. These categories reflect a theory developed by Habermas of the different ways in which knowledge is constructed:

● *Technical reflection* – for example, assessing and evaluating particular treatments. This emphasises that evidence-based practice and reflection can be linked.

● *Practical reflection* – which focuses less on the 'external' knowledge and more on the personal encounter within the process of the treatment (internal knowledge, feelings, and intuition, etc.).

● *Emancipatory reflection* – which involves looking at structures and power issues. 'In this type of reflection the learner is encouraged to look at the constraints on their practice and how to challenge them' (Thomas, 2004, p. 106).

This critical reflection overlaps with one other frequently cited concept in this area – that of reflexivity. This too emphasises the need for practitioners to question the basis of their assumptions, the political context in which they work and even the knowledge base they are drawing on:

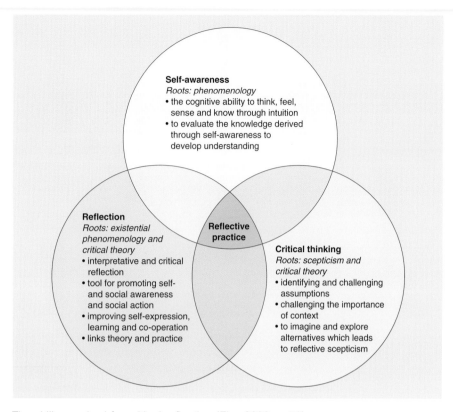

The skills required for critical reflection (Eby, 2000, p. 53)

Epistemology is the theory of knowledge, a branch of philosophy which is concerned with the nature and scope of knowledge (what we know and how we know it).

So reflexivity has an **epistemological** dimension: it involves a process of 'bending back' which allows the practitioner to analyse what they know and how they know it.

(Turney, 2007, p. 82)

One further dimension of reflexivity is the recognition that just as practitioners influence the practice encounter, so in turn they are influenced by it (Eby, 2000).

In order to maximise learning from practice experiences, reflection can be approached in a structured way. To achieve this, Thomas (2004) advocates the use of 'critical incident analyses'. A critical incident is a moment of practice that has important consequences for the practitioner, or those they are working with. Specific questions rather than open-ended discussion can draw out the knowledge, values and issues. It can be done as an individual exercise, but more can be gained by using it within teams or with 'critical friends' (Thomas, 2004).

## Practice box 6.5

Critical incident analysis

Practitioners are encouraged to choose one incident – a family interview, a drop-in session, a review of a Looked After child, a telephone call – then use these structured questions to start a reflective process. The questions could be adapted for use in any practice setting.

- Give a brief outline of the situation, what happened, who was involved, where it took place. Include any relevant issues of oppression or discrimination that you were aware of.
- Describe what you did or said, what action you took, and the responses of others.
- How were you feeling at the time and how do you think others were feeling?
- What were the main challenges for you?
- What went well and what did you do to enable this?
- What underpinning knowledge and theories did you use? What methods of intervention did you use? How were these informed by research and evidence-based practice?
- What values underpinned the work and how did you demonstrate or convey these?
- What value conflicts were you aware of and how did you deal with these?
- What skills did you draw on?
- If you were undertaking a similar piece of work again is there anything you would do differently? If so what? If not, why not?
- What do you think you learnt from the work?
- What have you learnt from reviewing the situation and your practice within it? (This question is posed after the incident has been discussed in small groups.)

(Adapted from Thomas, 2004, p. 107)

It is this team experience that can be useful for promoting reflection across disciplinary boundaries. Through this process, individual practitioners are making explicit the values and knowledge that underpin their practice. Many of the key processes for successful interagency working discussed in these chapters rely on exactly this type of process – understanding each other's cognitive and normative maps as suggested by Clark (2006) above. It is through the ability to reflect that a perspective on 'who am I and what do I know?' and also 'who are the others and what do they know?' can be achieved. The theory suggests that the process also creates new learning from the sharing of practice experience and identifying alternative approaches.

Many practitioners will feel that their practice is at least in part intuitive. Reflective practice can enable the implicit to be more explicit and open to critical questioning; however, some commentators argue that there may be limits to this. In dynamic and complex interactions, practitioners can respond without accessing explicit knowledge and it is possible that the value of intuition merits greater recognition. Atkinson and Claxton (2000) suggest that intuitive skills could also be developed alongside those of analysis and reflection.

## Learning organisations

As Thomas (2004) stresses when advocating critical incident analysis (see above), revisiting the initial incident can be emotionally demanding, and exposing practice in this in a team situation needs to be done in an environment safe enough to explore issues, doubts and problems. Frequently a problem for teams is protecting this time to learn together. While on the one hand all practitioners are encouraged to develop their knowledge and skills and acquire qualifications, on the other they can experience the pressured working environment reducing opportunities for learning. One child and adolescent mental health team described how important this time and space for development was in their successful transition to a well-functioning multi-disciplinary team:

> Despite pressures from increasing demand, clinical work was undertaken jointly in order to learn about each other's skills and abilities and establish best practice with regard to assessment and interventions. ...
>
> Progress was co-ordinated through a schedule of team days, where discussion and team building activities took place. The mixture of personalities, paces and an ability to contain differences of opinion, and even at times to value and celebrate differences, has led to considerable development.
>
> (Wiles, 2005, p. 49)

This question of whether practitioners have time to reflect inevitably relates partly to the organisations in which they work. As well as the onus on individuals to update their knowledge and skills, there has been considerable interest in the idea of the 'learning organisation'. How can organisations promote, enable and sustain such lifelong learning?

Are you aware of any ways in which your organisation (or one you know of) successfully promotes reflection or informal learning?

We have already noted how reflective practice requires time and space in order to be effective. The concept of communities of practice also raises issues for organisations to consider – how can informal learning in the workplace can be encouraged? Similarly, the advancement of research evidence in practice discussed above requires the organisation to find strategies to enable appropriate access to research by practitioners. Other formal mechanisms for learning discussed earlier can also be encouraged by the organisation itself.

Taylor (2004), considering the learning organisation in the increasingly interprofessional environment, argues that rapid change brings into question assumptions about what an organisation is, given the reality of changing structures, management structures and the arrangement of many practitioners in new 'cross-agency' configurations. She suggests that Wenger too assumes a certain degree of stability for the emergence of a community of practice. While organisations clearly have a key role in supporting the learning of practitioners, lack of research knowledge about how this operates makes it difficult to develop any clear model of the learning organisation supporting increasingly integrated working.

## Key points

1   Reflection is widely seen as a key skill in developing and integrating new learning into practice.

2   Critical reflection and reflexivity promote a more serious questioning of the assumptions within work with children and their families, and potentially supports a more empowering form of practice.

3   The success of 'learning together' can be enabled by the way in which organisations support both formal and informal learning.

## Conclusion

Analysing learning, particularly that supporting more integrated working, is multi-faceted with pre- and post-qualifying structures and formal and informal elements. A closer examination of the ways in which practitioners from different disciplines learn together should guard against any assumptions of guaranteed success. However, there is clearly the potential for learning together to support more effective working together and make a significant contribution to better practice and better services for children.

# References

Anning, A., Cottrell, D., Frost, N., Green, J. and Robinson, M., (2006) *Developing Multiprofessional Teamwork for Integrated Children's Services*, Maidenhead, Open University Press.

Atkinson, T. and Claxton, G. (eds) (2000) *The Intuitive Practitioner: On the Value of Not Always Knowing What One is Doing*, Maidenhead, Open University Press.

Birchall, E. and Hallett, C. (1995) *Working Together in Child Protection*, London, HMSO.

Braye, S. (2000) 'Participation and involvement in social care: an overview' in Kemshall, H. and Littlechild, R. (eds) *User Involvement and Participation in Social Care: Research Informing Practice*, London, Jessica Kingsley, pp. 9–28.

Brechin, A. and Siddell, M. (2000) 'Ways of knowing' in Gomm, R. and Davies, C. (eds) *Using Evidence in Health and Social Care*, London, Sage, pp. 3–25.

Children's Rights Officers and Advocates (CROA) (2000) *Total Respect: Ensuring Children's Rights and Participation in Care*, London, CROA and DH.

Clark, P.G. (2006) 'What would a theory of interprofessional education look like? Some suggestions for developing a theoretical framework for teamwork training', *Journal of Interprofessional Care*, vol. 20, no. 6, pp. 577–589.

Clark, A. and Moss, P. (2001) *Listening to Young Children: The Mosaic Approach*, London, National Children's Bureau.

Clark, A. and Statham, J. (2005) 'Listening to young children: experts in their own lives', *Adoption & Fostering*, vol. 29, no. 1, pp. 45–56.

Cleaver, H., Walker, S. and Meadows, P. (2004) *Assessing Children's Needs and Circumstances: The Impact of the Assessment Framework*, London, Jessica Kingsley.

Clyde, J.J. (1992) *Report of the Inquiry into the Removal of Children from Orkney in February 1991*, Edinburgh, HMSO.

Cooper, H. and Spencer-Dawe, E. (2006) 'Involving service users in interprofessional education narrowing the gap between theory and practice', *Journal of Interprofessional Care*, vol. 20, no. 6, pp. 603–617.

Davies, P.A. and Bynner, J. (1999) *The Impact of Credit-based Systems of Learning on Learning Cultures*, ESRC report of the Learning Society Programme, London, City University.

Davies, M. and Morgan, A. (2005) 'Using computer-assisted self-interviewing (CASI) questionnaires to facilitate consultation and participation with vulnerable young people', *Child Abuse Review*, vol. 14, no. 6, pp. 389–406.

Department for Education and Employment (DfEE) (1998) *The Learning Age: A Renaissance for a New Britain*, London, DfEE, available online at <http://www.lifelonglearning.co.uk/greenpaper>, accessed 20 January 2008.

Department for Education and Skills (DfES) (2005) *Common Core of Skills and Knowledge for the Children's Workforce*, Nottingham, DfES.

Department of Health (DH) (2002) *Learning from Past Experience – A Review of Serious Case Reviews*, London, DH.

Department of Health, Department for Education and Employment, Home Office (2000) *Framework for the Assessment of Children in Need and their Families*, London, The Stationery Office.

Eby, M. (2000) 'Understanding professional development' in Brechin, A., Brown, H. and Eby, M.A. (eds) *Critical Practice in Health and Social Care*, London, The Open University/Sage, pp. 48–70.

Engeström, Y. (2001) 'Expansive learning at work: toward an activity theoretical reconceptualization', *Journal of Education and Work*, vol. 14, no. 1, pp. 133–156.

Eraut, M. (1994) *Developing Professional Knowledge and Competence*, London, Falmer Press.

France, A. and Utting, D. (2005) 'The paradigm of "risk and protection-focused prevention" and its impact on services for children and families', *Children & Society*, vol. 19, no. 2, pp. 77–90.

Frost, N. (2001) 'Professionalism, change and the politics of lifelong learning', *Studies in Continuing Education*, vol. 23, no. 1, pp. 5–17.

Frost, N. and Lloyd, A. (2006) 'Implementing multidisciplinary teamwork in the new child welfare policy environment', *Journal of Integrated Care*, vol. 14, no. 2, pp. 11–17.

Frost, N., Robinson, M. and Anning, A. (2005) 'Social workers in multidisciplinary teams: issues and dilemmas for professional practice', *Child & Family Social Work*, vol. 10, no. 3, pp. 187–196.

Funkee Munkee (2007), *Young People's Participation*, available online at <http://www.funkeemunkee.co.uk/young_people_part.html>, accessed 19 September 2007.

HM Government (2006) *Working Together to Safeguard Children: A Guide to Inter-agency Working to Safeguard and Promote the Welfare of Children*, London, The Stationery Office.

Horwath, J. (ed.) (2001) *The Child's World: Assessing Children in Need*, London, Jessica Kingsley.

James, A. and Prout, A. (eds) (1997) *Constructing and Reconstructing Childhood: Contemporary Issues in the Sociological Study of Childhood*, London, Falmer Press.

Jarvis, P. (2007) *Globalisation, Lifelong Learning and the Learning Society: Sociological Perspectives*, London, Routledge.

Kellett, M. (2005) *Children as active researchers: a new research paradigm for the 21st century?*, available online at <http://www.ncrm.ac.uk/research/outputs/publications/methodsreview/MethodsReviewPaperNCRM-003.pdf>, accessed 2 November 2007.

Kolb, D.A. (1984) *Experiential Learning: Experience as the Source of Learning and Development*, Englewood Cliffs, NJ, Prentice Hall.

Laming, Lord (2003) *The Victoria Climbié Inquiry*, London, The Stationery Office.

Lattuca, L.R. (2002) 'Learning interdisciplinarity: sociocultural perspectives on academic work', *Journal of Higher Education*, vol. 73, no. 6, pp. 711–739.

Lave, J. and Wenger, E. (1991) *Situated Learning: Legitimate Peripheral Participation*, Cambridge, Cambridge University Press.

Macdonald, G. (2001) *Effective Interventions for Child Abuse and Neglect: An Evidence-based Approach to Planning and Evaluating Interventions*, Chichester, Wiley.

McInnes, K. (2007) *A Practitioner's Guide to Interagency Working in Children's Centres: A Review of Literature*, Ilford, Barnardo's.

Morgan, R. (2005) 'Finding what children say they want: messages from children', *Representing Children*, vol. 17, pp. 180–188.

National Evaluation of the Children's Fund (NECF) (2004) *Collaborating for the Social Inclusion of Children and Young People: Emerging Lessons from the First Round of Case Studies*, Research Report No. 596, London, DfES.

O'Brien, S. (2003) *Report of the Caleb Ness Inquiry*, available online at <http://www.nhslothian.scot.nhs.uk/news/annual_reports/publichealth/2005/ar2003/caleb/cnr.pdf>, accessed 21 September 2007.

244 Changing children's services: working and learning together

Payne, M. (2002) 'Social work theories and reflective practice' in Adams, R., Dominelli, L. and Payne, M. (eds) *Social Work: Themes, Issues and Critical Debates* (2nd edn), Basingstoke, Palgrave/The Open University.

Pollard, A. (2002) *Reflective Teaching: Effective and Evidence-informed Professional Practice*, London, Continuum.

Rabiee, P., Sloper, P. and Beresford, B. (2005) 'Doing research with children and young people who do not use speech for communication', *Children & Society*, vol. 19, no. 5, pp. 385–396.

RAW (2007) *April 2007 Newsletter*, available online at <http://www.raw4us.co.uk/newsletter/Spring%20newsletter%201.pdf>, accessed 19 September 2007.

Reder, P. and Duncan, S. (2003) 'Understanding communication in child protection networks', *Child Abuse Review*, vol. 12, no. 2, pp. 82–100.

Rogoff, B., Turkanis, C.G. and Bartlett, L. (eds) (2001) *Learning Together: Children and Adults in a School Community*, New York, Oxford University Press.

Ruch, G. (2005) 'Relationship-based practice and reflective practice: holistic approaches to contemporary child care social work', *Child & Family Social Work*, vol. 10, no. 2, pp. 111–123.

Salford Centre for Social Work Research (SCSWR) (2004) *Education and Training for Inter-agency Working: New Standards*, Manchester, Salford University.

Schön, D.A. (1987) *Educating the Reflective Practitioner: Toward a New Design for Teaching and Learning in the Professions*, San Francisco, Jossey-Bass.

Scottish Executive (2002) *It's Everyone's Job to Make Sure I'm Alright. Report of the Child Protection Audit and Review*, Edinburgh, The Stationery Office.

Scottish Institute for Excellence in Social Work Education (SiSWE) (2005) *Service User and Carer Involvement in Social Work Education: Good Practice Guidelines*, available online at <http://www.sieswe.org/files/IA33GoodPracticeGuidelines.pdf>, accessed 19 September 2007.

Sheldon, B. and Chilvers, R. (2000) *Evidence-based Social Care: A Study of Prospects and Problems*, Lyme Regis, Russell House.

Smith, M.K. (2003) 'Communities of practice', *Encyclopaedia of Informal Education*, available online at <http://www.infed.org/biblio/communities_of_practice.htm>, accessed 19 September 2007.

Social Care Institute for Excellence (SCIE) (2004) *Improving the Use of Research in Social Care Practice*, Bristol, The Policy Press.

Taylor, B. (2000) *Reflective Practice: A Guide for Nurses and Midwives*, Buckingham, Open University Press.

Taylor, I. (2004) 'Multi-professional teams and the learning organization' in Gould, N. and Baldwin, M. (eds) *Social Work, Critical Reflection and the Learning Organization*, Aldershot, Ashgate, pp. 75–86.

Thomas, J. (2004) 'Using "critical incident analysis" to promote critical reflection and holistic assessment' in Gould, N. and Baldwin, M. (eds) *Social Work, Critical Reflection and the Learning Organization*, Aldershot, Ashgate, pp. 101–116.

Trinder, L. (ed.) (2000) *Evidence-based Practice: A Critical Appraisal*, Oxford, Blackwell Science.

Turney, D. (2007) 'Practice' in Robb, M. (ed.) *Youth in Context: Frameworks, Settings and Encounters*, London, Sage/The Open University.

Utting, W. (1991) *Children in the Public Care: A Review of Residential Child Care*, London, HMSO.

Warmington, P., Daniels, H., Edwards, A., Brown, S., Leadbetter, J., Martin, D. and Middleton, D. (2004) *Learning in and for Interagency Working: Conceptual Tensions in 'Joined Up' Practice*, Teaching and Learning Research Programme, Bath, University of Bath. Also available online at <http://www.tlrp.org/dspace/retrieve/247/Daniels+full+paper.doc>, accessed 3 January 2008.

Waterhouse, S. (2000) *Lost in Care: Report of the Tribunal of Inquiry into the Abuse of Children in Care in the Former County Council Areas of Gwynedd and Clwyd Since 1974*, London, The Stationery Office.

Watson, D., Abbott, D. and Townsley, R. (2007) 'Listen to me too! Lessons from involving children with complex healthcare needs in research about multi-agency services', *Child Care, Health and Development*, vol. 33, no. 1, pp. 90–95.

Welsh Assembly Government (2004) *Safeguarding Children: Working Together under the Children Act 2004*, Cardiff, Welsh Assembly Government.

Wiles, C. (2005) 'Developing integrated mental health services for children and young people in Moray' in Glaister, A. and Glaister, B. (eds) *Inter-Agency Collaboration – Providing for Children*, Edinburgh, Dunedin Academic Press.

Zwarenstein, M., Reeves, S., Barr, H., Hammick, M., Koppel, I. and Atkins, J. (2001) 'Interprofessional education: effects on professional practice and health care outcomes', *Cochrane Database of Systematic Reviews*, Issue 1, available online at <http://www.cochrane.org/reviews/en/ab002213.html>, accessed 19 September 2007.

# Chapter 7

## Reflecting on skills for work with children

Pam Foley

## Introduction

Developing and expanding skills for work with children, while at the same time implementing a significant amount of structural and cultural change within children's services, is likely to lead to some difficult questions for practitioners as individuals. Children's services across the UK are working towards greater integration and coordination. They are also focused on early intervention and now aim to ensure that safeguarding children becomes the common responsibility of all those working with children, including those for whom this has been less of a focus in the past.

Practitioners need a range of skills, knowledge and values. Many of these will be shared by everyone working with children. Some of these qualities will be the kinds of thing you would look for when recruiting people – that they therefore bring to the job – and others would be developed. Some of these qualities are supported by policy and practice development, but other qualities, rather than being developed, may be gradually drained from people as their radicalism or commitment is dissipated and diluted. The more recent strategies of teaching practitioners together and of developing a common set of skills and knowledge are perhaps radical enough to lead to the development of a shared value base, breaking down friction between practitioners, groups and agencies. But this will also raise questions for practitioners about their core purpose: are practitioners becoming hybrid workers, and why would this necessarily improve outcomes for children?

Practitioners also now need to be able to work in a constantly changing environment (see Chapter 1), to work more systematically and consistently with parents (see Chapter 2), and to work effectively in interagency and interprofessional teams (see Chapters 3, 4 and 5). In order to examine how skills, knowledge and values are acquired, applied, challenged and changed, this chapter will use accounts from practitioners from across the children's workforce. These unedited accounts are written by a range of practitioners who we asked to reflect on their work with children and any changes they were experiencing in relation to interagency working; you may agree or disagree with the points they make. What we are aiming to do here is to focus specifically on practitioners and practice, and to use the tool of critical reflection: a deliberate, thoughtful consideration of what we do and how we do it that can improve practice and refocus and re-energise practitioners. Reflective practice as a concept, and as an essential part of practice, was discussed in the previous chapter, 'Learning together'. Reflective practice should enable us to study our own decision-making processes, be constructively critical of our relationships with colleagues, analyse hesitations and skill and knowledge gaps, face problematic and painful episodes, and identify learning needs (Bolton, 2001). And a factor of uncertainty is an important part of reflection:

> Reflective practice entails an embracing of: uncertainty as to what we are doing and where we are going; confidence to search for something when we have no idea what it is; the letting go of the security blanket of needing answers. This kind of work will lead to more searching questions, the opening of fascinating avenues to explore, but few secure answers.
>
> (Bolton, 2001, p. 15)

Reflection can happen, for example, alone or in team meetings, with peers, as part of supervision, or as part of an educational programme. We are using some written practitioners' accounts. Our aim here is to identify, examine, discuss and reflect upon processes and outcomes associated with the acquisition of skills, the application of knowledge and the examination of values that underpin work with children.

## Core questions

- What are the skills, knowledge and values essential for work with children?
- What are the skills involved in interagency work with children?
- Why is it important for practitioners to consider the role of care in their work with children?
- How can a range of different practice approaches, disciplines and theories come together to improve services for children?
- How can the use of the tool of critical reflection enable practitioners to improve work with children and services for children?

# 1 Working with children

Thinking point 7.1   What kinds of people work with children? What kinds of skills and values do we want them to have? What kinds of skills and values would children want them to have?

## A foster carer ...

A **Children's Hearing** (in Scotland) is a legal tribunal arranged to consider and make decisions on the cases of children who are having problems in their lives and who may need legal steps to be taken to help them.

Imagine if you will the scene one rather routine morning. My husband and I ate breakfast with our 'newly turned into Goth' foster lad. Goth had not communicated by voice or word since becoming a black clad figure three days previously, or for that matter, a teenager the week before ... except by ever so slight upward eyebrow movement, or deeply pained, long suffering sigh. The post arrives, and for some light relief I open the letter from the Social Work department. It informs me that we are now to be paid for our fostering skills. I rather proudly announce this fact. Goth, eyebrow raised, states in a good impersonation of Gollum, 'Skills! What skills? You two haven't got any skills.'

'More toast anyone?' offers my husband helpfully.

Before I go on to explain the significance (if only to me) of this domestic exchange, let me offer some definition and parameters. In Scotland, the term 'looked after children' is a legal one determined by the Children (Scotland) Act 1995. A child becomes looked after either as a result of appearing before a **Children's Hearing** or when the parent requests that the local authority provide care and accommodation. When the Children's Hearing makes a supervision requirement it decides where the child should live. For many children this may be at home; called home supervision.

However, where a child is to be accommodated the Children's Hearing may stipulate the type of care or placement, for example, foster care, family placement, children's home. The local authority will assume the role of corporate parent and support the child in whichever setting is decided to be in the child's best interests.

Foster care involves looking after other people's children sometimes for brief periods or sometimes for extended stays. Foster carers are required to provide a safe, secure environment and high quality care to ensure that all the needs of the child are met. These children are trying to cope with massive changes in their lives. As well as focusing on the child, foster carers are called on to work with the child's family or significant others who are important to the child and to facilitate contact where this is part of the plan. Working with social workers and other professionals from other agencies is required to promote the best interests of the child. This may often entail meetings where the carer may be asked to contribute to the planning for the care of the child.

Although in our Goth's view we had no skills, I'd like to think that there must have been something keeping him with us besides a Children's Hearing supervision requirement. It just seemed like yesterday that he took my hand crossing the road.

Considering the views of children and young people on a wider scale too is vital when discussing skills required for foster carers. It is essential to hear their voices (even if they are saying things we may not feel entirely comfortable with on a personal level). In a feedback report for the Scottish Executive's National Fostering and Kinship Care Strategy Consultation, children who had experienced foster care listed the following qualities for an 'ideal foster carer':

> A good carer should be able to talk to the child about their family without offending them.
>
> Be a nice and kind person.
>
> They should be able to listen to children without judging them or breaking their confidences.
>
> Someone who children can have a laugh with.
>
> Someone who can relate to children.
>
> Not to judge the children as they are on the outside, but what they're like on the inside.
>
> Adaptable, caring, acts well under pressure and willing to stand up for the child/young person's rights.
>
> To be understanding and sensitive to different backgrounds young people come from.
>
> The most frequently mentioned qualities were patience, caring, forgiveness and good listener.
>
> (Fostering Network Young People's Project, 2007, pp. 6–7)

Meanwhile, back to the letter from the Social Work department. They must think we had skills – they were paying us for them! What did this payment refer to? Luckily they had enclosed a skills list which included:

- the ability to accept children as they are;
- being able to provide stable and consistent care;
- an ability to communicate with children and to listen to them;
- an ability to stick with children when their behaviour is difficult or challenging;
- a flexible approach to meeting the child's needs;
- an ability to recognise when things are difficult and to get appropriate help; and
- a sense of humour.

(Aberdeen City Council, 2007, p. 2)

Good news at least in two quarters. Children and young people and social workers are looking for much the same things from foster carers. As I considered these, with a sinking heart, I realised that I did not display a sense of humour at all times; there were circumstances when my patience was wearing thin; and as I looked in our Goth's direction, no, I could not understand but I could accept him as he was. Another piece of Scottish research describes the views of foster carers in relation to how we feel about our lot.

> Foster carers should be involved at all stages of the care plan – all too often at present decisions are made out of the meetings – in social work supervision etc. ... and this creates a blinkered approach where social workers and managers already have a strategy and target in focus and are therefore less likely to take on board foster carers' and the child's opinions and wishes. Social services need to view carers as part of the team and a professional with valued knowledge and skills.
>
> (Scottish Executive, 2007, p. 128)

These and several other similar comments from carers were reported in the National Fostering and Kinship Care Strategy Consultation (Scottish Executive, 2007) and seem to suggest that the fostering role is undervalued. Perhaps there is a lack of clarity about what fostering involves or confidence about the worth of 'the job'. Taking a historic view it is certain that foster carers were seen as volunteers, or that fostering was a life style decision rather than a job or even a semi-profession. More recently there has been a move to professionalise 'the service'.

> Expectations of foster carers have risen sharply as their role has changed from volunteer to professional. In order to meet the challenge of the job, foster carers now need to be capable of handling difficult and complex tasks: ensuring children have contact with their families, attending court hearings or meetings with professionals and keeping detailed records. Foster carers are also expected to be skilled in child development and need to have an understanding of the impact of abuse.
>
> (Fostering Network, 2007, p. 2)

The word 'skills' demands attention. In considering the lists of skills from children and young people and social workers, a lot of what is required focuses on characteristics, traits, attributes. But what is a skill? Is 'sense of humour' a skill? Not one list talks about loving or even liking children. Are these concepts skills?

If in describing skills there is an effort to define a level of competence, of knowledge, of a value system, of a code of conduct, of precise and considered practice, of action which is informed and purposeful, then foster carers are 'well qualified'. We work with children and young people in demanding circumstances. Often dealing with children in desperate situations, we may work in isolation in that we lack the close support of colleagues in day-to-day experience. Our practice often springs from experience, intuition, emotion and critical thinking about raw, real-life situations. A half-day training session might not help you there, but let me be clear that I do recommend training heartily.

In thinking about what skills I think are required in fostering, I refer to reflective practice. Schön has captured for me the essential in this regard, to be able to care:

> The reflective practitioner will cope with uncertainty by putting the relationship with the client at the centre of practice with an attempt reflectively to develop negotiated and shared meanings and understandings as a joint process.
>
> (Schön, 1983, p. xx)

The children's workforce is large, with people, mainly women, working in the statutory or voluntary sector, in children's services, in the community and in their own homes. When we think about the qualities of 'people who work with children', what comes to mind? That they are particularly warm and friendly people, that they have very developed 'people skills', that they have no problem communicating with children, that they have a special rapport with children or that they don't mind about being poorly paid?

If we were to work backwards from a job description such as the fictional one opposite, what needs to be in place to produce the skills knowledge and values that are likely to lead to good outcomes for children?

> The Government's vision is of a world-class children's workforce that:
> - is competent and confident;
> - people aspire to be part of and want to remain in – where they can develop their skills and build satisfying and rewarding careers; and
> - parents, carers, children and young people trust and respect.
>
> (DfES, 2005a, p. 3)

Foster carers are a vital part of the children's workforce. Many are caring 24 hours a day for children who may come with high levels of need and some difficult behaviour. Over 80 per cent of children in care are living in foster care or adoptive placements (Commission for Social Care Inspection

### Green Valley District Council
*Children are the top priority in Green Valley*

**Every Child Matters in Green Valley.**
**Are you someone who could make a real difference for children?**

Our top class children's services are looking to constantly improve, we have a clear vision of what we want to achieve and we are looking to fill some key positions which will focus on delivering effective programmes.

• You'll have skills to ensure every child reaches their full potential.
• You'll be someone who is a genuine team player.
• You'll be able to drive performance.
• You'll be able to work with partners to regenerate our target communities.
• You'll bring strategic, flexible and innovative management and practice skills.

Working in our children's services means being responsible for a wide range of multi-agency programmes designed to intervene early and effectively. For these posts you will need to bring a thorough knowledge of all the issues that impact upon children with a commitment to making a lasting change. You'll be able to deliver our leading edge children's services through drawing on a strong background in working with children, working with a team of dedicated professionals, through exercising your proven problem-solving approach and through your strengths and experience in programme management.

Are you up for the challenge?  For further information about the role and how to apply please visit
www.greenvalleychildren.gov.uk

(CSCI), 2007); the number of children in foster placements has significantly increased since 2000. The profile of the foster care workforce has evolved in recent decades into something much more diverse in terms of age, ethnicity, culture, marital status and sexual orientation. Foster care has evolved from a dominantly full-time model to one that includes short-term and support foster care, treatment and long-term foster care. Foster carers are expected to provide a supporting and caring family environment and to contribute to good outcomes for the health and education of fostered children. They work with common standards that cover a range of topics from keeping children safe and supporting them in their education, to knowing how children form attachments.

We would suggest that the foster carer in the account above is describing some of the key qualities that would characterise the 'world-class children's workforce'; she seems to be both a competent and confident practitioner, with an occupation that people should aspire to and want to remain in, and where skills are developed in association with a role that parents, carers, children and young people can trust and respect (DfES, 2005a, p. 3). But she raises some quite deep-seated issues too. There are points she makes, as she takes a moment to consider her skills, that refer to the differences in status between different groups of practitioners, to the way some practitioners' knowledge is more highly valued than the knowledge of others, to the professionalisation of the voluntary sector, and to the role of advocate. A further vitally important point raised here is that work with children is about values as much as skills.

Luckock et al. (2006) found that children felt that effective communication had a lot to do with *being* as well as *doing*. Children said practitioners needed to be 'kind', 'friendly', 'gentle', 'fair', 'respectful', 'trustworthy', 'patient', 'reliable' and 'telling the truth' (Luckock et al., 2006, p. 5). When asked what adults needed to do to communicate effectively, listening, understanding, explaining well and getting things done were identified by children. Children also emphasised the need for practitioners to develop their skills, including the skills needed for them to be able to involve and consult with younger children and those with communication impairments. Children and young people want many of the same things that other people involved with care services want; seven qualities are particularly valued:

- choice
- flexibility
- information
- being like other people
- respect and being heard
- fairness and non-discrimination
- safety

(CSCI, 2007, p. 4)

Other children in care, when asked about how they wanted to be treated by those working with them, said to:

> 'treat each child as an individual; take what a child says as seriously as what an adult says; allow children to have a real say in decisions affecting them; have a sufficient range of places available for there to be a choice of which one suits the child best'

(CSCI, 2007, p. 4)

Almost all work with children is a mix of the individual, familial, social and cultural, and of emotional engagement and care. Practitioners need to engage children in frequent face-to-face social interactions; they need to respond to children's cries or other signs of distress by providing comfort; they need to support the social and relationship skills of children; they help children deal with conflict; they help children learn about their own and others' emotional lives; and they help children understand their own and others' behaviour (Knitzer and Lefkowitz, 2005). This is skilled work too, as skills are involved in the learning, application and evaluation of strategies to support positive relationships with and among children. We are referring here not to a rapport with children, although that is of course highly valuable in itself, but to a sustained connection with children for their benefit.

Care '*of* a person implies care *about* him or her ... it would be naïve to assume that giving care is completely "natural" or effortless. Care is a result of many small subtle acts, conscious or not' (Hochschild, 2003, p. 214). This is the kind of day-to-day work that practitioners engage in with children. It is the elemental thing that the foster carer noted was missing from her list of skills when she pointed out that not one list talks about loving or even liking children. The fluid boundaries between emotional engagement, care and care work are intrinsic to work with children. Care may also be related to emotional capital, the stock of emotional resources that can be built up in families and drawn upon by children, in that the care capital of the practitioner may be depleted (Reay, 2002). In Chapter 2, Leverett discussed the various kinds of capital a family can possess and looked at how the emotional capital of children, parents or families can be expended if a family has to deal with factors outside their control such as racism.

Care, and its gendered nature (that is, that most of it is carried out by women), is a key aspect of children's services. It is mostly women who work in the so-called 'pink collar jobs', pink collar jobs, as opposed to blue collar or white collar jobs, frequently involve care work. As the skills of the children's workforce are examined, developed and expanded, it will be important to re-examine care as work in order to support the quality of work with children. And perhaps a key question for parents will remain: 'How genuine is it possible for institutional care to be?'

In integrated settings, where practitioners are called upon to demonstrate their particular field of knowledge and particular skills, demonstrating skilled care work as part of routine working practice can be difficult. Simpson and Smith (2006) argued that the consideration of emotional work, alongside physical and mental work, needs to join other explicit judgements of work and organisations now growth in the service economy and the feminisation of labour markets have taken place to such a significant extent. They highlighted some crucial issues for emotional work:

- Work plays a central role in the construction of individual identity, including the construction of masculinity or femininity; the gendering of emotional work therefore has implications for the identity of emotional labourers.

- Unlike mental and manual labour, emotional labour can be especially resistant to centralisation, de-skilling or direct control; authentic emotional work demands an appreciation of the processes underlying emotional labour and the performance of emotional work.

- The assumed value of emotional work may not fully reflect the meanings ascribed to it by emotional labourers themselves or by the recipients of such work.

- There are ethical and moral considerations in the buying and selling of emotional work and in the **commodification** of this work between the employer, employee and service users.

(Simpson and Smith, 2006)

**Commodification** refers to the transformation of something not previously seen in economic terms into something that can be bought and sold.

Thinking point 7.2     How might workers, managers and workplaces address tensions within the commodification of care?

As Brannen and Moss (2003) point out, there are dangers to commodifying care as it is not a neutral market process; it reflects class relations and international relations. When care is commodified, care work is transferred from one group of women (unpaid) to another group of women (paid). However, the pool from which paid carers have been drawn is shrinking as other jobs in the service sector draw upon the same group. Current solutions put forward include expanding the pool by including underrepresented groups (including men), or increasing the supply of women from within a free-market globalised economy, or 'professionalising' the workforce. An examination of the concept of care focuses on the cared for and the relational aspects as applied to both families and the nature and quality of care which practitioners provide for children (Brannen and Heptinstall, 2003). Care and its relational dimensions remain central to our understanding of childhood and what children are. Care, emotional involvement and emotional work lie at the heart of many interactions between children and adults in children's services, where care encompasses a wide range of skills:

It involves physical, mental and emotional work – caring for and caring about. It involves feeling responsible and taking responsibility ... involves work that may be undertaken unpaid in the home by family members (usually female), or that may be commodified and undertaken as paid labour by public or private sector workers (usually women) ...

This conceptualization of care has great value, not least for its attention to the labour and costs of care ... and its recognition of the complexity of care including material, emotional and moral dimensions.

(Moss and Brannen, 2003, p. 6)

## Key points

1   Practitioners need skills and time to develop the critical self-awareness and reflection that are essential to quality of children's services and their innovation and evolution. They also need policies and management that recognise and support these skills.

2   Care and emotional work are at the core of many of the skills needed by practitioners who are working with children, although this is more implicitly than explicitly recognised. The element of care can be important when considering gender and work.

# 2 National policy and community action

A wide range of people work with children in the community and are central to contemporary integrated approaches to poverty reduction, the educational agenda and children's wellbeing generally.

## A community worker ...

When I first started work in the UK, coming from Germany, where I had trained and worked for several years, I was amazed at the lack of professional self-confidence of social work team colleagues. In Germany at that time (early eighties) social workers, including residential care staff, were all professionally qualified with at least a four-year degree, and possibly further professional training in a specialism, such as drugs counselling. Their professional status was seen to be on a par with that of a lawyer, teacher or medical doctor, and in terms of multi-professional working this made working together and challenging each others' professional agenda, judgement etc., much more straightforward.

So, I was amazed when I witnessed a UK social work colleague having to steel himself for a simple phone call to a psychiatrist who was to give an urgent assessment of a child. This society's ascribing of such low status for social care staff was a total surprise and, although I have got used to the media reinforcing this image, I still cannot believe how much the many professions in the social care field have internalised this. It will be interesting to see how the impact of the more recent social work degree in this country filters into people's consciousness (I am not holding my breath!).

To work successfully you must enjoy hanging out with kids and young people, and hang in there when the going gets tough. Investing time and energy in local 'multi-networks' on a routine basis pays off a hundredfold in times of crisis – when there is not the time or energy to build relationships – as you know how others work and 'tick': this means you can 'call in favours' and use well established channels of communication to get a quick reply/ assessment/result/report whatever ... The local grapevine also has great potential to alert staff and carers informally to new resources/potential funds in the pipeline or policy/legislation developments that might impact over time on children and families. As manager of a residential unit I was part of a local network for youth homelessness and young runaways in Stirling which made an enormous difference to staff and service users, be it quick turnarounds of bureaucracy, urgent benefit payments authorised because our service was known and respected, B and B provided without going through multiple assessments, or someone such as Women's Aid alerting us to a house clearance coming up where a youngster could get furniture.

When bringing up my elder step-daughter who has a learning disability, although as a carer I kept my 'social worker identity' under wraps, I was able to tap into professional communities of practice and informal networks with other parents/carers. The latter was especially valuable because we could coach and encourage each other in arguing the children's case for access to resources, and if something worked for someone, others found out quickly – in the eighties there were huge barriers here, including lack of information from local authority social services who were protecting their budgets, especially if a child did not cause disruption in school. Some of the parents went on to lobby the Scottish Office administration and had no small part in creating a much better legislative and policy setting for future generations.

Work for children and families that is primarily rooted in communities has a long history, and its latest manifestation, community-based children's services – a large number of children's centres and extended or community schools delivering 'wrap around' child, social and health care and parental support – is explicitly linked with better outcomes for children in policy documents from across the UK. What this practitioner describes here is the variety of interagency work that evolves within community work, including team working, networking and 'knot working', the more focused acute work that can be needed at times. Overall there has been a growing disposition to recognise and engage with expertise that is distributed across often rapidly shifting groups. The expertise sometimes lies outside practice, for example in the hands of some groups of parents. This may mean that one needs a flexible approach to leadership when it is recognised that another could perhaps do better in that role.

However, within government policy documents it can be easier to find more rhetoric than attempts to address the difficult questions that can arise from community-based approaches; a whole series of questions should surface about what kinds of interventions are likely to be effective and whether these are best directed at the level of child, family or community (Cummings et al., 2007). In their study of professionals working in multi-agency schools, Cummings et al. (2007) found that school-orientated and community-orientated broad perspectives still, unsurprisingly, divided education professionals from the other professionals now also working from schools:

> the school-oriented understanding rests on a whole set of social, economic and political assumptions – that educational achievement offers a reliable pathway out of disadvantage; that the effects of family and community background on achievement can be overcome by the sorts of interventions that community-oriented

schools can muster and that state institutions led by professionals with little local accountability are justified in making such interventions.

(Cummings et al., 2007, p. 197)

Of course, such viewpoints are open to criticism; the capacity of education to achieve economic wellbeing can be seen as overstated, and schools that work in isolation can have little impact on family and community disadvantage (Cummings et al., 2007). Or the impact can be unequal, as Schuller (2004) points out:

> In Willie Russell's play/film *Educating Rita*, is Rita's climbing of the Open University ladder, from working-class routine to a more educated but unpredictable new life, an overall good? Most of us would say yes, but there are downsides, and not only in the eyes of the husband left marooned in his traditional milieu; communities too pay the price of the modernisation and social mobility to which education adds such impetus. ... education can act as a kind of ballast or insurance, offering people a better chance of security in a changing world ... but it can also dispel certainties and accentuate feelings of insecurity.

(Schuller, 2004, p. 8)

Schools are, in reality, limited in what they can offer a community in terms of what difference they can make. The home–school divide, for example, with its corresponding divide in what is learnt at home and what is learnt in school, is only partially addressed by involving parents in school activities. Children deal with such conflicting factors in their lives. Schools can also be seen to replicate rather than challenge disadvantage. And of the three main statutory services, education, social care and health, it is education which has most clearly resisted respecting children's participation rights (Mayall, 2006). On the other hand, the increase in a person's self-esteem, with a corresponding sense of purpose, as a result of education is probably the most widely documented 'soft' outcome of learning (Hammond, 2004).

Thinking point 7.3    What do you think of children's centres and community schools or extended schools as the main conduit for delivering national policy directly to communities on the ground?

Jack's (2006) analysis of recent policy developments in the UK examined children's services community programmes as the latest in a long line of attempts to achieve a better combination of preventative, proactive and protective services for children. In his view, any improvement in social capital from community programmes such as these will be effective only in the long term, and:

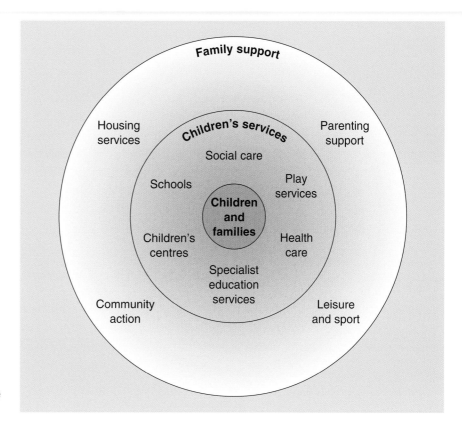

Policies need to be implemented by a range of support services

> Without major shifts in the culture and working practices of mainstream children's services, with a more central role given to prevention perspectives, incorporating the area and community elements of children's well-being, they are still liable to fail to identify situations ... where children are at serious risk because of a *combination of individual and area factors.*
>
> (Jack, 2006, pp. 336–337, emphasis in original)

As Jack (2006) points out, in practice drivers such as the *Common Core of Skills and Knowledge* (DfES, 2005b), with over 150 specific areas of skills and knowledge identified as essential for the children's workforce, any regard for the context in which work takes place is barely noticeable. In order for children's services, working through communities, to make a significant contribution to the government's wider social inclusion agenda, Jack argues that a skilled knowledge of the social and environmental context in which they work is crucial:

> What is needed is an understanding of the importance of working in partnership with vulnerable or disadvantaged groups and neighbourhoods, collecting and analysing information about the community circumstances in which they are living and developing

local area indices of child well-being, to complement continuing efforts to monitor high-risk individuals and families.

(Jack, 2006, p. 337)

This kind of approach and analysis leads us to another vital issue touched upon by our community worker here: the kind of breadth of skills and the kind of focus that may be highly relevant to work with children. There are some marked differences in the education and skills base for working with children in the UK and similar work in other parts of Europe.

Thinking point 7.4    The terms pedagogue and pedagogical practice are becoming more widely used in debates about the future of children's services. What do you understand these terms to mean?

The social pedagogical approach is one that is widespread in continental Europe and offers some challenging comparisons for those involved with building and working in a children's workforce and for those practitioners who wish to work with communities on a more committed and equitable basis. Social pedagogy has been defined within the UK as:

- a process of considering our practices
- a process of recognizing children as active agents who make choices
- a process that employs diverse learning contexts to support a variety of approaches to learning
- an approach that values the importance of play and is underpinned by knowledge of child development
- an approach based on the recognition that parents, children and professionals are a learning community and that professionals should continually review their practices.

(Learning and Teaching Scotland, 2006, p. 24)

A great number of newly emerging professions have continued to be set up in children's services (family support workers, children's centre managers, children's rights officers, for example) with little thought to the overall professional structure and with the consequence that training can be short and narrowly focused, and career opportunities are limited (Davies Jones, 1994). By contrast the social pedagogical groups in Europe have grown in numbers, status and versatility, emerging as a widely ranging professional force in the sector, supported by a 3- to 4-year education programme primarily rooted in the social, pedagogical and behavioural sciences (Davies Jones, 1994). And this is distinctly different from many of the contemporary children's services in the UK:

> The emphasis of this professional model is on learning, care and upbringing being inseparable, inter-connected parts of life. The child is seen as a social being, connected to others and at the same time with his or her own distinctive experiences and knowledge.
>
> (DfES, 2005a, p. 36)

Social pedagogical approaches, an essentially holistic way of working, might be now considered to be more appropriate to increasingly integrated children's services and to the care and education for children in the UK. They put emphasis on building relationships through practical engagement, working with groups and using groups for support, sharing practice, identifying goals and can involve regularly reminding people of what brought them into working with children in the first place. Pedagogic training involves:

- theoretical subjects in the behavioural and social sciences;
- skills training such as group work, working with conflict and challenging behaviour, and teamwork;
- creative and practical subjects ... media through which pedagogues can relate to children. Arts and practical subjects are also valued for their general therapeutic effect; they can help children enjoy life and feel good about themselves.

> (DfES, 2005a, p. 48)

Clearly, policy makers as well as practitioners are increasingly recognising that examining how other countries respond to similar challenges to our own can be a source of inspiration and can constructively challenge conventional thinking. (Another example of this was the appointment of Children's Commissioners for the UK.) The pedagogue does not see herself or himself as an isolated practitioner working for or with children; this approach is *relational*. This has the potential to support further growth in skills and knowledge for a wide range of children's services with a corresponding impact on the quality of services for children. It also could have, perhaps, a corresponding impact on their status and self-confidence, and this could improve recruitment, practice and retention. As theories and practices become more interactive and interwoven across education, healthcare, play and other fields, might this result in something different, something better, something more than the sum of its parts (Brannen and Moss, 2003)? The European experience of social pedagogy is one of practitioners involved in a dynamic process in which groups are coalescing, forming working alliances, redefining roles, and shaping new identities that can be of benefit to practice, practitioners and the people they work with (Davies Jones, 1994). Central to the pedagogical approach is that the pedagogue sees herself or himself as having a relationship with the child and with groups of children which is both personal and professional, relating to the child at the level of the person rather than focusing on attaining certain adult goals (Moss and Petrie, 2002).

## Practice box 7.1

### Developing pedagogic practice

In the Early Years' curriculum in Denmark, emphasis is on nurturing children's social and emotional development, inter- and intra-personal. ... Competence, in terms of the Danish curriculum, represents the abilities – social, emotional and cognitive – and proficiencies that can be fostered and developed in children. ... The view is that it isn't enough to have 'knowledge' – to know how to read, write and add – alongside knowledge, children need the skills and competences to use the knowledge they have. ... The careful balance between the curriculum, the activities and the educators' awareness of facilitating children's emerging skills and competences is the key to developing pedagogic practice ... The pedagogical training of educators combines the theoretical and the practical with the development of the educator's own self-awareness through physically and mentally challenging activities.

(Williams-Siegfredsen, 2007, pp. 64–66)

This is an example of a quite different kind of children's services and a new kind of practitioner for work with children and there are of course others. But if work with children needs to become increasingly highly skilled, with practitioners able and willing to encourage each other to draw upon a wide range of theoretical understandings and practical strategies, working within 'communities of practice' (see Chapter 6), some of this more fundamental thinking has to take place.

## Key points

1   National policies need local implementation. It is essential for practitioners to acquire, develop and apply knowledge of the familial, environmental and social context of work with children.

2   Other models of education and training for the children's services workforce may be more appropriate and more effective than those we currently use. With the changes underway in children's services, rethinking of services and practices using examples such as the European social pedagogical model may be informative for policy makers, managers and practitioners.

# 3 More than the sum of its parts? Integrated working for children

The children's workforce is undergoing radical expansion, reorganisation and up-skilling to improve children's services and to address flaws in systems that have led to fragmentation and both overlapping and underlapping services. Joined-up, even integrated working is an explicit policy aim across the four nations of the UK. A range of practitioners can now be recruited or seconded into a team with common goals, with an integrated management structure, and perhaps co-located to offer children's services usually from an early years or school setting (see Chapters 3 and 4).

Policy now links specific outcomes to key national targets and indicators, themselves linked to a range of inspection criteria, in an attempt to define better outcomes for children and translate this throughout the system. The success of this is believed to depend on a clear strategic direction, dissemination of good practice, and inspection and regulation (DfES, 2005b). However, evaluation relating to interagency working reports common dilemmas associated with merging different professional approaches and practices, managing teams of workers on different payscales, combining funding streams, and the lack of joint training and professional development (Anning et al., 2006; see also Chapter 3).

Integrated teams may be made up of people who have been trained to think about children and childhood in different ways

Little evidence exists relating to outcomes for service users – children – of multi-agency work in children's services (Jack, 2006). There has also been criticism of a rationale of multi-agency working that the wellbeing of parents and children is invariably the same thing, whereas it may be more accurate to see the interests of individuals within families as only sometimes coinciding (Warin, 2007). This lack of clarity is thought to lead to confusion about the primary beneficiaries of various services – children, parents, mothers, fathers, the child within the family, the whole family or the extended family – and is believed to amount to a serious flaw in multi-agency working (Warin, 2007).

There is some support for the proposition that everyone working with children and families should have a common set of skills and knowledge. The *Common Core of Skills and Knowledge for the Children's Workforce* (DfES, 2005b) identified six areas of expertise: effective communication and engagement, child and young person development, safeguarding and promoting the welfare of the child, supporting transitions, multi-agency working, and sharing information. The underlying idea that it is possible, indeed necessary, to identify common skills for all those working with children, could affect all pathways of education and training in the children's workforce. Children's services will continue to need to draw upon many disciplines to interrogate issues, identify problems and seek explanations. One such discipline is described by our next practitioner.

## An educational psychologist ...

I am an educational psychologist, a practitioner working with children, their families and schools and the head of a multi-professional service comprising three teams of educational psychologists, and three teams of specialist teachers in Northern Ireland supporting children with dyslexia, hearing impairment or developmental difficulties.

Currently, the core skills of an educational psychologist sit within the scientist practitioner approach to problem solving. This approach emphasises that practice is guided by, and operates within the framework of the general scientific method. This requires the use of a range of data collection methods such as, observation and recording, interview, use of diagnostic and standardised assessments which inform clear descriptions of problems, and the development of alternative hypotheses informed by psychological knowledge and theory. These hypotheses are then tested using the processes of observation, monitoring and evaluation. This methodology is used when working with children in order to determine the reasons for their difficulties in learning and offering solutions for addressing these difficulties. For example, a child may be referred to an educational psychologist because of a reading difficulty. The psychologist's job is to collect information and data through the assessment process in order to determine the reasons for the child's failure and to offer solutions. A range of hypotheses may spring to mind – has the child dyslexia or a language difficulty or a hearing impairment or a visual impairment or a memory difficulty or a mental impairment or autism or a mental health problem such as depression or anxiety – or indeed, a combination of any of these? Perhaps the child has been abused or has been neglected by his parents or carers or his teaching in school has been disrupted or poor? The work of the educational psychologist is to use his or her skills and perspective of applied psychology in an educational context, to bring clarity in understanding the barriers to learning for the child and to inform solutions for addressing these barriers.

A key problem in arriving at well-informed explanations for children's problems is that they tend not to be simple but rather are complex, layered and multi-factorial. The implication of this is that no one person or professional group has all the skills necessary to get the full picture. Over the years professionals have followed the practice of referring cases to one and other in order to get a more comprehensive picture of a child's problems. This usually meant that children were seen in school or at home or in the various clinics or offices of social care, educational, medical and paramedical professionals. This approach tended to 'fragment' the child's problems and sometimes made it difficult to get a holistic and agreed picture.

The context in Northern Ireland, within which services for children and their families are delivered, is rapidly changing. Ongoing is a major review of public administration. This review, when it is completed, will affect significantly the organisational structures through which education, health and social care are provided. As with the emerging structures in England and Wales, in Northern Ireland there is a greater than ever emphasis on multi-agency and multi-disciplinary working arrangements for services for children. The driver of these changes is a major report published by the Office of the First Minister and Deputy First Minister. This report, *A Ten Year Strategy for Children and Young People in Northern Ireland 2006–2016*, is the Northern Ireland equivalent of *Every Child Matters*, the implementation of which is currently influencing the organisation and delivery of services across England and Wales.

As a direct consequence of this report and its outcomes framework, many services previously provided in community settings will be delivered directly to children in schools and within a multi-professional service delivery model. For example, many services provided by speech and language therapists, occupational therapists, physiotherapists and nurse behaviour therapists, previously provided in community clinics will, for the first time, be provided to children and their families in their local schools. Services offered by the five Education and Library Boards in Northern Ireland are mainly provided to children and their families in schools and a key challenge for education managers is to ensure these services integrate and coordinate and cooperate with the new external services in ways that improve the outcomes for children. The challenge inherent in these processes is a key driver for professionals, their services and employing bodies striving to develop their skills in order to work better together.

The emerging context of multi-agency/multi-professional/trans-disciplinary working will change this way of working and, as a practising educational psychologist, my core/essential skills will need to broaden to accommodate to the demands of this emerging picture. The new skills that I will have to develop will be in the area of clearly understanding the different theoretical perspectives, values and ethics of others and fully appreciating the conditions and processes that lead to more effective professional, interprofessional and interagency working and in adjusting my practice accordingly. As a service manager as well as a practitioner I have the additional challenge of providing the leadership to my colleagues to ensure that our collective practice is moving in the right direction so that together we can better meet the outcomes embraced by the 'Ten Year Strategy'.

Thinking point 7.5   If you can look back over some years as a practitioner working with children, what would you identify as the most significant change you have experienced? Is the direction of change to policy and practice you have experienced one for the better?

This practitioner's account raises some more dilemmas and issues for consideration. Within this account there is a description of the evolution of the working life of a professional. Here we see that critical thinking is very much part of this practitioner's approach. Critical thinking describes an attitude to present experience and practice:

> Critical thinking enables us to speak of questions and possibilities rather than givens and necessities. It shows us there are choices to be made between possibilities, that the usual way of proceeding is not self-evident, that there is no one 'best practice' or 'standard of quality' to be found (since such concepts are always value-laden and relative) ... The choices are more fundamental, and require us first to formulate questions: 'what do we want for our children?',

> 'what is a good childhood?', 'what is the place of children in society?', 'who do we think children are?', 'what are the purposes of institutions/services/spaces for children?', 'what is education for?', 'what do we mean by care?' – and so on.
>
> (Moss and Petrie, 2002, p. 11)

These would seem to remain crucial questions for practitioners to visit and revisit. While some things remain constant, such as the application of a body of knowledge (the one identified by this practitioner is of a specific scientific nature), this practitioner also discusses the necessity of acquiring new skills for what will be new territory, interagency working. A major issue for workplaces is the successful blending of specialists and generalists in teams particularly where hierarchical structures, tiers of assessment, diagnosis and treatment are embedded (Anning et al., 2006).

> Multi-agency working is about different services, agencies and teams of professionals and other staff working together to provide the services that fully meet the needs of children, young people and their parents or carers. To work successfully on a multi-agency basis you need to be clear about your own role and aware of the roles of other professionals ... These behaviours should apply across the public, private and voluntary sectors.
>
> (DfES, 2005b, p. 18)

The skills and knowledge required for more integrated working include not only communication and teamwork skills but also the assertiveness and judgement that team working necessarily demands. And as this quote indicates, it also needs to be underpinned by knowledge of your own role and the procedures and working methods associated with it, alongside a general knowledge and understanding of the range of organisations and individuals who work with children. However, there is a tension between expertise, sharing expertise and developing expertise in sharing.

Craig's (2004) report into interprofessional working in schools led him to comment:

> Connections between public sector professionals therefore mean that they are increasingly caught in a bind ... On the one hand, in the wake of the Climbié Inquiry, the professional judgements of teachers and other professionals are seen as more and more important. On the other, they are being called on to work in contexts where they are outside of their professional tradition and open to contradiction from all angles. As a result, too often professionals feel overloaded, confused or held back by the information they receive or are required to share with others.

This experience is emblematic of a deeper tension in the self-image of many professionals in contemporary Britain.

(Craig, 2004, p. 21)

Thinking point 7.6   If you work in children's services, have you experienced these kind of changes within practice? Are people now willing to relinquish claims to specialist knowledge and give way to others when appropriate? And is a specialist practitioner's or a generic practitioner's knowledge more highly valued by the team?

Anning et al. (2006) identified some basic requirements for teams to work together:

All team members need to be line managed and to have their work coordinated with other members of the team. All team members also need to have appropriate support for personal and professional development. Above all, team members need to have absolute clarity about who is performing each of these tasks for themselves and for their team colleagues. All agencies need to develop formal structures for liaison with other agencies responsible for a multi-agency team and to agree collectively about how the team and its members will be managed.

(Anning et al., 2006, p. 46)

The development of common skills and knowledge could have a significant impact on working together. This could, in part, be a means of creating a common language.

Education and training together could also be indispensable (see Chapter 6). Education is essentially a critical activity that supports people to think independently, to question, to investigate. The account above from an educational psychologist was considering the use of and perhaps increase in interdisciplinary work. Work with children has supported the blurring of boundaries between the body, biology, culture and society. Interdisciplinarity has therefore long been a driving feature of childhood studies. There has been significant creative cross-fertilisation of ideas between the educational, social, medical, psychiatric and psychological disciplines. Interdisciplinarity can lead to more creative work than is possible within a single discipline, and is more likely to address any incorrect assumptions, but this should not lead to the loss of disciplinary-based studies: 'Interdisciplinarity does not imply non-disciplinarity but rather traffic between two or more disciplines' (Prout, 2005, p. 146).

Some of the benefits and barriers of interprofessional working are discussed in the next account.

## A healthcare worker ...

I've been working as a health visitor for several years so multi-agency working is not entirely new to me. Health visitors have been working in the community focusing on preventive healthcare and monitoring the growth and development of young children. However, the emphasis on community working and working in core teams with continual input from other agencies within a community is new and has the potential to help many more families.

We have contact with families at a very important time, when children are very young. There are lots of important decisions to be made and that's where we can help. We work closely with families focusing on health promotion and child health and we are essentially preventive healthcare practitioners. We work in people's homes, clinics and community settings and we are working in day care centres, schools and children's centres now too. Child and adolescent health is one of the most important areas of public health and it has been given a much higher profile in recent government documents including *Every Child Matters*.

What a family needs varies a great deal. Sometimes it is a family we see regularly, sometimes it is a family we haven't seen for years, but we can start a relationship that goes on for a long time and it is important to start things off in the right way. What we do is give advice and help or bring in someone else from the team to work with them. Now we are able to take a look at the whole child and recognise and respond to many more issues that act on a child and their family. Sometimes the root of the problem is not strictly a health issue – maybe much more to do with housing or transport or childcare – and now we are able to cross boundaries and this is crucial.

There are several different ways multi-agencies work. The Common Assessment Framework is key to making everyone work towards the same outcomes for children and families. This is the first time real information sharing can be something we can work towards.

With the *Every Child Matters* report there is much more working together, sharing of work and sharing of information. The National Service Framework also made public health work and preventative work much more at the forefront. I now work in a multi-disciplinary team and have come to realise just how much more effective we are if we pool knowledge. The aim is not to create a one size fits all service but to link up and coordinate the universal and specialist services that we have. Team meetings are important to how we work together. Children and families will benefit from this since we can now get a fuller picture.

However, there are times when there are problems. For example there are particular issues about which particular practitioners feel they hold the greatest knowledge. It can be difficult to let go of some things. We all need to start using the same jargon and we need to know the triggers and drivers for each of the different agencies that you work with. Someone asked me the other day what I did and I found this hard to answer. Was I still a health visitor or a health visitor working in a multi-agency team or something else? I am still not sure what the answer should be or whether it matters!

A challenge for all practitioners working in multi-agency teams is to reflect on the models they draw upon to underpin their practice with service users (Anning et al., 2006). Theoretical models have been developed to support practice frameworks and these in turn become allied to practitioner identities. What this practitioner is describing here are some of the advantages and disadvantages to multi-agency working, specifically introducing some ambiguity into her role and her practitioner identity. Identity is central to Wenger's (1998) model of a community of practice in that practice and identity can be inseparable (see Chapter 6). A professional identity with its underpinning ideologies and knowledge base, its orientation towards clients and its status is something that may feel hard won and maybe difficult to let go of. Indeed, professional identity (how professionals understand themselves and their roles), professional status (how professional hierarchies and different distributions of power are generated) and professional discretion and accountability (how professionals exercise discretion on a day-to-day basis) may constitute formidable barriers to interagency and integrated working (Anning et al., 2006).

Children can spend a great deal of their lives with the people who are providing services for them. The kinds of services provided by practitioners are profoundly influenced by the spaces in which these services are provided. The use of the word 'space' here should have a particular significance:

> The use of 'space' connotes not just a physical space, but a social space (combining social practices and relationships), a cultural space (where values, rights and cultures are created and changed), and a discursive space (where there is room for dialogue, confrontation, deliberation and critical thinking). The idea of children's spaces fundamentally changes the conceived relationships between professionals and service users, adult responsibilities and children's rights. Professionals are facilitators rather than technicians and both children and adults are co-constructors of knowledge and expertise. Participative relationships are thus fundamental to the idea of children's spaces.
>
> (Hill et al., 2004, p. 84)

A pivotal children's space remains the school.

## A teacher ...

My work as a primary teacher covers 32 years, including 8 years as a teaching head in a small school. In the early years of my career, I experienced little multi-agency working. On the few occasions when a pupil attended a speech therapist or an educational psychologist, I had to ask parents and/or head teacher for information about the outcome of these visits. As a class teacher I did not automatically receive written reports from other agencies working with the pupils I taught and I did not attend multi-agency meetings.

However, in more recent years I have benefited from multi-agency input into school and classroom. I have attended and also chaired multi-agency meetings. Through working with other professionals I have gained insights into pupils' strengths and areas of difficulty. I have been introduced to new approaches to help pupils in their learning. At the heart of this professional learning are the insights that come from understanding new perspectives on the children I teach.

A powerful example of multi-agency work in developing new understanding for teachers is the provision of 'visual-impairment workshops'. In these workshops, staff who work with visually impaired children in mainstream school are invited to complete reading and writing tasks wearing various sets of goggles to simulate different visual impairments. Participants are always amazed by this opportunity to 'see the world as the child sees it' and readily appreciate the need to adapt classroom practices.

Successful multi-agency working requires those involved to be open to learn from each other. This sometimes means professionals making a conscious effort to put aside stereotypes and look for common ground. For example, I can remember discovering that my speech and language therapist colleagues did not see their job merely in terms of providing techniques for overcoming 'speech defects', but were in fact deeply interested in developing language and communication. From that point I recognised that the value of their input was not limited to specific children and regularly engaged in fruitful discussion with them.

Similarly I learned that educational psychologists did not spend all their time withdrawing children to undertake batteries of psychometric tests and then writing up the results of these tests. I have found it extremely useful to have an educational psychologist observe an individual pupil in my class and give me feedback on how I am catering for that pupil's needs. Psychologists and others who observe children in a realistic classroom situation have a greater understanding of the needs of the child and of the rest of the class. Their recommendations are more useful because they are tailored to specific class situations.

Vygotsky's **Zone of Proximal Development** (within the theoretical framework of 'social constructionism') describes the gap between a learner's developmental level as determined by their independent problem solving level and their potential level of development.

I have also found much shared understanding with educational psychologists, for example the use of Vygotsky's concept of the **Zone of Proximal Development** in developing dynamic assessment. Discussions around the use of dynamic assessment help to shape my own ideas about scaffolding learning and the importance of formative feedback on assessment. Talking with other professionals is very valuable in developing new perspectives, as well as in finding practical ways to help particular children.

Mutual understanding and professional respect allows multi-agency working to be creative and effective. Each agency is better placed to appreciate and value the work of others and to be proactive in seeking an appropriate input. Multi-agency in-service sessions are very useful in developing shared understandings. At a shared in-service with social workers on supporting 'looked after and accommodated children', I noticed that both teachers and social workers developed increased respect for each other's practice. Shared in-service is also useful in developing the informal networking that helps to support productive multi-agency meetings.

On the negative side, I have experienced multi-agency meetings where lack of shared understandings leads to unrealistic expectations of what others could offer or where participants' own needs for professional recognition interfered with considering the needs of the child who was the focus of the meeting. On one such occasion two professionals spent time debating the wording of the diagnosis of the child's difficulties, an issue that provided little insight into how that child might be helped to overcome those difficulties.

The issue of language can be important. Each agency will have its own specialised language, its own discourse of practice, and it is important for others to make an effort to understand this. Sometimes it is useful to make use of the specialised language of other agencies. Sometimes it is important to recognise that terms may be used differently by different agencies and to take this into account in spoken and written communication.

Benefits of multi-agency working can be great. Having access to a variety of expertise is invaluable in finding ways to support the inclusion of children with special needs into mainstream schools. Together, the various agencies are able to highlight the strengths and needs of the individual child. When it is successful, multi-agency working creates a sense of team work that is extremely positive. Individual professionals listen to each other and learn from each other, developing new perspectives, new keys to unlock children's learning. Together they develop their understanding and awareness of factors which affect children's learning and wellbeing. I would say that the most important things are:

- being a reflective practitioner, engaging in regular and systematic reflection on all aspects of your work

- seeking out reading and research that will help to develop your practice

- having an open attitude to new ideas

- willingness to listen to the suggestions of others
- willingness to appreciate the perspectives of others and to work within multiple perspectives
- having respect for others – children as well as adults
- creativity in generating ideas and in synthesising the ideas of others
- a positive, problem-solving approach, seeking to move forward towards solutions, not dwell on difficulties
- a sense of humour
- a caring attitude
- most important of all, the ability to put the child or children at the centre of your thinking.

What this teacher is describing here is linked with the long-term, careful working out of how good relationships with children develop, and she gives some clear examples of how much children can benefit from this.

Thinking point 7.7   A range of qualities of practitioners have been demonstrated, described and discussed in this chapter. What would be on your list of qualities?

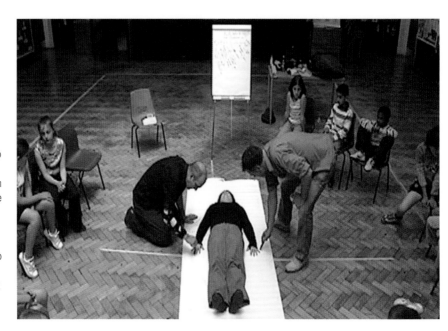

Children at a primary school were prompted to discuss the qualities of practitioners working with children by using a figure that was drawn around their actual teaching assistant. They thought she needed to be kind, to listen, to act upon what children told her and not to be distracted from doing her job.

**Practice box 7.2**

When asked about how to be a talking and listening sort of adult with children, children involved in a report about *Every Child Matters* said:

'talk to them, find out what they think'

'speak to us nicely'

'by taking the time to talk and listen to what people my age think'

'by talking, listening, and waiting for people to talk'

'by going to training and with the way you react or speak'

'do things that people my age like to do'

'they could talk to us and being nice about it. Saying that the children don't have to say anything if they don't want to'

'by being a bit more understanding and widening their horizons'.

(Morgan, 2005, p. 21)

The practitioners who have reflected on practice here, and the research and the examples we have given from practice, describe work that is developing through finding and applying theories, experience and good practices for work with children. These practitioners show a level of self-awareness that reflects their knowledge of the adoption of multiple identities:

Rather than a technician, a worker in a children's space is understood to be a reflective practitioner, a researcher, a critical thinker, and a co-constructor of knowledge, culture and identity ... The work and worker need to be suited to groups of children of varying ages in many types of setting, to relating to the whole child, and to being open to many and unpredictable possibilities. The worker needs to be comfortable in many fields – from ethics to children's culture, from learning to health – and with adopting varied identities, including reflective practitioner, researcher and co-constructor.

(Moss, 2006, p. 188)

So a final point that may be emerging here is that work with children needs a practitioner to be sometimes a carer, sometimes a community worker, sometimes an educational psychologist, sometimes a healthcare worker, sometimes a teacher and sometimes something else entirely. In other words, just as *externally* the practitioner will be combining her or his skills with those of others, the practitioner also needs to be developing a broad range of skills, knowledge and skills *internally* with the understanding that learning is a constant feature of work with children.

## Key points

1   Interagency working may need considerable time and effort to be effective but it can open out settings and practice to innovation.

2   Knowledge for work with children is drawn from a variety of disciplines and from interdisciplinary thinking and working. Learning and training together, drawing on 'communities of practice' and other models, could make significant improvements to work with and for children.

3   Practitioners working in the children's workforce are able to contribute to and benefit from the evolution of services and the evolution of practice.

# Conclusion

'People and organisations are all the time learning something that is not stable, not even defined or understood ahead of time. In important transformations of our personal lives and organisational practices, we must learn new forms of activity which are not yet there. They are literally learned as they are being created'

(Engeström, 2001, quoted in Anning et al., 2006, p. 84)

There is a pressing need for those working with children to have the time and space and the skills to think about, talk about, read about, and evaluate what they are doing every day with children, not least because this kind of work involves simultaneously doing and learning. At the same time practitioners will be working within a milieu in which they will be absorbing and responding to the ambiguities and shifting of ideas about children in society that are reflected in the media, or academic or political arenas. And as these practitioners' accounts emphasise, any development of knowledge, skills and values needs to be rooted in the realities and issues within children's lives.

The implementation of policy within children's services may be a formidable driver of practice, but if practitioners become so absorbed in policy directives, inspection and evaluation, and if practitioners are directed towards a specific set of prescribed skills, where will the more grass roots practice innovation, where will the 'thinking outside the box' of the future come from that will remain essential for good practice and change in children's services? Critical reflection using empirical research, experience, exploration, innovation and enquiry, rooted in the understanding that practitioners are all learning, is therefore likely to remain an essential part of the evolution of policy, of skilled practice and of good services for children.

# References

Aberdeen City Council (2007) *Thinking about Fostering? Information on Being a Foster Carer*, available online at <http://www.aberdeencity.gov.uk/ACCI/nmsruntime/saveasdialog.asp?lID=5567&sID=628>, accessed 26 November 2007.

Anning, A., Cottrell, D., Frost, N., Green, J. and Robinson, M. (2006) *Developing Multiprofessional Teamwork for Integrated Children's Services*, Maidenhead, Open University Press.

Bolton, G. (2001) *Reflective Practice: Writing and Professional Development*, London, Paul Chapman.

Brannen, J. and Heptinstall, E. (2003) 'Concepts of care and children's contribution to family life' in Brannen, J. and Moss, P. (eds) *Rethinking Children's Care*, Buckingham, Open University Press, pp. 183–197.

Brannen, J. and Moss, P. (2003) 'Some thoughts on rethinking children's care' in Brannen, J. and Moss, P. (eds) *Rethinking Children's Care*, Buckingham, Open University Press, pp. 198–209.

Commission for Social Care Inspection (CSCI) (2007) *Children's Services: CSCI Findings 2004–07*, available online at <http://www.csci.org.uk/PDF/childrens_services_csci_findings.pdf>, accessed 19 September 2007.

Craig, J. (2004) *Schools Out: Can Teachers, Social Workers and Health Staff Learn to Live Together?*, available online at <http://www.schoolsofambition.co.uk/sofa/files/Schools%20Out.pdf>, accessed 19 September 2007.

Cummings, C., Todd, L. and Dyson, A. (2007) 'Towards extended schools? How education and other professionals understand community-oriented schooling', *Children & Society*, vol. 21, no. 3, pp. 189–200.

Davies Jones, H. (1994) 'The social pedagogues in Western Europe – some implications for European interprofessional care', *Journal of Interprofessional Care*, vol. 8, no. 1, pp. 19–29.

Department for Education and Skills (2005a) *Children's Workforce Strategy: A strategy to build a world-class workforce for children and young people*, available online at <http://www.everychildmatters.gov.uk/_files/7805B4A312A144238AED77508DCFED9B.pdf>, accessed 19 September 2007.

Department for Education and Skills (2005b) *Common Core of Skills and Knowledge for the Children's Workforce*, available online at <http://www.everychildmatters.gov.uk/_files/37183E5C09CCE460A81C781CC70863F0.pdf>, accessed 19 September 2007.

Engeström, Y. (2001) 'Expansive learning at work: toward an activity theoretical reconceptualization', *Journal of Education and Work*, vol. 14, no. 1, pp. 133–156.

Fostering Network (2007) *Can't Afford to Foster: A Survey of Fee Payments to Foster Carers in Scotland*, available online at <http://www.fostering.net/resources/documents/financial/payments_report_scotland2007.pdf>, accessed 19 September 2007.

Fostering Network Young People's Project (2007) *Feedback Report for the Scottish Executive's National Fostering and Kinship Care Strategy Consultation*, available online at <http://www.fostering.net/resources/documents/young_people/young_people_consultation_scotland_feb07.pdf >, accessed 25 November 2007.

Hammond, C. (2004) 'The impacts of learning on well-being, mental health and effective coping' in Schuller, T., Preston, J., Hammond, C., Brassett-Grundy, A. and Bynner, J., *The Benefits of Learning: The Impact of Education on Health, Family Life and Social Capital*, London, Routledge Falmer, pp. 37–56.

Hill, M., Davis, J., Prout, A. and Tisdall, K. (2004) 'Moving the participation agenda forward', *Children & Society*, vol. 18, no. 2, pp. 77–96.

Hochschild, A.R. (2003) *The Commercialisation of Intimate Life: Notes from Home and Work*, Berkeley, University of California Press.

Jack, G. (2006) 'The area and community components of children's well-being', *Children & Society*, vol. 20, no. 5, pp. 334–347.

Knitzer, J. and Lefkowitz, J. (2005) *Resources to Promote Social and Emotional Health and School Readiness in Young Children and Families: A Community Guide*, available online at <http://www.nccp.org/publications/pdf/text_648.pdf>, accessed 19 September 2007.

Learning and Teaching Scotland (2006) *Let's Talk about Listening to Children: Towards a Shared Understanding for Early Years Education in Scotland*, available online at <http://www.ltscotland.org.uk/earlyyears/images/listeningtochildren_tcm4–324433.pdf>, accessed 19 September 2007.

Luckock, B., Lefevre, M., Orr, D., Jones, M., Marchant, R. and Tanner, K. (2006) *Teaching, Learning and Assessing Communication Skills with Children and Young People in Social Work Education*, London, Social Care Institute for Excellence.

Mayall, B. (2006) 'Child–adult relations in social space' in Tisdall, E.K.M., Davis, J.M., Prout, A. and Hill, M. (eds) *Children, Young People and Social Inclusion: Participation for What?*, Bristol, The Policy Press, pp. 199–216.

Morgan, R. (2005) *Younger Children's Views on 'Every Child Matters'*, available online at <http://rights4me.org/content/beheardreports/14/young_views_on_everychildmatters_report.pdf>, accessed 19 September 2007.

Moss, P. (2006) 'From children's services to children's spaces' in Tisdall, E.K.M., Davis, J.M., Prout, A. and Hill, M. (eds) *Children, Young People and Social Inclusion: Participation for What?*, Bristol, The Policy Press, pp. 179–198.

Moss, P. and Brannen, J. (2003) 'Concepts, relationships and policies' in Brannen, J. and Moss, P. (eds) *Rethinking Children's Care*, Buckingham, Open University Press, pp. 1–22.

Moss, P. and Petrie, P. (2002) *From Children's Services to Children's Spaces: Public Policy, Childhood and Children*, London, Routledge Falmer.

Prout, A. (2005) *The Future of Childhood: Towards the Interdisciplinary Study of Children*, London, Routledge Falmer.

Reay, D. (2002) *Gendering Bourdieu's Concept of Capitals? Emotional Capital, Women and Social Class*, Paper presented at the Feminists Evaluate Bourdieu Conference, Manchester University, 11 October 2002, available online at <http://www.bristol.ac.uk/education/research/esrc_seminar/papers/2_1ReayEmotlabour.doc>, accessed 19 September 2007.

Schön, D.A. (1983) *The Reflective Practitioner: How Professionals Think in Action*, New York, Basic Books.

Schuller, T. (2004) 'Studying benefits' in Schuller, T., Preston, J., Hammond, C., Brassett-Grundy, A. and Bynner, J., *The Benefits of Learning: The Impact of Education on Health, Family Life and Social Capital*, London, Routledge Falmer, pp. 3–11.

Scottish Executive (2007) *National Fostering and Kinship Care Strategy Consultation*, individual responses from workers, available online at <http://www.scotland.gov.uk/Publications/2007/04/25144002/0>, accessed 20 January 2008. See also *Analysis of Consultation Responses to Inform a National Fostering and Kinship Care Strategy*, available online at <http://www.scotland.gov.uk/Publications/2007/07/05133153/17>, accessed 20 January 2008.

Simpson, R. and Smith, S. (2006) *Emotional Labour and Organisations: A Developing Field*, available online at <http://www.inderscience.com/www/newsletter/2006/article_winter2006.pdf>, accessed 19 September 2007.

Warin, J. (2007) 'Joined-up services for young children and their families: papering over the cracks or re-constructing the foundations?', *Children & Society*, vol. 21, no. 2, pp. 87–97.

Wenger, E. (1998) *Communities of Practice: Learning, Meaning, and Identity*, Cambridge, Cambridge University Press.

Williams-Siegfredsen, J. (2007) 'Developing pedagogically appropriate practice' in Austin, R. (ed.) *Letting the Outside In: Developing Teaching and Learning Beyond the Early Years Classroom*, Stoke on Trent, Trentham Books.

# Acknowledgements

Grateful acknowledgement is made to the following sources:

## Tables

Page 104: Hudson, B. (2005) 'Partnership Working and the Children's Services Agenda: Is it Feasible?', *Journal of Integrated Care*, vol. 13, no. 2, April 2005, Pavilion; Page 130: Department for Education and Skills, (2006) *Common Assessment Framework for Children and Young People: Managers' Guide*. Crown copyright material is reproduced under Class Licence Number C01W0000065 with the permission of the Controller of HMSO and the Queen's Printer for Scotland.

## Illustrations

Page 16: Copyright © Maggie Murray/Photofusion; Page 23: Bloom, A. (2006) 'Fears new nursery staff will squeeze out teachers', *The Times Educational Supplement*, 1st December 2006; Page 30: Copyright © Swindon Children's Fund; Page 33: Copyright © 2005 TopFoto; Page 47: Copyright © John Phillips/Photofusion; Page 53: Copyright © Clarissa Leahy/Photofusion; Page 56: Copyright © Karen Robinson/Panos Pictures; Page 58: Copyright © Anwar Hussein/Getty Images; Page 73: www.JohnBirdsall.co.uk; Page 74: Tiers of Need, from *DfES Children's Services: The Market for Parental and Family Support Services*, 2006, PriceWaterhouseCoopers; Page 75: Mapping provider types against different tiers of need, from *DfES Children's Services: The Market for Parental & Family Support Services*, 2006, PriceWaterhouseCoopers; Page 78: Copyright © samc/Alamy; Page 88: www.JohnBirdsall.co.uk; Page 91: 'Paul's Family' from *Paul: Death Through Neglect*, The Bridge Child Care Consultancy Service. Copyright © Islington Area Child Protection Committee 1995; Page 109: Copyright © Crispin Hughes/Photofusion; Page 114: Copyright © Karen Robinson; Page 128: Office of the First Minister and Deputy First Minister, *The Super Six: A Publication from the Children and Young People's Unit*. Crown copyright material is reproduced under Class Licence Number C01W0000065 with the permission of the Controller of HMSO and the Queen's Printer for Scotland; Page 131: Department for Education and Skills, (2005) *Statutory guidance on inter-agency co-operation to improve the wellbeing of children: children's trusts*. Crown copyright material is reproduced under Class Licence Number C01W0000065 with the permission of the Controller of HMSO and the Queen's Printer for Scotland; Page 138: Department for Education and Skills, (2006) *Common Assessment*

# Index